T5-BQA-368

THE LIBRARY OF WORLD AFFAIRS

Editors:

George W. Keeton

and

Georg Schwarzenberger

Number 33

THE TRUSTEESHIP SYSTEM OF THE UNITED NATIONS

THE TRUSTEESHIP SYSTEM OF THE UNITED NATIONS

BY

CHARMIAN EDWARDS TOUSSAINT

M.SC. (ECON.), PH.D.

GREENWOOD PRESS, PUBLISHERS

WESTPORT, CONNECTICUT

Library of Congress Cataloging in Publication Data

Toussaint, Charmian Edwards.
The trusteeship system of the United Nations.

Reprint of the 1956 ed. published by Praeger, New York under the auspices of the London Institute of World Affairs, which was issued as no. 33 of The Library of world affairs.
Bibliography: p.
Includes index.
1. International trusteeships. I. Title.
II. Series: The Library of world affairs ; no. 33.
JX4021.T6 1976 341.2'7 75-27689
ISBN 0-8371-8460-6

This edition published in 1956 by Frederick A. Praeger, Inc., New York under the auspices of The London Institute of World Affairs

Reprinted with the permission of Praeger Publishers, Inc.

Reprinted in 1976 by Greenwood Press, a division of Williamhouse-Regency Inc.

Library of Congress Catalog Card Number 75-27689

ISBN 0-8371-8460-6

Printed in the United States of America

TO MY MOTHER

PREFACE

WHILST the Trusteeship System of the United Nations forms only a part of the world organisation established in 1945, it is nevertheless one of the most important parts. Even as the education and guidance of youth to take its place in the national society is recognised as of vital concern to the modern State government—indeed, at the height of the Second World War the British Parliament passed the 1944 Education Act, considering it a sufficiently important matter to justify the temporary diversion of attention from the waging of the War—so is the education and guidance of youthful nations to take their places as adult members of the international society of vital concern to a present-day comprehensive international organisation. This is especially obvious when one considers the important role played in international affairs today by India, Pakistan, Israel and other Eastern and Middle Eastern States which were dependent territories a generation ago.

In singling out the Trusteeship System of the United Nations for special treatment in this study, it is not intended to imply that this System is the only, or indeed the most progressive, system in existence for dealing with colonies. The colonial systems of some Powers have much to commend them; indeed, the international treatment of colonialism developed out of the practice of individual States. The importance of the Trusteeship System is that it complements, rather than replaces, national colonial administration. It tackles the problem of colonial rivalry between States and thus contributes to the maintenance of international peace and security. Furthermore, it attempts to raise the level of the more backward colonial rule. This operates in three ways: by focusing attention on colonial areas it brings to light problems and conditions that might otherwise be overlooked; through international supervision it can bring pressure to bear on unwilling States to improve the lot of their subject peoples; and it provides an international standard of colonial treatment. The international standard has been set by the United Nations in its Declaration Regarding Non-Self-Governing Territories, but it is the Trusteeship System that embodies the supervisory machinery and which provides the most comprehensive international treatment of colonialism to date.

The present study is an analysis of the legal and institutional aspects of the Trusteeship System. The provisions of the Charter are set against their historical background, and examined and interpreted in the light of the practice of the United Nations. Frequent reference has been made to the provisions and practice of the League of Nations Mandates System, to show the origin of some of the trusteeship provisions, to provide a comparison with the Trusteeship System, and to suggest practices which the United Nations might usefully employ.

The study is divided into six parts. The purpose of Part I is to sketch the historical background which led up to the drafting of the Trusteeship provisions of the Charter at San Francisco, and to illustrate how the individual and often different attitudes of the Great Powers towards the solution of the colonial problem were reconciled and embodied into a single international instrument. This at the same time helps to explain the subsequent attitudes of individual States in the practice of the Trusteeship System.

Parts II–VI provide an analysis of the System in theory and practice. To place the System in perspective, consideration is given first to its scope and aims. Then follows an examination of the Trust Agreements which, inasmuch as they form the basis for the application of the System to the trust territories, provide the real core of the System. The negotiation, conclusion, contents and alteration of these agreements receive detailed attention, showing the way in which intentional and unintentional ambiguities in the Charter provisions have contributed to difficulties in the conclusion of these agreements; unless some attempt at interpretation is made, these ambiguities may prove stumbling blocks to the alteration or termination of the agreement.

In Parts IV and V the machinery of supervision and administration receive detailed attention. The separation of supervision and administration is stressed throughout, illustrating how the Charter did not intend to establish a system of international colonial administration, but rather machinery to supervise national administration. The purpose of the final Part is to explain how, in spite of the confusion which has arisen over it, the United Nations Declaration Regarding Non-Self-Governing Territories remains separate and does not fall within a study of the Trusteeship System established by the Charter. What supervisory machinery does exist for non-self-governing territories—other than trust territories—is a product not of the Charter but of the practice of the United Nations.

In its initial form, this work was presented as a thesis for the Ph.D. degree of the University of London. Whilst I take full responsibility for its contents and shortcomings, what merit the work may possess is due in no small part to the valuable help and encouragement I received from many people. I am particularly indebted to the members of the Faculty of Laws at University College, London. First among these is Dr. Georg Schwarzenberger, my teacher and supervisor, who first introduced me to the field of international law and relations and who guided me throughout my university career. His suggestions and criticisms, always constructive and challenging, were invaluable in the preparation of this work. My sincere appreciation is due to Mr. L. C. Green who devoted many hours of an overcrowded life to offering helpful advice on the manuscript from its inception to completion, and to Dr. B. Cheng, who together with Mr. Green, personally took time to read the two final drafts. I should like to mention Professor B. A. Wortley of Manchester University who read my Ph.D. thesis and whose comments and suggestions assisted me in preparing the work for publication.

Especially I should like to mention the help and understanding I received from my husband, a fellow political scientist. Besides reading and constructively criticising the manuscript in its various drafts, and helping with the preparation of the work for publication, he encouraged me to complete the task when often I would have laid it aside.

I am deeply grateful for the experience and insight gained whilst serving as the United Kingdom Interne to the United Nations Secretariat in the summer of 1951. I should also like to acknowledge the courteous assistance rendered by the staffs of the following libraries: The London School of Economics, the United Nations Information Centre in London, the Bodleian Library at Oxford University, Manchester Public Library, and the Stanford University and Hoover Libraries at Stanford, California.

C. E. TOUSSAINT

Washington, D.C.
August, 1956

CONTENTS

PART FIVE

ADMINISTRATION

PART SIX

TRUSTEESHIP AND NON-SELF-GOVERNING TERRITORIES

APPENDIX

ADDENDUM

New paragraph for insertion into page 52 immediately before final paragraph (after line 17 of the text).

A further question that has arisen from the 1950 Advisory Opinion concerns the admissibility of oral petitions from South West Africa. In order to clarify the matter, the General Assembly, in December 1955, submitted the following question to the International Court: 'Is it consistent with the advisory opinion of . . . 1950 for the Committee on South West Africa . . . to grant oral hearings to petitioners on matters relating to the Territory of South West Africa?'[17] In its Opinion, handed down on June 1, 1956, the Court replied in the affirmative.[18] In arriving at its conclusion, the Court drew attention to the fact that procedure for dealing with petitions under the Mandates System had been introduced originally by the League Council in 1923 in the form of additional Rules of Procedure.[19] Although oral petitions were not provided for, 'the Council having established the right of petition, and regulated the manner of its exercise, was, in the opinion of the Court, competent to authorise the Permanent Mandates Commission to grant oral hearings to petitioners, had it seen fit to do so.'[20] Since the League Council had the right to authorise oral hearings, its successor in the role of supervising authority for South West Africa, the General Assembly, also possessed this right. Moreover, the lack of co-operation from the Union of South Africa necessitated 'an alternative procedure for the receipt and treatment of petitions.' In delivering this Opinion, the Court was sanctioning a practice which the General Assembly had employed in the past.[21]

17 Official Records of the General Assembly, Tenth Session, Resolution 942A (X).

18 *Admissibility of Hearings of Petitioners by the Committee on South West Africa,* Advisory Opinion: *I.C.J. Reports 1956,* p. 23.

19 See below, p. 194.

20 *I.C.J. Reports 1956,* p. 29.

21 At the Fourth Session of the General Assembly, the Rev. Michael Scott, appearing on behalf of the Herero Tribe of South West Africa, was granted an oral hearing by the Fourth Committee.

PART ONE

THE ORIGINS OF THE TRUSTEESHIP SYSTEM

Chapter 1

HISTORICAL BACKGROUND

The Trusteeship System of the United Nations represents the most recent attempt at the international control of colonial government. For the first time the principle of 'trusteeship' is recognised as applying to all non-self-governing peoples, it is restricted neither geographically nor to territories formerly ruled by defeated States. Whilst the *International Trusteeship System* as formulated in Chapter XII of the United Nations Charter is of restricted application, the principle of trusteeship is stated in Chapter XI—the *Declaration Regarding Non-Self-Governing Territories*. By Article 73 of this Chapter, 'Members of the United Nations which have or assume responsibilities for the administration of territories whose peoples have not yet attained a full measure of self-government recognise the principle that the interests of the inhabitants of these territories are paramount, and accept as a sacred trust the obligation to promote to the utmost . . . the well-being of the inhabitants of these territories.' Whilst it is true that it is only the United Nations Members who accept the principle of the 'sacred trust,' in view of the fact that the United Nations was originally conceived of as a universal organisation, it can be held that the Charter attempted to apply the trusteeship principle to all non-self-governing territories no matter under what flag they were administered. In practice, not all colonial States did become Members of the United Nations during its first decade, and therefore not all non-self-governing territories were subject to the trusteeship principle. This defect has since been rectified by the admission of sixteen States to Membership in the Organisation on December 14, 1955, and it is now true to say that the principle of the 'sacred trust' is applicable to all non-self-governing territories.

The problem of colonial peoples today stems from the founding of the 'crusading' empires of the sixteenth and seventeenth centuries by Spain, Portugal and France, and of the commercial empires by British and Dutch trading companies. The professed aim of the former was the spreading of Christianity and Western Civilisation,[1] an additional purpose being undoubtedly a desire for trade,[2] whilst the latter were to a large extent founded for the purpose of providing markets and raw materials and were thus a direct result of the Industrial Revolution.[3] In neither case was much attention paid to the interests of any one but the occupying Power or company until the second half of the eighteenth century,[4] from which time the growth of national and international concern for colonialism can be traced. This led to the inclusion of various aspects of colonialism within the field of international regulation and ultimately to the over-all international machinery provided by the United Nations Charter. Essentially, the historical background of the United Nations Trusteeship System and the Declaration Regarding Non-Self-Governing Territories is the development of specific principles to be applied to colonialism to a stage at which they could be regulated by a single international instrument, such as the United Nations Charter.

[1] *e.g.,* The right granted by Pope Nicholas V in 1452, to King Alphonse of Portugal to acquire dominion over American territory not already possessed by any other Christian prince, and to subjugate the non-Christian natives therein (see E. Nys, *Les Origines du Droit International* (1894), p. 370). It is interesting to note the definition of Portuguese colonial policy found in the Colonial Act of Portugal, a part of the present Portuguese Constitution: 'It is the essential attribute of the Portuguese nation to fulfill the historic function of possessing and colonising overseas dominions and of civilising the native populations inhabiting them' (Paragraph 2 of the Act, see A. J. Peaslee, *Constitutions of Nations* (1950), Vol. 3, p. 26).

[2] See B. A. Wortley, *Idealism in International Law: a Spanish View of the Colonial Problem* (24 *Transactions of the Grotius Society,* 1938, pp. 147–167 at p. 148).

[3] The third type of colony, the settlement colony, is not considered here since this in general did not involve the establishment of alien rule over indigenous peoples (see further, G. Schwarzenberger, *Power Politics* (1951), p. 648).

[4] It is true that the problems raised by the establishment of Spanish rule over the Indians in America received some attention from Spanish philosophers, notably Francisco de Vitoria (1480–1549), and as a result some enlightened colonial legislation was enacted in Spain. The Spanish colonists, however, resisted this legislation, and distance and lack of communications made it difficult for Spain to control her colonists, with the result that enlightened thinking in Spain had little effect on practice in Spanish America (see further, B. A. Wortley, *Idealism in International Law: a Spanish View of the Colonial Problem* (24 *Transactions of the Grotius Society,* 1938, pp. 147–167); J. B. Scott, *The Spanish Conception of International Law and Sanctions* (1934); and G. Schwarzenberger, *Power Politics* (1951), pp. 32–34).

Principle of the 'Sacred Trust'—Humanitarian Aspect of Colonialism

The revival of the theory of natural law in the late seventeenth and the eighteenth centuries by Rousseau, Locke and other writers, with its emphasis on equality and the natural rights of the individual,[5] inaugurated a period of revolutionary liberalism. The American and French Revolutions both rejected the concept of the 'Divine Right of Kings' or of any imposition of government from above. 'Governments are instituted among Men, deriving their just powers from the consent of the governed,' affirmed the American Declaration of Independence, and this was followed by the even more revolutionary theory of the French Revolution which, unsatisfied with the idea of mere representative government, affirmed that the people was the supreme authority—the sovereign.[6] Whilst it is true that these egalitarian concepts were applied only to peoples of European stock,[7] it was inevitable that the impact of this new liberalism would eventually fall on colonialism. Some moral justification had to be found for imposing the rule of one people over another, for ignoring the natural right of peoples to govern themselves or freely to delegate this right to representatives. The answer found was that the subject peoples were incapable of governing themselves and that therefore it was to their benefit to be under the control of an advanced nation. This in itself logically meant that the rule of the imperial power must be of such a nature that it would benefit the subjected peoples. No longer could it be held that colonies existed merely to be exploited for the benefit of the imperial power.

The lead in this new era of colonialism was taken by Great Britain where certain prominent liberal thinkers strove to drive home the lessons of the American Revolution. In the British Parliament, Edmund Burke agitated for the application of the new democratic ideas to India, which was at that time subject to the rule of the East India Company. Burke is generally credited with the formulation for the first time of the 'trustee-

[5] J. J. Rousseau, *Discours sur l'Inegalité* (1754), *Contrat Social* (1762); J. Locke, *Second Treatise on Civil Government* (1685), Chap. 2.

[6] Alfred Cobban, *National Self-Determination* (1945), p. 5.

[7] This is especially true in the case of the new United States of America where neither the Indians nor the Negro slaves were accorded citizenship rights.

ship' concept of colonialism,[8] a concept which has been at the basis of all enlightened colonial thinking since then. Speaking in the House of Commons on December 1, 1783, during the consideration of Fox's India Bill, Burke expressed the 'trusteeship' principle of colonialism in the following manner:

> 'All political power which is set over men, and . . . all privilege claimed or exercised in exclusion of them, being wholly artificial, and for so much a deregation from the natural equality of mankind at large, ought to be in some way or other exercised ultimately for their benefit.
>
> 'If this is true with regard to every species of political dominion, and every description of commercial privilege, none of which can be original self-derived rights, or grants for the benefit of the holders, then such rights or privileges, or whatever else you choose to call them, are all, in the strictest sense, a trust; and it is of the very essence of every trust to be rendered accountable; and even totally to cease, when it substantially varies from the purposes for which alone it could have a lawful existence.'[9]

Thus did Burke insist that the possession of political power implied a duty towards the subjected people, a duty to exercise this political power for their benefit. Locke's conception of political power being in the nature of a trust was being applied to colonial rule. By 1788, the idea of the colonial trust had gained sufficient acceptance in England for Burke, at the conclusion of his opening speech for the House of Commons in the Impeachment Trial of Warren Hastings, to include what amounted to the violation of the colonial trust among the charges against Hastings:

> 'Therefore, it is with confidence, that, ordered by the Commons,
>
> 'I impeach Warren Hastings, Esquire, of high crimes and misdemeanours,
>
> 'I impeach him in the name of the Commons of Great Britain in Parliament assembled, whose Parliamentary trust he has betrayed,

[8] See M. F. Lindley, *The Acquisition and Government of Backward Territory in International Law* (1926), p. 330.

[9] Hansard, *Parliamentary History*, Vol. 23 (1783), cols. 1316–1317.

'I impeach him in the name of all the Commons of Great Britain, whose national character he has dishonoured,

'I impeach him in the name of the people of India, whose laws, rights, and liberties he has subverted, whose properties he has destroyed, whose country he has laid waste and desolate.'[10]

Not only was Hastings being impeached for violating the trust of Parliament but also for subverting the laws, rights and liberties of the people of India. As the chosen representative of the British House of Commons, Burke was giving official recognition to the possession of rights by colonial peoples. Thus the 'sacred trust' of colonial government was a trust to exercise power for the benefit of the native inhabitants and in so doing to protect their natural rights.

The development of the 'sacred trust' principle in the United States came by way of the assertion of the duty of the Government to protect the Indians. Whilst denying to them the status of sovereign nations,[11] their national status was nevertheless kept intact and Chief Justice Marshall referred to them as 'domestic dependent nations' looking to the United States Government for protection.[12] Likewise the treaty between the United States and the leaders of the Cherokee Nation in November 1786, contained the following clause: 'The Indians for themselves and their respective tribes and towns, do acknowledge all the Cherokees to be under the protection of the United States.'[13] When the United States began to acquire territory for other than settlement purposes, the concept of trusteeship began to be mentioned frequently. On December 3, 1900, President McKinley referred to the newly acquired possession of the Philippines as a 'trust which should be unselfishly discharged,' and he stated that towards the Philippines, the United

[10] *The Writings and Speeches of Edmund Burke* (1901), Vol. 10, pp. 144–145 (Pub. Little, Brown and Co.).

[11] See *Cherokee Nation v. Georgia* (1831) 5 Peters 17. This case was cited with favour in the *Cayuga Indian Claim* (1926), decided by an American and British Claims Arbitration Tribunal (see Nielsen's report, p. 203 at p. 327). See also *Johnson and Graham's Lessee* v. *William M'Intosh* (1823) 8 Wheaton 543.

[12] *Cherokee Nation* v. *Georgia* (1831) 5 Peters 17.

[13] See Article III of the Treaty (1 Laws U.S. 322). In 1847 the Supreme Court asserted, with respect to the Indians, that the United States Government was '*in loco parentis*' (*Howell* v. *Fountain* (1847) 3 Ga. 176).

States Government had 'a moral as well as national responsibility.'[14] The following year the Supreme Court held that Cuba was a 'territory held in trust for the inhabitants of Cuba.'[15]

The earliest attempts at the international regulation of aspects of colonialism were made with regard to the slave trade. During the eighteenth century, anti-slavery societies began to be formed in England, France and the United States.[16] The greatest effect of these societies was felt in England where the lead was definitely established, and slavery within the British Isles was abolished in 1772. In 1807 the slave-trade was forbidden, in 1811 it was made a transportable offence for any British subject to be concerned with the slave-trade,[17] and in 1824 slave-trading by British subjects was established as constituting the crime of piracy under English law.[18] The final step was taken in 1833 when Great Britain purchased the freedom of all slaves throughout the British Empire. As a result of British insistence at the Congress of Vienna, a clause agreeing in principle to the abolition of the slave-trade was inserted into the Treaty of Paris of 1815.[19] But not until 1885 was it officially recognised that the slave-trade was forbidden by international law. The General Act of the Berlin Conference recognised that the slave-trade was forbidden not merely by national legislation, but by 'the principles of international law as recognised by the signatory powers.'[20] This Act provided the first real international treatment of matters concerning colonial peoples. It 'aimed at the extension of the benefits of civilisation to the natives, the promotion of trade and navigation on a basis of perfect equality for all nations, and the preservation of the territories affected from the ravages of war.'[1] Its weakness lay in the fact that it was territorially limited to the area

14 See Richardson, *Messages and Papers of the Presidents,* Vol. 10, p. 222.
15 *Neeley* v. *Henkel* (1901) 180 U.S. 109.
16 *e.g., Aborigines Protection Society* in England.
17 51 Geo. 3, c. 23.
18 5 Geo. 4, c. 113. Cf. the judgment of Sir William Scott in the case of *The Le Louis* (1817) 2 Dods. 210, see L. C. Green, *International Law Through the Cases* (1950), p. 412 *et seq.,* decided by the High Court of Admiralty prior to the passing of this Act. Sir William said that the occupation of slave-trading was not piracy (pp. 415–416).
19 See G. Schwarzenberger, *Power Politics* (1951), p. 212, and *The Protection of Human Rights in British State Practice* (1 *Current Legal Problems,* 1948); also see T. Clarkson, *The History of the Abolition of the African Slave Trade by the British Parliament* (1808).
20 Article 9 of the Berlin Act.
1 See Lord Keith's analysis of the Act (African Society, *Journal,* July 1918, pp. 248–261 at p. 250).

comprising the Conventional Basin of the Congo, and there was no means of enforcement.[2] The General Act of Brussels of 1890, attempted to regulate additional matters affecting colonial peoples, and it extended the area covered to all the territories of Africa under European control. Once more the slave-trade came in for attention, the signatory States agreeing to take common action for the suppression of the slave-trade and declaring their 'firm intention of putting an end to the crimes and devastations engendered by the traffic in African slaves.'[3] Also included in the Act was the regulation of the import of arms and trade spirits into Africa. The welfare of colonial peoples was now definitely a matter of international concern.

The colonial question was prominent among the problems facing the peacemakers in 1919. It had been agreed among the victorious powers that Germany was to lose her colonial possessions, and in addition, militant nationalism in Eastern Europe and the Middle East demanded the detachment of certain territories from Russia, Austria-Hungary and Turkey. In the fifth of his Fourteen Points, President Wilson held that 'the interests of the populations concerned' should have 'equal weight with the equitable claims of the government whose title is to be determined' in the adjustment of various colonial claims. In 1918, General Smuts put forward his proposals for a League of Nations which introduced for the first time the plan for a mandatory system.[4] Although General Smuts foresaw his proposal as applying only to the territories detached from the Austro-Hungarian, Russian and Turkish Empires, considering annexation more suitable for the former German African dependencies, nevertheless this plan laid the foundation-stone for the Mandates System which finally emerged and which was to apply to certain Middle Eastern areas, and to all the former German colonies in Africa and the Pacific.[5]

Article 22 (1) of the Covenant of the League of Nations gave

[2] Machinery for enforcement consisting of an international commission was set up, but it did not function since representatives to sit on this commission were never nominated by the signatory Powers (see *ibid.*, p. 250, and G. Schwarzenberger, *Power Politics* (1951), p. 651).

[3] Great Britain, H.M.S.O. C. 6048 (1890).

[4] J. C. Smuts, *The League of Nations, a Practical Suggestion* (1918).

[5] For details of the establishment of the Mandates System, see David Hunter Miller, *The Drafting of the Covenant* (1928), Vol. 1, pp. 101–117.

expression to the principle of the 'sacred trust.' With regard to colonies and territories detached from the enemy and inhabited by peoples not yet able to stand by themselves 'there should be applied the principle that the well-being and development of such peoples form a sacred trust of civilisation.' 'The tutelage of such peoples should be entrusted to advanced nations . . . [and] should be exercised by them as Mandatories on behalf of the League.'[6] The great weakness of the Mandates System was that it applied only to ex-enemy territory, although a rather vague clause concerning colonial areas was included in Article 23 of the Covenant. By this article, League Members undertook 'to secure just treatment of the native inhabitants of territories under their control.'[7]

The next step was taken at San Francisco. This was the recognition of the 'sacred trust' principle as applying to all dependent territories. By Article 73 of the United Nations Charter, 'Members of the United Nations which have or assume responsibilities for the administration of territories whose peoples have not yet attained a full measure of self-government recognise the principle that the interests of the inhabitants of these territories are paramount, and accept as a sacred trust the obligation to promote to the utmost, within the system of international peace and security established by the present Charter, the well-being of the inhabitants of these territories.' This is further elaborated in paragraph (a) of Article 73, by which Members agree 'to ensure, with due respect for the culture of the peoples concerned, their political, economic, social, and educational advancement, their just treatment, and their protection against abuses.' In the case of territories brought under the Trusteeship System, one of the basic objectives is said to be the encouragement of human rights and fundamental freedoms on a non-discriminatory basis.[8]

In less than two hundred years, therefore, the principle of the 'sacred trust,' first concretely stated in Great Britain, had grown to such an extent that it is now recognised as being universally applicable.

[6] Article 22 (2).
[7] Article 23 (b).
[8] Article 76 (c). See further below, Chap. 4, pp. 66–68.

The Principle of International Accountability

The principle of accountability for colonial rule was originally introduced in the form of accountability of the administering body of the colony to the government or people of the home State. Stating that the exercise of political power over colonial peoples is a trust, Burke further held that 'it is of the very essence of every trust to be rendered accountable.'[9] 'To whom, then, would I make the East India Company accountable? Why, to parliament, to be sure; to parliament, from whom their trust was derived.'[10] In the case of India, to which Burke was referring, the governing body was the East India Company to which authority had been delegated by the British Parliament in the Company's Charter, therefore the East India Company was accountable to Parliament.

The extension of national accountability into international accountability was the result of the application of international regulation to colonialism in the humanitarian sphere,[11] and of the development of the second principle of the 'dual mandate'[12]—colonial administration for the benefit of the world at large. A concrete proposal to apply the principle of international accountability was put forward by President Theodore Roosevelt in 1906. He proposed that France and Spain should hold a joint 'mandate' for Morocco and that they should report to Italy, as the supervising authority on behalf of all the Powers, with the right of inspection and verification.[13] This never materialised, however. The League of Nations Mandates System supplied the first real example of international accountability in practice. The Powers entrusted with the administration of the mandated territories, known as mandatories, were to exercise this power 'on behalf of the League.' The mandatories were required to render annual reports on the territories to the League Council, and a permanent commission was established to receive and

[9] See debate on Fox's India Bill in the House of Commons (Hansard, *Parliamentary History,* Vol. 23, (1783), col. 1316).

[10] *ibid.,* col. 1317.

[11] See above, p. 5 *et seq.*

[12] The 'Dual Mandate' was the expression used by Lord Lugard which comprised the sacred trust for the native peoples and the sacred trust for the world (see Lord Lugard, *The Dual Mandate in British Tropical Africa* (1923)).

[13] See Pitman B. Potter, *Origin of the System of Mandates Under the League of Nations* (16 *American Political Science Review,* November 1922, p. 563 *et seq.*).

examine the reports and to advise the Council on matters concerning the mandates.[14] When the Trusteeship Council was established after the Second World War, the practice of the League with regard to international accountability was followed, the administering Powers being made accountable to the General Assembly or Security Council, as the case might be, for the administration of the territories under trusteeship. At the same time the broad outline of the principle was extended to all colonies held by United Nations Members, for which information is required to be transmitted to the United Nations.[15]

Colonial Administration for the Benefit of the World at Large

As a result of the Industrial Revolution, rivalry developed between the more advanced industrial countries for the control of markets and raw materials. The possession of sovereignty over vast portions of undeveloped territory became of distinct commercial advantage. Being no longer satisfied with the territories they possessed, the industrial nations sought to acquire additional areas which resulted in the 'scramble for Africa' in the late nineteenth century. But the territory remaining to be colonised was not inexhaustible, and therefore the industrial nations began to have commercial designs on the colonies of other States. The result was the conclusion of bilateral agreements between the Powers concerned for the application of the 'open-door' on a reciprocal basis, for the settlement of boundary disputes, and for other mutually advantageous matters. With the expansion of these bilateral agreements into multilateral agreements, it came to be accepted that colonial matters had both a commercial and a political significance to States other than the sovereign. This marked the beginning of the recognition of the interest of the world-at-large in colonial matters.

The beginning of international regulation for the benefit of the outside world came with the Berlin Act of 1885. This provided that the principle of the open-door for the trade and navigation of all countries was to be applied in the area comprising the 'Conventional Basin of the Congo.'[16] These pro-

14 See Article 22 of the League Covenant.
15 Article 73 (e) of the Charter of the United Nations.
16 See Further B. Gerig, *The Open-Door and the Mandates System* (1930).

visions were limited by the 1919 Convention on the Revision of the Berlin and Brussels Acts, signed at St. Germain-en-Laye,[17] to the signatories of this Convention and to Members of the League of Nations. The open-door principle was also incorporated into the Mandates System where it was made an integral part of the B Mandates.[18] The doctrine that Lord Lugard called the 'Dual Mandate' had come to be accepted internationally. 'For the civilised nations have at last recognised that while on the one hand the abounding wealth of the tropical regions of the earth must be developed and used for the benefit of mankind, on the other hand an obligation rests on the controlling power not only to safeguard the material rights of the natives but to promote their moral and educational progress.'[19] The 'sacred trust' principle had come to be recognised as a trust for the inhabitants of the colonial territories and a trust for the world-at-large. Defining the 'open-door' principle in terms of the dual mandate, Lord Lugard stated that 'the policy of "the open-door" has two distinct though mutually dependent aspects—*viz.*, equal opportunity to the commerce of other countries, and an unrestricted market to the native producer. The tropics can only be successfully developed if the interests of the controlling Power are identical with those of the natives of the country, and it seeks no individual advantage, and imposes no restriction for its own benefit.'[20]

By the time the Charter of the United Nations came to be drawn up in 1945, a further reason for stressing the interests of the world in colonialism had come to be recognised. The strategic importance of colonial areas for military bases had shown itself during the Second World War. Colonies were a potential threat to international peace and security, and experience in Asia had shown that undefended colonies were an invitation to aggression by an imperialist Power. The United States, was especially alive to the security aspect of colonialism with her experience of the use of a mandate by the Japanese to prepare the attack against the United States. Likewise was the Soviet Union which was imbued with the Marxist theory of colonialism. This characterises the colonial question 'as a dual

17 See M. O. Hudson, *International Legislation,* Vol. 1, pp. 344–352.
18 Article 22 (5) of the League Covenant.
19 Lord Lugard, *The Dual Mandate in British Tropical Africa* (1923), p. 18.
20 *ibid.,* p. 61.

tendency—the struggle between advanced capitalistic nations and colonies and the struggle among capitalistic powers over the redivision of the colonies.'[1] This latter struggle is considered responsible for imperialistic wars, such as the two World Wars, which, according to Marxist theory, break out 'as the sole means of redividing the world and restoring the equilibrium.'[2] In this way colonialism is seen as a threat to international peace and security and as such of concern to the world. These attitudes of the United States and Soviet Union caused them to stress the security aspect of colonialism when the Charter was being drafted. As a result, in addition to its being stated as the primary aim of the United Nations itself, the furtherance of international peace and security was included in the Charter of the United Nations among both the purposes of the Trusteeship System[3] and among the obligations of United Nations Members towards all non-self-governing territories.[4] Indeed it was made the primary aim of the International Trusteeship System.

In giving prominence to the security aspect of the international concern with colonialism, the United Nations Charter has not ignored the commercial interests of States in colonialism. Under the Declaration Regarding Non-Self-Governing Territories, Members of the United Nations administering non-self-governing territories agree to take into account 'the interests and well-being of the rest of the world, in social, economic, and commercial matters.'[5] Furthermore, one of the basic objectives of the Trusteeship System is the 'equal treatment in social, economic, and commercial matters for all Members of the United Nations and their nationals.'[6]

The Temporary Nature of the Colonial 'Trust'

In his parliamentary speech on colonial trusteeship,[7] Burke included the possibility of the colonial trust being of a non-permanent nature. He stated that it was of the essence of a

[1] See Joseph John Sisco, *The Soviet Attitude Towards the Trusteeship System* (University of Chicago Dissertation, 1950), p. 11.

[2] Historicus, *Stalin on Revolution* (27 *Foreign Affairs*, No. 2, January 1949, p. 175 *et seq.* at p. 184). The source of this statement by Historicus is Stalin, *Voprosy Leninizma* (1945), 11th ed., pp. 3, 17.

[3] Article 76 (a), see below, Appendix.

[4] Article 73 (c), see *ibid.*

[5] Article 74, see *ibid.*

[6] Article 76 (d), see *ibid.*

[7] See above, p. 6.

trust 'totally to cease, when it substantially varies from the purposes for which alone it could have a lawful existence.'[8] This concept justifies both the revolt of colonial peoples on account of misrule by the governing State, and the transfer of political power from one entity to another if the 'sacred trust' is violated. The American Revolution had been justified on this basis, the Declaration of Independence naming the various ways in which the colonies had been misruled.

The nineteenth century witnessed the development of the idea of eventual self-government or independence for dependent territories. Once this was accepted, colonialism became a temporary status leading to self-government. The idea of guardianship was introduced into colonial administration, the dependent territory resembling a ward which was to be guided towards self-government.[9] In 1831 Chief Justice Marshall used this concept of guardianship to describe the relationship of the Indian communities to the United States.[10] By the turn of the century, the principle of ultimate self-government was becoming well-established in both British and American colonial practice. Beginning with the British North America Act of 1867, which set Canada on the road to independence, the temporary nature of colonial trusteeship gained increasing prominence in Great Britain until it became officially accepted policy in 1926. It was officially recognised by the British Government at the Imperial Conference in 1926, that all British colonies were in a temporary status leading to self-government. 'The climbing process is common to all the communities which form part of the Empire. Each of them, whether the population is predominantly white or predominantly coloured, is gradually . . . passing upward from the stage in which the community is wholly subject to control exercised from London to that in which the measure of control diminishes, and so on to that in which the control has ceased entirely.'[11] Likewise, the United States was recognising that her overseas possessions were destined for independence.[12] Even in French

[8] Hansard, *Parliamentary History,* Vol. 23 (1783), col. 1317.

[9] See Quincy Wright, *Mandates Under the League of Nations* (1930), p. 11.

[10] See *Cherokee Nation* v. *Georgia* (1831) 5 Peters 17.

[11] Sir Cecil Hurst, *Great Britain and the Dominions* (1928), p. 12.

[12] In the *Jones Act* (1916) the United States announced its intention to withdraw from the Philippine Islands and 'to recognise their independence as soon as a stable government can be established therein' (U.S.

colonial thinking, where independence was not considered as a goal for French colonies, the temporary nature of the colonial trust was recognised, full rights of French citizenship being considered the goal for all colonial peoples.[13]

By 1919, the idea of eventual self-government for colonies—either in the form of assimilation or of independence—had gained general recognition. The Mandates System incorporated the idea in both its forms. Class A Mandates were described as those communities whose 'existence as independent nations can be provisionally recognised subject to the rendering of administrative advice and assistance by a Mandatory until such time as they are able to stand alone.'[14] They were destined for, and have since reached full independence. The goal for B Mandates was not stated.[15] In the case of the C Mandates, 'territories, such as South West Africa and certain of the South Pacific Islands,' it would appear that their destiny lay in assimilation, but not absorption, into the territory of the Mandatory. It was considered that they could 'be best administered under the laws of the Mandatory as integral portions of its territory.'[16]

Finally, in the United Nations Charter, the temporary nature of the colonial trust has been recognised in the case of all non-self-governing territories. All Members of the United Nations administering non-self-governing territories 'accept as a sacred trust the obligation . . . to develop self-government.'[17] In the case of trust territories, one of the aims of trusteeship administration is 'the progressive development towards self-government or independence.'[18]

Thus the four roots of the United Nations Charter's colonial

Statutes at Large, 64th Congress, Session 1, Vol. 39, Part 1, Chap. 416, p. 545). This was followed by the *Tydings-McDuffie Act* (1934), which provided that ten years from the date of the formation of a government under the new constitution provided for in this Act, the Philippine Islands should be declared independent. This was duly carried out on July 4, 1946 (see *ibid.,* 73rd Congress, Session 2, Vol. 98, Part 1, Chap. 84, p. 463).

13 The Constitution of the French Republic, adopted in 1946, states that 'all nationals of the overseas territories shall have the status of citizens, in the same capacity as French nationals of metropolitan France or the overseas territories' (Section 3, Article 80 of Constitution, see A. J. Peaslee, *Constitutions of Nations* (1950), Vol. 2, p. 17).

14 Article 22 (4) of the League Covenant.

15 Article 22 (5).

16 Article 22 (6).

17 Article 73, see below, Appendix.

18 Article 76 (b), see *ibid.*

provisions—the principles of the 'sacred trust,' of international accountability, of the temporary nature of the colonial trust, and the concept of colonial administration for the benefit of the world-at-large—have been developed in less than two hundred years. For the first time, an international organisation has attempted to deal with the whole problem of colonialism: not just with particular colonial areas, but with *all* colonial areas. However, the most comprehensive and recent system of international colonial control, the Trusteeship System of the United Nations, still applies only to a selected group of colonial areas. But in view of the fact that it is the most comprehensive international system, it deserves special attention. It is this Trusteeship System which forms the subject of this present study.

CHAPTER 2

THE SAN FRANCISCO CONFERENCE

THE Four Sponsoring Powers of the San Francisco Conference had agreed to accept the Dumbarton Oaks Proposals,[1] together with the Yalta Voting Formula,[2] 'as affording a basis' for the Charter.[3] These, however, did not include any proposals on trusteeship although it was understood that the subject would be introduced at San Francisco.[4] The United States was anxious that the system of Four-Power Consultation should continue, and that the Sponsoring Powers should show some semblance of agreement when the proposals on trusteeship were introduced at the San Francisco Conference. With this in mind, the Department of State, in a memorandum to the British, Soviet and Chinese Embassies in Washington of March 28, 1945, proposed 'that the four sponsoring governments should agree among themselves that any substantial changes which any of them may have to suggest to the Conference should only be brought forward after consultation among the four governments.'[5] This was readily agreed to, Mr. Stettinius stressing that it was only an 'agreement to consult' not an agreement to agree in advance. In pursuance of this agreement, the Foreign Ministers of the Four Sponsoring Powers held consultations from April 23 until May 4, 1945,[6] during which time the San Francisco Conference itself opened. Due to lack of time, the matter of trusteeship was not discussed in substance, but it was agreed that the Powers should present individual national, rather than joint, proposals on the

1 Cmd. 6560, Miscellaneous No. 4 (1944).

2 See U.S. Department of State *Bulletin*, March 11, 1945, pp. 394–395.

3 See U.N.C.I.O. Doc. 3, G/2, April 26, 1945 (*United Nations Conference on International Organisation, Documents*, Vol. 1, p. 1).

4 It was agreed at Yalta, that the five States which were to become permanent members of the Security Council would consult together on the subject of territorial trusteeship prior to the San Francisco Conference. A formal statement was issued, limiting the territories to which trusteeship might be applied and prohibiting discussion of actual territories at either the preliminary consultations or at the San Francisco Conference (see Cmd. 7088 (1947), and U.S. Department of State, *The Conferences at Malta and Yalta 1945*, Part 2, pp. 820–821 (Pub. March 1955)).

5 *Post-War Foreign Policy Preparations 1939–1945*, Department of State Publication No. 3580, p. 679, Appendix 60.

6 *ibid.*, p. 439 *et seq.*

subject to the Conference, in order that the Conference committee on trusteeship would not be left without any proposals from the major powers.[7] Consultations on the specific question of trusteeship were also held between the delegations of the Four Sponsoring Powers and France at San Francisco, but again time did not permit agreement on a common draft.[8] Thus, when the committee on trusteeship at the Conference met, it was faced not with a basic draft from which to work but with a number of individual proposals presented by national delegations. This was in contrast to most of the work of the San Francisco Conference which had the Dumbarton Oaks proposals as a convenient basis of discussion.

In addition to the interest shown by the Sponsoring Powers in the subject of trusteeship, many of the opening speeches from other delegations before the Plenary sessions of the Conference mentioned trusteeship in a general way. The most detailed consideration of the matter came from Mr. Francis Forde of the Australian Delegation. Mr. Forde specifically envisaged the creation of a special trusteeship organ: 'We also wish to see the setting up of an expert organ of the United Nations, the function of which will be to inform the world organisation of the welfare and progress of the peoples of mandated territories and such other dependent territories as may be determined upon by appropriate action.'[9] Although it would appear that Mr. Forde was thinking more along the lines of a specialist body similar to the Permanent Mandates Commission, the important point is that he did consider that the matter deserved a separate body.

When the organisation of the Conference was undertaken, Commission II was set up to concern itself with the proposed General Assembly of the new organisation. This Commission in turn established a technical committee, referred to as Committee II/4, 'to prepare and recommend to Commission II, and to Commission III[10] as necessary, draft provisions on principles and mechanism of a system of international trusteeship for such dependent territories as may by subsequent agreement be placed thereunder.'[11]

7 *ibid.*, p. 445.
8 *ibid.*, p. 445 *et seq.*
9 U.N.C.I.O. Doc. 13, P/2 (*U.N.C.I.O. Docs.*, Vol. 1, p. 177).
10 Commission III dealt with the Security Council.
11 U.N.C.I.O. Doc. 42, P/10 (a) (*U.N.C.I.O. Docs.*, Vol. 1, p. 404).

Separate proposals on trusteeship were presented to the Conference by the United States,[12] the United Kingdom,[13] France,[14] China,[15] and Australia [16]—the Soviet Union presented a paper entitled *Amendments of the Soviet Delegation to the United States Draft on Trusteeship System.*[17] The Chinese and French proposals were modelled on those of the United States, and the similarity between the British and Australian proposals gave evidence of prior consultations. Other States contented themselves with making comments and suggestions upon one of these papers or upon the Working Paper on the subject, which was subsequently drawn up.[18] It is worth while examining the initial papers that were put forward and comparing the various proposals, in order to determine the origin of the various Charter provisions on trusteeship. Such an examination, by throwing light on the kind of trusteeship system originally envisaged by the various States, may help to explain their subsequent attitudes with regard to the interpretation of the Charter provisions on trusteeship.

Comparison of the Five Drafts

The main distinction between the British and Australian proposals on the one hand and the other three States' on the other, was the inclusion in the former of a declaration on policy to be adopted towards dependent peoples in general—no similar provisions being found in the others. Although this study is concerned only with the International Trusteeship System, it is important to bear in mind the fact that the British and Australian proposals were concerned with *all* dependent peoples, regardless of whether they were inhabitants of trust territories or of some other colonial area.

Objectives and Purposes

Concerning the objectives and purposes of the system, the United Kingdom (Article 1)[19] and Australian (Article 1) drafts

[12] U.N.C.I.O. Doc. 2, G/26 (c) (*U.N.C.I.O. Docs.*, Vol. 3, p. 607).
[13] U.N.C.I.O. Doc. 2, G/26 (d) (*U.N.C.I.O. Docs.*, Vol. 3, p. 609).
[14] U.N.C.I.O. Doc. 2, G/26 (a) (*U.N.C.I.O. Docs.*, Vol. 3, p. 604).
[15] U.N.C.I.O. Doc. 2, G/26 (e) (*U.N.C.I.O. Docs.*, Vol. 3, p. 615).
[16] U.N.C.I.O. Doc. 2, G/14 (1) (*U.N.C.I.O. Docs.*, Vol. 3, p. 543).
[17] U.N.C.I.O. Doc. 2, G/26 (f) (*U.N.C.I.O. Docs.*, Vol. 3, p. 618).
[18] U.N.C.I.O. Doc. 323, II/4/12 (*U.N.C.I.O. Docs.*, Vol. 10, p. 677).
[19] See also paragraph 1 of the explanatory note of the draft submitted by the United Kingdom Delegation, which was annexed to the draft (*loc. cit.*).

stressed the primary object as being the welfare of the inhabitants, whilst the French, American and Chinese (Article 2 (a) in each case) stressed the furtherance of international peace and security. All drafts mentioned economic, social, and political advancement with the exception of the United Kingdom's (Article 1 (1)) where the 'political' was missing. Both the United States (Article 2 (b)) and the United Kingdom (Article 1 (11)) put the goal of the Trusteeship System as self-government; the French and Australian drafts did not mention this, whilst the Chinese introduced the phrase, which was later to arouse much controversy, of 'independence or self-government' (Article 2 (b)). It is possible to argue that the United States and United Kingdom considered that 'self-government' might take the form of independence and that therefore it was superfluous to mention the latter specifically, especially as the United Kingdom's draft envisaged 'self-government in forms appropriate to the varying circumstances of each territory.' The Chinese phrase of 'independence or self-government' is a little strange as it is hard to see how the alternative of 'independence' can be achieved without self-government.[20] France (Article 2 (c)), China (Article 2 (c)) and the United States (Article 2 (c)) all mentioned some kind of open-door policy to be pursued in the territories, whilst the United Kingdom's draft (Article 1) merely made some vague references to the fact that due account should be taken of the interests and well-being of other States in economic, social, security and commercial matters. This can be partially explained by the fact that the United Kingdom, as Australia, envisaged these principles and objectives as applying to *all* dependent territories, whereas the other three Powers were thinking only of territories which would be specifically placed under the future Trusteeship System.

20 In its original League context 'self-government' meant democratic self-government. If the same meaning is attributed to self-government in the United Nations Charter, then 'independence or self-government' means independence involving self-government which is not necessarily of a democratic nature, or self-government alone in its democratic sense. However, since by Article 73 (b) of the Charter, all non-self-governing territories are to be guided towards self-government, the achievement of independence by a trust territory *must* also include democratic self-government (see further below, Chap. 4, pp. 57–58, and Chap. 12, p. 237).

Scope of the System

As regards the scope of the application of the Trusteeship System, in accordance with the Yalta Agreement, no mention of actual territories was made. The United States (Article 3), the United Kingdom (Article 2) and China (Article 3) envisaged the System as applying to three categories of territories: former League Mandates, territories detached from the enemy as a result of the Second World War, and any other territory voluntarily placed under the System by the State responsible for its administration. The French draft (Article 3) included only former Mandates and territories detached from the enemy—it made no provision for other dependent areas. The Australian draft, which was much vaguer, did however make provision for other dependent areas. The Australian draft (Article 3) stated that the territories to come under the System were those declared by voluntary action of the administering Power, and those declared by the General Assembly acting upon the basis of the recommendations of a conference composed of colonial Powers.

Method of bringing territories under the System

The United Kingdom's draft did not specify the method of bringing territories under the Trusteeship System. China (Article 5), France (Article 4), and the United States (Article 4), however, considered that this should be accomplished in each case by a trusteeship agreement between the States directly concerned, France and the United States going on to state that these agreements should be subject to approval by the General Assembly or Security Council. The Australian proposals (Article 5) differed somewhat in that they envisaged a trusteeship agreement between the administering authority and the General Assembly, no mention being made of other States which might be concerned. According to this plan, the process of bringing a territory under the Trusteeship System would commence either through voluntary action of the administering Power, or by the General Assembly acting upon the recommendation of a conference of colonial Powers which the United Nations would convene.

Type of administering authority

Neither France nor the United States made any suggestions

as to the type of authority which might undertake administration of a trust territory. The United Kingdom (Article 3) considered that administration should be exercised by advanced nations on behalf of the General Assembly, Australia (Article 4) thought that it should be exercised by a specified Member of the United Nations. China (Article 4) had in mind the plan which was ultimately adopted, that of administration either by the United Nations itself or by one or more Member States.

Obligations of the administering authority

The proposals were unanimous concerning the obligation of the administering authority to make annual reports on its administration, but there were differences of opinion as to whom these reports should be made. The United States (Article 11) and France (Article 11) considered that they should be made to the General Assembly, China (Article 14) to the General Assembly or Security Council, Australia (Article 2) to an expert advisory commission, and the United Kingdom (Article 7) to the Economic and Social Council. Here, one very basic difference between the Australian and United Kingdom proposals on the one hand, and those of the United States, France and China on the other, becomes apparent. The former considered that the special trusteeship body should be an expert commission under the Economic and Social Council, and that it should limit itself to matters of an economic, social and humanitarian nature and have no concern with political affairs. The other States were thinking of a supervisory body under the General Assembly. China, France and the United States were specific about the annual reports and proposed that they should be compiled on the basis of a questionnaire formulated by the Trusteeship Council, China holding that the Security Council should formulate the questionnaire for territories under its authority.

Although the United States, China and France had been the only ones to stress the maintenance of international peace and security as being the basic objective of the Trusteeship System, they made no mention of the obligations of the administering authority of a trust territory in this respect; this matter was dealt with only in the United Kingdom draft (Article 5). According to this, it was to be the duty of the administering Power to ensure that the trust territory played its part in the maintenance of international peace and security; for this purpose, it was to be empowered to make use of local forces and facilities for local defence and for the maintenance of law and order within the territory, as well as for carrying out the administering authority's obligations towards the Security Council. All this was a long way from the non-fortification principle of the Mandates System.[1]

The nature of the Trust Agreement

All the drafts proposed that the terms of the trust should be embodied in some kind of trusteeship agreement. The United Kingdom (Article 4) specified that this agreement should be between the administering authority and the United Nations, while Australia (Article 5) went still further and stated that the agreement should be between the administering authority and the General Assembly. These proposals of both Australia and the United Kingdom did indicate what they meant by 'agreement': it was to be an agreement between the two parties which they specified. This is interesting in view of the fact that the Trusteeship Chapter as written into the Charter—as with the proposals of the other three Powers—gives no definition of what is meant by agreement,[2] using it at one moment to mean the kind of agreement mentioned by the United Kingdom and Australia and at the next moment some kind of understanding between the 'States directly concerned.'

Composition of the Trusteeship Organ

All drafts agreed that there should be a special trusteeship organ. On the question of the composition of this organ, there was a distinct difference of opinion between Australia (Article 2) and the United Kingdom (Article 8) on the one hand, and France (Article 9), China (Article 12) and the United States (Article 9) on the other. The former were thinking of a commission of experts along the lines of the Permanent Mandates Commission

[1] The basic principles of the Mandates System were the 'sacred trust' of colonialism, international accountability, administration for the benefit of the international community, the temporary nature of the 'trust,' non-annexation, tutelage by advanced nations, and military non-exploitation —which included non-fortification of the Mandates. See above, Chap. 1, and G. Schwarzenberger, *Power Politics* (1951), pp. 652–660. pp. 652–660.

[2] See below, Chap. 5, p. 77 *et seq.*

with nothing but advisory functions. The latter envisaged a Council composed of representatives of States rather than experts on the subject, and there was to be equality of representation as between administering Powers and non-administering Powers. China (Article 14) introduced the idea of associating the peoples of the trust territories directly in the work of the United Nations: the Chinese draft proposed that a representative of the people of the trust territory should be entitled to attend meetings of the Trusteeship Council when matters relating to that particular territory were under discussion.

Functions of the United Nations with regard to Trusteeship

In the same way that there was lack of agreement over the kind of trusteeship body which should be established, so there was lack of agreement over the functions which this and other organs of the United Nations would perform with respect to trusteeship. While the United Kingdom and Australia considered that the trusteeship body should have merely advisory functions, the United States, France, and China advocated supervisory functions. In the Australian (Article 2) and United Kingdom (Article 8) view, the trusteeship body would advise the Economic and Social Council on trusteeship matters, while in the views of the United States (Article 10), France (Article 10) and China (Article 13), the trusteeship body would have specific functions to undertake together with and under the authority of the General Assembly and it would also undertake the formulation of the questionnaire. All three drafts thought that the specific functions should include that of examining the reports from the trust territories and of exercising other functions which would be defined in the trust agreements. The United States and Chinese drafts went further in that they empowered the General Assembly and the Trusteeship Council to institute investigations and to accept petitions. These two drafts thus incorporated all the specific functions which were later written into the Charter: these consisted of the receiving and examining of annual reports, the formulation of the questionnaire, the acceptance of petitions, and the dispatch of visiting missions.

The problem of security

Two entirely different methods of dealing with the security

problem were advocated in the five original drafts. The French (Articles 6 and 7), United States (Articles 6 and 7), and Chinese (Articles 8 and 10) drafts proposed two distinct categories of trust territories—strategic and non-strategic. The strategic areas would be designated in the trust agreements and all functions of the United Nations with regard to them would be exercised by the Security Council. Thus any of the five permanent members of the Security Council would have a veto over United Nations action with regard to strategic areas.

A completely different system was proposed in the United Kingdom's draft (Articles 5 and 6) which made no distinction between the different kinds of trust territory. This draft stated that it was the duty of the administering authority to see that the territory played its part in the maintenance of international peace and security. For this purpose and for local defence, the administering authority was to be empowered to make use of local forces, facilities and assistance. At the same time the administering authority was to be required to furnish to the Security Council such information on this as the latter, on the advice of the Military Staff Committee, might require. The United States, French and Chinese method of dealing with the security problem stressed the security element from the point of view of the administering Power, whereas the method adopted by the United Kingdom was concerned with security from the point of view of the international community.

The Australian plan (Articles 6 and 7) tended towards that of the United Kingdom. The requirement of reporting on a trust territory was not to apply to such bases or areas as the General Assembly, on the recommendation of the Security Council, would declare to be specially important for the maintenance of international peace and security. The General Assembly, on the recommendation of the Security Council, might also remove any existing military restrictions on a trust territory which were prejudicial to the security of that territory. Thus, as in the United Kingdom draft, the emphasis on the security element was from the international point of view, the difference being that whereas the United Kingdom envisaged the trust territory as being automatically required to play its part in maintaining international peace and security, the Australian draft envisaged the United Nations making a specific declaration that a certain area was needed for that purpose.

Welfare of the inhabitants

As regards welfare matters in the trust territory, the United Kingdom (Articles 7 and 8) and Australia (Article 2) thought that these things should be the responsibility of the Economic and Social Council, while the other three Powers (Article 11 of Chinese draft, Article 8 of French and United States' draft) thought they should come within the scope of the General Assembly.

Termination of the Trusteeship Status

No proposals were put forward on the question of the termination of a trust. This point was brought up in subsequent discussions on these drafts.

Conclusion

The fundamental difference which emerges from an examination of these five drafts for a trusteeship system is that, while the United Kingdom and Australia had in mind the establishment of a commission under the authority of the Economic and Social Council, the other States were thinking in terms of a special trusteeship organ which would have a status equal to that of the Economic and Social Council, and which would itself make annual reports to the General Assembly as does the Economic and Social Council. To the United Kingdom and Australia, trusteeship was merely one of the social problems with which the United Nations was faced, whereas the other three States saw it as a problem affecting international peace and security.

As has already been mentioned, the Soviet Union presented a paper on trusteeship to the Conference at San Francisco which was officially stated as being an amended form of the United States draft. The United States draft was reproduced in its entirety, the points over which the Soviet Union differed from the United States being indicated at the appropriate places on the draft.[3] For this reason it is unnecessary to comment on the Soviet view with regard to each aspect of trusteeship discussed. Except for the points about to be indicated, it may be assumed that the Soviet Union advocated the same trusteeship provisions as did the United States.

[3] U.N.C.I.O. Doc. 2, G/26 (f) (*U.N.C.I.O. Docs.*, Vol. 3, p. 618).

The main alterations to the American draft which were made by the Soviet Union were as follows: The proposal was introduced that all permanent members of the Security Council should have seats on the special trusteeship organ, whether or not they administered a trust territory (Article 9 (a)). In common with the Chinese proposals, the Soviet Union mentioned 'independence' among the objectives of the trusteeship system Article 2 (b))—'full national independence' being the phrase used. The designation of the administering authority for a trust territory would be a matter of subsequent agreement. On the question of the designation of a strategic area within a trust territory, the Soviet Union put the initiative firmly into the hands of the Security Council: such areas were to be designated on the recommendation of the Security Council (Article 6). On the question of the General Assembly's power to 'institute investigations,' no doubt was left as to what this was to mean: the Soviet amendment stated that it included sending 'representatives and inspectors to the trust territories' (Article 10).

Committee Consideration of the Draft Proposals

The draft proposals were discussed at length in Committee II/4 and several governments presented written observations on them. Comments were made upon the lack of any proposals for the termination of the trusteeship status. Ecuador suggested that the General Assembly should be empowered to declare a trust territory independent under specified conditions,[4] while Venezuela favoured the elaboration of conditions necessary for independence.[5] Serious misgivings concerning the 'open-door' proposals were expressed by the Delegate of the United Kingdom, who held that this principle, which had been applicable to all B Mandates, had not always operated to the benefit of the dependent peoples concerned. At the same time he warned against applying the trusteeship system compulsorily to existing colonies since this would amount to interference in the internal affairs of Member States.[6] The Delegate of France voiced similar

[4] U.N.C.I.O. Doc. 2, G/7 (p), p. 12 (*U.N.C.I.O. Docs.*, Vol. 3, p. 393 at p. 405).

[5] U.N.C.I.O. Doc. 2, G/7 (d) (1), p. 34 (*U.N.C.I.O. Docs.*, Vol. 3, p. 189 at p. 222).

[6] See *Summary of Fourth Meeting of Committee* II/4 (*U.N.C.I.O. Docs.*, Vol. 10, p. 439).

fears.[7] The Soviet Delegate seized upon a phrase which was subsequently to cause much dispute in the United Nations[8]: he suggested that the 'States directly concerned' in the trust agreements should be more precisely defined.[9]

On the basis of the general discussion in the Committee and of the draft proposals which had been submitted to the Conference, the United States Delegation presented a Working Paper to the Committee as requested by the Chairman. This had been prepared under the direction of Commander Harold Stassen and was accepted by Committee II/4 as a basis for drafting the provisions for an international trusteeship system.

The Working Paper[10]

The Working Paper presented to Committee II/4 was divided into two parts. Section A was taken from the Australian-United Kingdom proposals and consisted of a statement of general policy to be adopted by Member States towards their dependent territories.[11] The wording followed closely that found in the original United Kingdom draft. Section B, entitled 'Territorial Trusteeship System,' bore great similarity to the original United States draft, particularly as regards the nature of the special trusteeship organ and the method of dealing with the security factor. It is this section which provided the basis for the International Trusteeship System as found in the Charter in Chapters XII and XIII and which therefore requires examination.

The basic objectives of the system followed the pattern set down in the original United States proposals although the wording was slightly altered. These objectives comprised the furtherance of international peace and security, the political, economic and social advancement of the trust territory and its inhabitants towards the goal of self-government—no mention was made of educational advancement, and the maintenance of the 'open-door' in the trust territory.

The system was to apply to three kinds of territories: Mandates, ex-enemy territories, and territories voluntarily placed

7 See *Summary Report of Third Meeting of Committee* II/4 (*U.N.C.I.O. Docs.*, Vol. 10, p. 433).
8 See below, Chap. 5, p. 80 *et seq.*
9 See *Summary of Fourth Meeting of Committee* II/4 (*loc. cit.*).
10 U.N.C.I.O. Doc. 323, II/4/12, May 15, 1945 (*U.N.C.I.O. Docs.*, Vol. 10, p. 677).
11 This became Chapter XI of the Charter.

under the system by the administering State. Two limitations, however, were to operate. The system would apply only to such territories as were brought thereunder by means of subsequent trusteeship agreements, and it would not apply to territories which had become Members of the United Nations.

Territories would be brought under the system by means of trusteeship agreements which would be agreed upon by the States directly concerned and approved by the Security Council or General Assembly. At this point a conservatory clause was introduced which had not appeared in any of the original draft proposals. This was to the effect that nothing in the trusteeship provisions of the Charter should be interpreted as altering the rights of any State or people in any territory, except as might be agreed on in the trust agreements. This provision was aimed at protecting the rights of the Mandatory and of any other States or people with an interest in the mandated territories. It was subsequently made use of with regard to South-West Africa, when the Union of South Africa claimed that the trusteeship provisions of the Charter could not be held to alter the rights which she had enjoyed under the Mandate—rights which included administering South-West Africa as an integral part of the Union.[12]

There was provision for a single State or for the United Nations itself to become the administering authority but not for any form of joint administration. The administering authority was to be obligated to present an annual report to the General Assembly upon the basis of a questionnaire drawn up by the Trusteeship Council. The trust agreements were to include the terms under which the territories were to be administered.

The Australian-United Kingdom conception of an expert advisory trusteeship body was rejected in favour of a supervisory political organ which was to operate under the authority of the General Assembly. This organ was to have equality of representation as between administering and elected non-administering States. The Soviet demand for the automatic representation of all the five permanent members of the Security Council had not yet been met. The functions of the General Assembly,

[12] This conservatory clause was also important during the Palestine discussions in the General Assembly. See *Official Records of the General Assembly,* Second Session, Supplement No. 11, Vol. 3, p. 66; *Official Records of the General Assembly,* First Special Session, Vol. 1, pp. 70, 107, 109; *ibid.,* Vol. 2, p. 108; *ibid.,* Vol. 3, pp. 110, 195.

and under its authority the Trusteeship Council, were to include the consideration of annual reports, the acceptance and examination of petitions, and the carrying out of periodic visits to the trust territories. This last function of conducting visits was stated in more specific terms than in the original United States proposals.

As regards the security factor, the method proposed for dealing with it was that put forward by the United States, France, and China in their original drafts. At the same time attention had been paid to the British idea that the trust territories should be made to play their full part in the maintenance of international peace and security. There was to be a distinction between strategic and non-strategic areas, the former were to be designated in the trust agreements and were to come under the control of the Security Council rather than the General Assembly. In dealing with strategic areas, the Security Council was to have the right to avail itself of the assistance of the Trusteeship Council as the General Assembly did for non-strategic areas, the difference being that for the Security Council it was a permissive right while for the General Assembly it was mandatory. In accordance with the British draft proposals, the administering authority was to be permitted to employ local volunteer forces, assistance and facilities, for carrying out its obligations towards the Security Council, for the maintenance of law and order in the trust territory and for local defence.

As with all the original draft proposals, no mention was made of the termination of a trust.

Discussions on the Working Paper

Discussions in Committee II/4 proceeded on the basis of the Working Paper which was examined and amended article by article. Although these discussions resulted in many changes in the wording of the Working Paper, its form and content remained basically the same. During the general discussion, many delegations expressed their views and fears on the whole question of a trusteeship system. The French expressed concern lest the system result in interference in the domestic affairs of any State, and subsequently a special statement by the Delegation of France was annexed to the Report of the Rapporteur of Committee II/4.[13] According to this statement, none of the

13 U.N.C.I.O. Doc. 1115, Annex D (*U.N.C.I.O. Docs.*, Vol. 10, p. 622).

provisions adopted by the Committee for a trusteeship system implied a renunciation of the right of the French Government to invoke the 'domestic jurisdiction' clause which was being adopted in another section of the Charter.

The South African Delegate stressed his view that the terms of existing Mandates could not be altered in any way without the consent of the existing Mandatory Power.[14]

The Soviet Delegate was anxious that the aims of the trusteeship system should include 'self-determination of peoples,' and that all the permanent members of the Security Council should be represented on the Trusteeship Council.[15]

The Guatemalan Delegation proposed that the trusteeship system should not apply to any territory which was the subject of litigation between States,[16] a proposal which was not accepted. The proposal was due to the dispute which Guatemala had with the United Kingdom over the title to the territory of British Honduras (Belize).

Many Delegates commented on the lack of provision in the Working Paper for the termination of the trusteeship status, and they tried unsuccessfully to have such provisions inserted. The Egyptian Delegation was in favour of giving the General Assembly the power to terminate the trusteeship status and declare a territory independent. At the same time the Egyptian Delegation expressed a desire that there be some provision for the transfer of a trust territory to another administering authority should the original administering State violate the terms of the trust agreement, cease to be a Member of the United Nations, or have its Membership suspended.[17] Had such provisions been adopted, it would have been difficult subsequently to have appointed non-Member Italy as an administering authority. Lengthy discussions on the points raised by the Egyptian Delegation ensued, with the result that the Chairman of the Committee asked the United States and United Kingdom Delegates to prepare an authoritative statement on the matter, which was

[14] See *Summary of Fourth Meeting of Committee II/4* (*U.N.C.I.O. Docs.*, Vol. 10, p. 439).
[15] *ibid.*
[16] Amendment proposed by the Delegation of Guatemala, Doc. 386, II/4/15 (*U.N.C.I.O. Docs.*, Vol. 10, p. 463).
[17] See *Summary Report of Fourteenth Meeting of Committee II/4* (*U.N.C.I.O. Docs.*, Vol. 10, p. 543).

then annexed to the Rapporteur's Report.[18] The main theme of this statement was that the action to be taken against an administering Power who committed an act of aggression, violated its trust, or withdrew from the United Nations, could only be decided 'at the time and in the light of all relevant circumstances.' According to this, there was no reason why the system of annual reports, petitions and visiting missions could not continue and the administering Power be permitted to attend meetings of the Trusteeship Council.[19]

The Main Alterations to the Working Paper

The discussions in Committee II/4 resulted in a set of draft proposals which were finally recommended to Commission II. These draft proposals embodied several changes to the provisions of the Working Paper. One was the inclusion of independence as an alternative goal to self-government among the objectives of the trusteeship system. This change was the result of compromise: the Chinese Delegation had proposed the insertion of the goal of independence into the statement of general principles for all dependent territories, both trust and other non-self-governing territories.[20] This proposal was finally withdrawn on the understanding that it would be included among the objectives of the trusteeship system. A further alteration in the objectives of the trusteeship system was the addition of the 'educational advancement of the inhabitants of the trust territories' to the provisions existing for political, economic and social advancement. Finally, a completely new paragraph was added to the proposed article on the objectives of the trusteeship system. This was 'to encourage respect for human rights' and fundamental freedoms on the basis of non-discrimination, and to 'encourage recognition of the interdependence of the peoples of the world.' In addition, a slight clarification of the meaning of the 'States directly concerned' was made to the extent that it was to include the Mandatory Power in the case of territories held under Mandate by one of the Members of the United Nations.

Two changes were made to the provisions concerning the Trusteeship Council. Firstly, it was to include all the permanent

18 U.N.C.I.O. Doc. 1115, Annex C (*U.N.C.I.O. Docs.*, Vol. 10, p. 620).
19 See below, Chap. 11, p. 206 *et seq.*
20 See Journal of the Conference for June 1, 1945 (*U.N.C.I.O. Docs.*, Vol. 2, p. 111).

Members of the Security Council, whether or not they administered any trust territories; and secondly, it was to be recommended to Committee I/2 that the Trusteeship Council be included among the principal organs of the United Nations and be so designated in the Charter. With regard to strategic trust areas, the provisions were altered to include the approval of the strategic trusteeship arrangements and their alteration or amendment within the powers of the Security Council.

A few changes in wording were made in these proposals after they were presented to Commission II by Committee II/4, but the provisions that were finally approved and became part of the United Nations Charter were the same in essence.

The Establishment of the Trusteeship System

The Charter entered into force on October 24, 1945, but not so the operation of the International Trusteeship System. This section of the Charter required the conclusion of trusteeship agreements before it could come into operation. The International Trusteeship System was to be concerned only with trust territories, and, until the agreements were drawn up and approved, no trust territories existed. Apart from this, the special organ of the International Trusteeship System, the Trusteeship Council, was to be composed of an equal number of administering and non-administering Members, including all the permanent members of the Security Council: therefore it was necessary for sufficient trust agreements to be in operation to enable the Trusteeship Council to be established with the specified membership. This fact was noted with concern by the Preparatory Commission of the United Nations when it met to deal with interim arrangements of the United Nations. Its Executive Committee recommended the establishment of a Temporary Trusteeship Council which would carry out the functions specified in the Charter and would help in speeding the conclusion of trusteeship agreements. This proposal met violent opposition from the representatives of the Soviet Union, Byelo-Russia and the Ukraine, who contended that such a course was not mentioned in the Charter and would therefore be unconstitutional.[1]

As a result the matter was not pursued. However, this con-

[1] United Nations, *Official Records of the Preparatory Commission,* Committee 4, November 24–December 24, 1945, pp. 3–4, 6, 10.

troversy marked the beginning of the East-West split in the United Nations over the question of trusteeship.

The Trusteeship System finally came into being at the Second Part of the First Session of the General Assembly in December 1946, following the approval of eight trust agreements; immediately thereon, the Trusteeship Council was established.

The establishment of the Trusteeship Council was held to be illegal by the Soviet Union, on the grounds that the trust agreements approved by the General Assembly were not in conformity with the Charter.[2] The Soviet Union held that they violated the Charter on three matters: the 'States directly concerned' had not been defined, and therefore Article 79, requiring the 'States directly concerned' to agree on the terms of trusteeship, had not been complied with[3]; the provisions in the agreements allowing for the administration of the territories as an integral part of the territories of the administering authorities amounted to annexation, therefore they were contrary to Article 76 (b) which required development towards self-government: the draft agreements permitted the establishment of military bases in the trust territories without the Security Council's consent, which was contrary to Article 83 of the Charter. For these reasons the Soviet Union held that in approving the agreements the General Assembly was acting illegally, and the Trusteeship Council could not be established on the basis of illegally approved agreements.

However, in the Report of the Rapporteur of Committee IV/2 at San Francisco, it was stated that 'in the course of the operation from day to day of the various organs of the Organisation, it is inevitable that each organ will interpret such parts of the Charter as are applicable to its particular functions.'[4] In exercising its function of approving the trust agreements, the General Assembly was thus entitled to interpret the provisions of Article 79 of the Charter so far as they concerned that organ. In approving the trust agreements, the General Assembly was establishing that they were legal, and since the General Assembly itself was the competent organ to undertake this approval, its own action in approving the agreements was legal.

[2] See *Official Records of the General Assembly*, Second Part of the First Session, Plenary Meetings, pp. 1276–1283.
[3] See below, Chap. 5, p. 80 *et seq*.
[4] *U.N.C.I.O. Docs.*, Vol. 13, p. 700. Committee IV/2 was concerned with legal problems.

PART TWO

SCOPE AND AIMS OF THE TRUSTEESHIP SYSTEM

CHAPTER 3

TERRITORIES SUBJECT TO THE TRUSTEESHIP SYSTEM

THE Trusteeship System applies only to such territories as are specifically brought thereunder by means of trusteeship agreements.[1] Until such agreements are concluded, the territories in question remain subject only to the more limited provisions of Chapter XI of the Charter, which apply to all non-self-governing territories. Thus, the Trusteeship System does not apply automatically to any territory, and the provisions of Chapters XII and XIII of the Charter are not brought into operation until and unless a trust agreement is concluded.[2]

Three categories of territories are eligible for trusteeship: former Mandates, ex-enemy territories, and 'territories voluntarily placed under the system by states responsible for their administration.'[3] Only territories within the first two categories have so far been placed under the Trusteeship System, and the majority of these have been former Mandates.[4] Thus, although the Trusteeship System is theoretically of wider application than the Mandates System,[5] in that it makes provision for any dependent territory to be brought under it, in practice this has been of no importance. The use of the word 'voluntarily' in category (c) of territories eligible for trusteeship has clearly ruled out any interpretation of legal compulsion, although it has been suggested in the General Assembly that a moral obligation exists to make

[1] Article 77 (1) of the Charter.

[2] See Advisory Opinion of the International Court of Justice on the *International Status of South-West Africa* (1950) (*I.C.J. Reports 1950*, pp. 138–139).

[3] Article 77, paragraphs 1 (a), 1 (b), and 1 (c).

[4] The only offer to place a territory in the third category under trusteeship came from the United Kingdom, who, at one stage in the discussions over the disposal of the former Italian territories, offered to place British Somaliland under trusteeship. It was proposed that Italian Somaliland should be placed under trusteeship with the United Kingdom as administering authority, and for this purpose British Somaliland would be united with Italian Somaliland to form a single trust territory. Nothing came of this proposal (see *Official Records of the General Assembly*, Second Part of the First Session, Fourth Committee, Part 3, p. 40).

[5] The Mandates System applied only to ex-enemy territories.

this provision a reality.[6] In the case of the former Mandates, all those which have not achieved independence, either before the inauguration of the Trusteeship System or subsequently, have been brought under the System, with the exception of South-West Africa. Only one ex-enemy territory has been placed under trusteeship, and this has been accorded the rather odd treatment of being given its old ruler as administering authority. However, political considerations, which were not anticipated at San Francisco, were responsible for the selection of Italy to be the administering authority for Somaliland.[7]

The eligibility for trusteeship of territories within the three categories mentioned is subject to the limitation that such territories must not be Members of the United Nations.[8] Since, to be eligible for membership in the United Nations a territory must be a State according to the Charter,[9] and, it appears, a sovereign State,[10] this limitation would seem to be superfluous. However, in actual fact there were Members of the United Nations in 1945 which were not sovereign States. India and the Philippine Republic were original Members of the Organisation although they did not obtain their complete independence until 1947 and 1946 respectively; the same was true of Syria and the Lebanon, in which cases the Mandate treaties with France had not been terminated, and of the Ukraine and Byelo-Russia. Thus Article 78 served to protect these political entities which were not sovereign States, in that it ruled out the possibility of States responsible for their administration submitting trust agreements for them.

It might be questioned whether only non-self-governing territories are eligible for trusteeship inasmuch as this is not specifically

[6] India argued that it was the clear intention of the Charter that the System should apply to other non-self-governing territories besides former Mandates (see *Official Records of the General Assembly*, Second Session, Fourth Committee, Annex 5a, pp. 217–218; and 106th Plenary Meeting, pp. 655–657).

[7] See further, G. Schwarzenberger, *Power Politics* (1951), pp. 407–411.

[8] Article 78.

[9] Article 3 states that 'the original Members of the United Nations shall be the states which . . . ,' and Article 4 says that 'Membership in the United Nations is open to all other peace-loving states . . .' Thus, according to the Charter, *all* Members of the United Nations must be States—both original Members and those subsequently admitted to Membership.

[10] Article 2 (1): 'The Organisation is based on the principle of the sovereign equality of all its Members.'

stated in Article 77. Whilst States which have become Members of the United Nations are excluded from trusteeship by Article 78, there is no similar provision to exclude non-Member States. However, two considerations would rule out this possibility: a State, by definition, must be self-governing and independent, and since trusteeship is an intermediary stage towards this end,[11] the final goal of the Trusteeship System could not be applied to a State.[12] In addition, a territory other than a former Mandate or ex-enemy territory must be placed under the System by the State responsible for its administration, which would amount to a State placing itself under trusteeship and thus voluntarily surrendering its sovereignty—an improbable if not impossible event. Whilst it would appear that only a non-self-governing territory is eligible for trusteeship, the territory need not have been always non-self-governing: it need only be non-self-governing at the time when it is submitted to trusteeship. Thus, when Germany came under the control of the Allied Powers in 1945, it would have been legally possible for them to have submitted all or part of German territory to United Nations trusteeship, since Germany as a State had ceased to exist and with the signing of the Instrument of Surrender had become non-self-governing.[13]

[11] During discussions in the Trusteeship Council over a Statute for the City of Jerusalem, the Iraqi Delegate held that permanent trusteeship for the City would be illegal since trusteeship was an intermediary stage leading to self-government (*Official Records of the Trusteeship Council*, Second Session, 46th Meeting). In the case of a State, this intermediary stage could not apply since the State is already self-governing.

[12] According to Article 76 (b), the final goal of the Trusteeship System is 'self-government or independence.' It could be argued that by definition a State may, by treaty, limit or destroy its self-government or independence and then submit to trusteeship. Two points arise. Firstly, the entity in question would no longer be a State at the time of its submission to Trusteeship. Secondly, it would make a farce of the Trusteeship System for a State to extinguish its independence or self-government in order to submit to a System the professed aim of which is to develop these very things.

[13] 'By the impetus of the war effort of the United Nations, Germany had broken down, its government had disintegrated and Germany ceased to exist as a subject of international law' (G. Schwarzenberger, *International Law*, Vol. 1, (1949), p. 142). 'By abolishing the last Government of Germany the victorious powers have destroyed the existence of Germany as a sovereign state. Since her unconditional surrender, at least since the abolishment of the Doenitz Government, Germany has ceased to exist as a state in the sense of international law' (H. Kelsen, *The Legal Status of Germany According to the Declaration of Berlin*, 39 *American Journal of International Law*, 1949, pp. 518–526 at p. 519). 'The Declaration of Berlin . . . means that a so-called *deballatio* of Germany has taken place' (*ibid.*, p. 520). For an opposite view, see the opinion of the British Foreign Office, upheld by the Court

Voluntary Nature of Trusteeship

There was a great deal of discussion in the General Assembly over the question whether there existed any compulsion to bring certain or all territories mentioned in Article 77 under the Trusteeship System. This is clearly ruled out in the case of category (c) where the placing of such territories under trusteeship is specified as being voluntary. It is not stated in Article 77 whether the placing of territories in the other categories under trusteeship is compulsory or voluntary.[14] The question arose in the General Assembly over the case of South-West Africa. During the First Part of the First Session of the General Assembly, a resolution was adopted inviting States administering former Mandates to draw up trusteeship agreements for submission to the United Nations.[15] In due course, trust agreements were submitted to the General Assembly or Security Council, as the case might be. There were, however, two exceptions: Palestine and South-West Africa. For the former, the United Kingdom Government requested the Secretary-General to place the question of the future of Palestine on the agenda of the next session of the General Assembly and in the meantime the Government would submit a report on its administration to the General Assembly for its consideration. Palestine was subsequently partitioned and two independent States emerged, one of which is now a Member of the United Nations. This left South-West Africa as the only remaining Mandate.

At the Second Part of the First Session of the General Assembly, the Union of South Africa submitted a proposal to the effect that the territory of South-West Africa be incorporated into the Union. Although the Union Government did not press

of Appeal in the case of *R.* v. *Bottrill, ex p. Kuechenmeister* [1947] 1 K.B. 41. In upholding the decision of a Divisional Court, the Court of Appeal accepted as conclusive the certificate of the Secretary of State for Foreign Affairs to the effect that, in consequence of the declaration of the unconditional surrender of Germany, 'Germany still exists as a State and German nationality as a nationality.'

14 But see the opinion of Mr. Huntington Gilchrist, Executive Officer of Commission II (dealing with the General Assembly) at San Francisco and formerly Assistant Director of the League of Nations Mandates Section, who, in an article entitled *Colonial Questions at the San Francisco Conference,* said of the Trusteeship System that 'its first characteristic is that it is voluntary' (39 *American Political Science Review,* October 1945, pp. 982–992).

15 *Resolutions adopted by the General Assembly during the First Part of its First Session, Resolution* 9 (I), p. 13.

its point at this time, the proposal unleashed a controversy which was to occupy a great deal of the General Assembly's time. The subject of the controversy was whether or not it was compulsory to bring any territories under the Trusteeship System. It was argued that since the voluntary aspect was mentioned only with regard to the third category of Article 77, it must therefore be compulsory to bring territories in the other two categories under trusteeship.[16] This view was so generally held that it was possible for the General Assembly's Fourth Committee to adopt a resolution holding that it was 'the clear intention of Chapter XII of the Charter of the United Nations that all territories previously held under Mandate, until granted self-government or independence, shall be brought under the trusteeship system.'[17] This, however, did not appear in the resolution which the General Assembly meeting in plenary session finally approved. This resolution merely expressed the hope that the Union of South Africa would submit a trusteeship agreement to the next session of the General Assembly.[18] The Union Government clung throughout to its original contention that nothing in the Charter could be held to establish that a government was compelled to place a territory under trusteeship.[19] The conservatory clause in Article 80 (1) would support this contention when it states that 'nothing in this Charter shall be construed in or of itself to alter in any manner the rights whatsoever of any states or any peoples or the terms of existing international instruments to which Members of the United Nations may respectively be parties.' As the United States pointed out at San Francisco, the effect of this clause was to establish that rights under existing international instruments were neither increased nor diminished

[16] See the views of the Haitian and Chinese Delegates to the General Assembly (*Official Records of the General Assembly,* Second Session, 105th Plenary Meeting, pp. 608, 601).

[17] *Official Records of the General Assembly,* Second Session, Plenary Meetings, Vol. 2, p. 1541. See also the view of the Soviet Delegate to the Trusteeship Council, who held that there existed only two alternatives to deal with the former mandated territory of South-West Africa: either it should be declared independent or it should be placed under trusteeship (*Official Records of the Trusteeship Council,* Third Session, 31st Meeting, Doc. T/P.V. 104, p. 17).

[18] *Official Records of the General Assembly,* Second Session, Resolution 141 (II), p. 47 (Doc. A/519).

[19] See *Official Records of the General Assembly,* Second Part of the First Session, Fourth Committee, Part 3: Summary Records of Meetings of Sub-Committee 2, p. 55.

by the United Nations Charter.[20] Thus the Union Government was neither obliged to present a trust agreement for South-West Africa nor was she permitted to abrogate the Mandate treaty by proceeding with the incorporation of the territory into the Union of South Africa. It would appear that the use of 'voluntarily' in category (c) was not to imply compulsion in the other two, but rather it was a case of including the word for extra emphasis and in order to reassure the colonial powers. This interpretation is supported by the Advisory Opinion of the International Court of Justice on the *International Status of South-West Africa* (1950).[1]

The wording of the preamble to Article 77 (1) certainly does not suggest that it is obligatory for all territories in any category to be placed under trusteeship. It merely says that 'the trusteeship system shall apply to *such* territories in the following categories as *may* be placed thereunder by means of trusteeship agreements.'[2] If it was meant to impose a positive obligation on the administering powers to place territories under trusteeship, 'such' and 'as may be' should have been omitted from the article. Furthermore, paragraph 2 of Article 77 states that 'it will be a matter for subsequent agreement as to *which* territories in the foregoing *categories* will be brought under the trusteeship system and upon what terms . . .'[3] It does not say that it will be a matter for subsequent agreement as to which territories in *category* (*c*) will be brought under the System.

The proceedings of the San Francisco Conference do not indicate that it was the intention of the drafters of the Charter to create a compulsory Trusteeship System. In Committee II/4, the Delegate of Egypt proposed the deletion of 'such territories

20 See U.N.C.I.O. Doc. 580, p. 2, *Summary Report of Tenth Meeting of Committee II/4* (*U.N.C.I.O. Docs.*, Vol. 10, p. 486). See also *Report of the Rapporteur of Committee II/4*, Doc. 1115, p. 5 (*U.N.C.I.O. Docs.*, Vol. 10, p. 611). The importance of this conservatory clause is for purposes of interpreting the Charter provisions where such are not clear. In the case where a provision of the Charter quite clearly increases or diminishes the rights of Members under another international instrument, the Charter provisions over-rule the other by Article 103 (Article 103 reads: 'In the event of a conflict between the obligations of the Members of the United Nations under the present Charter and their obligations under any other international agreement, their obligations under the present Charter shall prevail.'

1 *I.C.J. Reports 1950*, p. 139.

2 Italics added.

3 Italics added.

in the following categories as may be placed thereunder by means of trusteeship arrangements' from the provisions of the Working Paper, so that the preamble to the future Article 77 (1) would read as follows: 'The Trusteeship System shall apply to:' The Egyptian Delegate went on to suggest the insertion of 'all' into paragraph (a) so that this would read: 'all territories now held under mandate.'[4] Had these proposals been adopted, they would have established a clear obligation on the part of the Mandatory Powers to place all Mandates under trusteeship. The proposals were rejected by Committee II/4, and among the objections to them put forward by other Delegates was that they would have the effect of creating a compulsory system and would thus go beyond the competence of the San Francisco Conference.[5]

That the placing of a territory under trusteeship is not compulsory has now been determined by the Advisory Opinion of the International Court of Justice on the *International Status of South-West Africa* (1950). The Court was of the opinion that the Charter did not impose an obligation on the Union of South Africa to place South-West Africa under the Trusteeship System. It considered that the language used in Articles 75 and 77 was permissive. 'Both refer to subsequent agreements by which the territories in question may be placed under the Trusteeship System. An "agreement" implies consent of the parties concerned, including the mandatory Power in the case of territories held under Mandate (Article 79). The parties must be free to accept or reject the terms of the contemplated agreement. No party can impose its terms on the other party. Article 77, paragraph 2, moreover, presupposes agreement not only with regard to its particular terms, but also as to which territories will be brought under the Trusteeship System.'[6] What can be held to apply in the case of South-West Africa, applies similarly to all other territories which fall within categories (a) and (b) of Article 77.

[4] See *Summary Report of the Eighth Meeting of Committee II/4,* Doc. 512, II/4/21 (*U.N.C.I.O. Docs.,* Vol. 10, pp. 468–469).
[5] *ibid.*
[6] *International Status of South-West Africa,* Advisory Opinion: *I.C.J. Reports 1950,* p. 128 at p. 139.

Mandates under the United Nations

The problem of deciding to which territories the System was to apply did not face the League of Nations with regard to the Mandates System. The Covenant made provision only for ex-enemy territories to be placed under trusteeship and the task of allocating these territories to an administering Power was undertaken by the Allied Supreme Council. Thus each territory in question was handed over to its administering Power for the express purpose of being administered as a Mandate; there could be no question as to whether or not the administering Power was bound to administer the territory as a Mandate. Furthermore, the territories had already been allocated by the time the League Covenant came into force; all that remained was for the League Council to inform the Mandatory of its having been charged with the responsibility of the administration of the Mandate, and thereupon for the terms of the Mandate to be decided upon. Thus the possibility which the Soviet Delegate pointed out with regard to the Trusteeship System, that 'a situation might arise under which no country would place its territory under trusteeship,'[7] did not arise in the case of the Mandates System.

The fact that the International Court of Justice settled that there is no compulsion to place a former Mandate under the United Nations Trusteeship System,[8] revealed a serious gap in the provisions of the Charter. There was no system to supervise those Mandates which had not been terminated either through being declared independent or through being placed under the Trusteeship System voluntarily. At the last meeting of the Assembly of the League of Nations on April 18, 1946, a resolution was adopted recognising that the League's functions with regard to Mandates would cease upon the termination of the League itself. It noted that Members of the League still administering Mandates had expressed the intention of continuing to administer them in accordance with the terms of the respective Mandate treaties 'until other arrangements have been agreed between the United Nations and the respective mandatory

[7] *Official Records of the General Assembly,* Second Part of the First Session, Fourth Committee, Part 1, p. 188.

[8] *International Status of South-West Africa,* Advisory Opinion: *I.C.J. Reports 1950,* p. 128.

Powers.'[9] No machinery was suggested to supervise the Mandates until those 'other arrangements' should be concluded, and indeed the resolution did not consider what should happen if 'other arrangements' were *never* concluded. All it did was to recognise that the Trusteeship System did not automatically apply to the Mandates, but that arrangements would have to be made between the United Nations and the respective Mandatory Powers in order to bring the territories under the Trusteeship System. The League Assembly's resolution did recognise that a Mandate could be terminated through agreement between the United Nations and the Mandatory on other arrangements,[10] but it did not specify that these other arrangements had to take the form of a trust agreement. Presumably these arrangements could provide for the annexation of the territory by the Mandatory Power. However, should no arrangements be agreed upon between the United Nations and the Mandatory, there is no authority in the League Assembly's resolution for the unilateral termination of the Mandate. Moreover, the Advisory Opinion of the International Court of Justice on the *International Status of South-West Africa* (1950), specifically rejected the idea of the unilateral alteration of the Mandate. 'The international status of the Territory results from the international rules regulating the rights, powers and obligations relating to the administration of the Territory and the supervision of that administration, as embodied in Article 22 of the Covenant and in the Mandate. It is clear that the Union has no competence to modify unilaterally the international status of the territory or any of these international rules.'[11]

There is nothing in the United Nations Charter which could be held to authorise the unilateral termination of a League of Nations Mandate, in fact the idea is specifically rejected. Article 80, paragraph 1, says that 'nothing in this Chapter [Chapter XII] shall be construed in or of itself to alter in any manner the rights whatsoever of any states or any peoples or the terms of existing international instruments to which Members of the

[9] League of Nations Doc. A.33 (1946), p. 6. See paragraph 4 of the resolution on Mandates adopted by the Assembly on April 18, 1946 (League of Nations: *Official Journal* (Special Supplement 194); Records of the 20th (conclusion) and 21st ordinary sessions of the Assembly, p. 58).

[10] *ibid.*

[11] *I.C.J. Reports 1950*, p. 141.

United Nations may respectively be parties.' The parties to the Mandates treaties, the Principal Allied and Associated Powers, have rights under the Mandates.[12] Moreover, each of the Mandate treaties included the provision that 'the consent of the Council of the League of Nations is required for any modification of the terms of this mandate.'[13] Bearing in mind this provision, the International Court argued that since the League Council was the same organ as exercised supervision over the Mandates, and since, in the case of the United Nations, the General Assembly is the supervisory organ and the organ which approves the trusteeship agreements and any subsequent alterations of them, it can be inferred by analogy that the consent of the General Assembly is required for any alteration of the Mandate treaty.[14] The Court was of the opinion that 'the competence to determine and modify the international status of the Territory rests with the Union of South Africa acting with the consent of the United Nations.'[15]

For those Mandates which are not terminated by independence or by the conclusion of a trusteeship agreement, the question arises as to how supervision is to be exercised over them. Under the Mandates System the main method of supervising the Mandates was through the receipt and examination of annual reports from the Mandatory Powers. These reports were received by the League Council who then handed them over to the Permanent Mandates Commission for examination. After the dissolution of the League, the problem was to find a successor for these tasks. With regard to the Mandated territory of Palestine, the United Kingdom Government stated that it would submit its annual report on this territory to the General Assembly.[16] Although this was done in connection with the United Kingdom's declaration that it intended placing the whole question of the future of Palestine in the hands of the General Assembly, it was

12 The Union of South Africa has offered to negotiate with the three remaining Principal Allied and Associated Powers on the South-West Africa question (see Report to the General Assembly of the *ad hoc* Committee on South-West Africa, Doc. A/1901, October 8, 1951, p. 6).

13 Article 7 of the Mandate for South-West Africa (see United Nations Doc. A/70, *Terms of League of Nations Mandates*). The exact wording of this clause varies in some of the Mandate treaties.

14 *I.C.J. Reports 1950*, pp. 141–142.

15 *ibid.*, p. 144.

16 *Official Records of the General Assembly*, First Special Session, Vol. 1, Plenary Meetings, p. 183 (Doc. A/286).

at the same time a recognition of the General Assembly's succession to the League's functions with regard to annual reports from mandated territories.

The Union of South Africa presented its report on the administration of South-West Africa during 1946 to the General Assembly, who then handed it over to the Trusteeship Council for examination. The legality of this action of the General Assembly may be questioned, for, as the Soviet Delegate to the Trusteeship Council pointed out, the Trusteeship Council is authorised to examine reports only under Article 87 (a) of the Charter. This paragraph authorises the examination of reports from trust territories and from no others.[17] There is no authority for the Trusteeship Council to examine a report from any other non-self-governing territory, indeed to do so would be to assimilate that territory into the Trusteeship System without having complied with the legal requirements of Chapter XII. The only remaining body of the United Nations which could be considered competent to examine a report from a Mandate is the General Assembly itself, which derives this competence from Article 10 of the Charter.[18] With respect to the Mandate for South-West Africa, the International Court of Justice was of the opinion that 'the General Assembly of the United Nations is legally qualified to exercise the supervisory functions previously exercised by the League of Nations with regard to the administration of the Territory, and that the Union of South Africa is under an obligation to submit to supervision and control of the General Assembly and to render annual reports to it.'[19]

The Advisory Opinion of the International Court on the *International Status of South-West Africa* (1950) was adopted by the General Assembly on December 13, 1950,[20] and thereupon an *ad hoc* Committee of Five was established 'to confer with the Union of South Africa concerning the procedural measures necessary for implementing the advisory opinion of the Inter-

[17] See Report of the Trusteeship Council covering its Second and Third Sessions (*Official Records of the General Assembly,* Third Session, Supplement No. 4, p. 42).

[18] 'The competence of the General Assembly of the United Nations to exercise such supervision and to receive and examine reports is derived from the provisions of Article 10 of the Charter' (*International Status of South-West Africa,* Advisory Opinion: *I.C.J. Reports 1950,* p. 137).

[19] *I.C.J. Reports 1950,* p. 137.

[20] *Official Records of the General Assembly,* Fifth Session, Resolution 449 (V), A.

national Court of Justice.'[1] At the same time the *ad hoc* Committee was authorised 'to examine the report on the administration of the territory of South-West Africa covering the period since the last report, as well as petitions and any other matters relating to the territory that may be transmitted to the Secretary-General.'[2] The negotiations between the Committee and the Union of South Africa, however, proved unsuccessful.

In 1953,[3] the General Assembly established a Committee on South-West Africa and authorised it to exercise the same supervisory functions as the *ad hoc* Committee, with the important proviso that such supervision should, as far as possible, be in accordance with the procedure of the League Mandates System. In particular, the information and documentation examined must be within the scope of the Permanent Mandates Commission's Questionnaire of 1926. The Committee on South-West Africa was also asked to 'prepare for the consideration of the General Assembly, a procedure for the examination of reports and petitions which should conform as far as possible to the procedure followed in this respect by the Assembly, the Council and the Permanent Mandates Commission of the League of Nations.'[4] Two sets of rules were prepared, one set forming the Committee's Rules of Procedure for the examination of reports and petitions relating to South-West Africa,[5] the other prescribing the procedure to be followed by the General Assembly in its consideration of the reports and observations of the Committee on South-West Africa. This latter set of Rules was adopted by the General Assembly on October 11, 1954.[6] Amongst these Rules was Rule F which provided that 'decisions of the General Assembly on questions relating to reports and petitions concerning the Territory of South-West Africa shall be regarded as important questions within the meaning of Article 18, paragraph 2, of the Charter of the United Nations.' Thus decisions of the General

[1] *ibid.*, paragraph 3.
[2] *ibid.*, paragraph 4.
[3] *Official Records of the General Assembly,* Eighth Session, Resolution 749 (VIII).
[4] *Official Records of the General Assembly,* Eighth Session, Resolution 749 (VIII).
[5] See *Report of the Committee on South-West Africa to the General Assembly* (*Official Records of the General Assembly,* Ninth Session, Suppl. No. 14), p. 8, Annex II.
[6] *Official Records of the General Assembly,* Ninth Session, Resolution 844 (IX).

Assembly on questions concerning reports and petitions on South-West Africa were to be taken by a two-thirds majority of the Members present and voting, whereas under the Mandates System, such decisions were taken by a unanimous vote of the League Council thus providing a Mandatory Power with a veto over Council decisions affecting its Mandate.[7]

In its Advisory Opinion on the *International Status of South-West Africa* (1950), the International Court expressed the opinion that South-West Africa was still to be considered a territory held under the Mandate of 1920, and that 'the degree of supervision to be exercised by the General Assembly should not therefore exceed that which applied under the Mandates System, and should conform as far as possible to the procedure followed in this respect by the Council of the League of Nations. These observations are particularly applicable to annual reports and petitions.'[8] The question arises as to whether, by means of this opinion, the General Assembly is required to take its decisions on questions relating to reports and petitions on South-West Africa by unanimous vote. However, nowhere in the Charter is the General Assembly authorised to do this; it is authorised to vote in two ways only—by a two-thirds majority on important questions and simple majority on all other matters. As a result of the lack of agreement on this in the General Assembly, the matter was referred to the International Court for an advisory opinion.[9]

The exact question put to the Court by the General Assembly was whether Rule F of the Rules of Procedure adopted by the General Assembly for dealing with the supervision of South-West Africa[10] was a correct interpretation of the Advisory Opinion of 1950. The Court's Opinion, given on June 7, 1955, stated that the interpretation was correct.[11] The reasoning of the Court was that 'the degree of supervision' as used in the Court's

7 All Mandatories were, in the practice of the League, afforded representation and voting rights in the Council when matters affecting their mandates were under discussion, even though they might not be members of the Council (see League of Nations, *The Council of the League of Nations: Composition, Competence, Procedure* (1938), p. 57).

8 *I.C.J. Reports 1950*, p. 138.

9 *Official Records of the General Assembly*, Ninth Session, Resolution 904 (IX).

10 *ibid.*, Resolution 844 (IX).

11 See *South-West Africa–Voting Procedure*, Advisory Opinion of June 7, 1955: *I.C.J. Reports 1955*, p. 67 at p. 78.

previous opinion referred to the 'extent of the substantive supervision thus exercised, and not to the manner in which the collective will of the General Assembly is expressed.'[12] It was intended to prevent the General Assembly using methods of supervision which were inconsistent with the Mandate Treaty or with the supervision applied by the League Council.[13] In recognising that the General Assembly's competence to exercise supervision over South-West Africa was based on Article 10 of the Charter,[14] the Court was also implicitly recognising that the supervision must be exercised in accordance with the provisions of the Charter.[15] These provisions include Article 18 on voting procedure of the General Assembly. This view of the Court is reinforced when it is considered that any alteration in the voting procedure of the General Assembly provided by the Charter would necessitate an amendment to the Charter,[16] and nowhere in the Court's 1950 Opinion is such a drastic course hinted at, nor can it be presumed that it was intended by the Court.

(A further question that has arisen from the 1950 Advisory Opinion concerns the admissibility of oral petitions from South-West Africa.[17])

Although from a legal point of view the gap has been closed, there still remains the problem of persuading the Union of South Africa to comply with the opinion of the International Court. Had the possibility of a Mandate not being terminated been envisaged by the League of Nations, and had other arrangements for the supervision of such a Mandate been made by the League, the controversy over South-West Africa need never have arisen. The attempts to force the Union of South Africa to place this Mandate under the Trusteeship System have so alienated her, that the chances of her complying with the course of action recommended by the International Court remain remote.

12 *ibid.*, p. 72.
13 *I.C.J. Reports 1955*, p. 73.
14 *I.C.J. Reports 1950*, p. 137.
15 *I.C.J. Reports 1955*, p. 74.
16 This was disputed by Judge Lauterpatcht in his Separate Opinion on *South-West Africa–Voting Procedure* (1955) (see *I.C.J. Reports 1955*, p. 108 *et seq.*
17 See Addendum, *ante*, p. xiv.

Chapter 4

THE OBJECTIVES OF THE TRUSTEESHIP SYSTEM

The basic objectives of the International Trusteeship System are to be found in Article 76 of the Charter, which embodies the principle of the dual mandate much more clearly than did the League of Nations Mandates System. Thus the purposes of the System as far as both the international community and the inhabitants of the trust territories are concerned appear in this article. At its face value, it would appear that more stress was being laid on the interests of the international community than on the welfare of the inhabitants of the trust territories. This can be partially explained by the fact that Article 73, which sets forth the principles in accordance with which non-self-governing territories should be administered, is not limited to colonial territories but applies to all non-self-governing territories including those which have been brought under the Trusteeship System. The only exception to this is Article 73 (e) which specifically exempts trust territories from those territories concerning which information is to be transmitted to the Secretary-General. Thus the provisions regarding the welfare of dependent peoples which appear in Article 73, apply equally to trust territories and supplement the rather meagre provisions of Article 76.

At the same time it might be taken into account that, so far as the African trust territories are concerned, there are numerous international conventions in force which protect the native inhabitants against abuses, conventions which have grown up since the General Act of the Berlin Conference of 1885. In the case of the non-African trust territories, the trust agreements themselves contain provisions similar in essence to these international conventions.[1] Apart from the fact that all these supplementary ways of ensuring the welfare of the inhabitants exist, the primary emphasis which Article 76 gives to the interests of the international community can be understood in the light of the main purpose of the United Nations Organisation—the

[1] For details, see below, pp. 107, 115–116.

maintenance of international peace and security. Looked at from this aspect, all the other functions of the United Nations were intended to be subsidiary to this primary purpose and were considered important only because of their effect on international peace and security.

The Furtherance of International Peace and Security

Paragraph (a) of Article 76 states that one of the basic objectives of the Trusteeship System is the furtherance of international peace and security. This coincides with the primary purpose of the United Nations Organisation as a whole which is stated in Article 1 (1). This fact is not surprising, since the preamble to Article 76 states that the objectives of the Trusteeship System are in accordance with the purposes of the United Nations as laid down in Article 1. Furthermore, Article 1 states the purposes of the whole United Nations Organisation and these purposes are therefore automatically purposes of the Trusteeship System. Leaving aside Article 1, the objective of the Trusteeship System stated in Article 76 (a) is also identical with Article 73 (c), and it would thus be applicable to the Trusteeship System whether or not it were specifically mentioned in Chapter XII. The only difference between this aim of furthering international peace and security in the Trusteeship System as compared with its inclusion in the Declaration Regarding Non-Self-Governing Territories, is the position of the phrase within the relevant articles: in Article 73 it is the third paragraph, whilst in Article 76 it appears first. Thus it is arguable that for reasons of international peace and security a particular territory should be transferred from its colonial status and be placed under the Trusteeship System. Of course, in reality such reasoning carries no weight since the administering Power would have to agree to place the territory under trusteeship.

A further indication of the primary importance which the drafters of the Trusteeship System attached to the security aspect is evident from the way in which trust territories are divided into categories. Whereas under the League Mandates System territories were divided into A, B and C Mandates according to their stage of development, under the Trusteeship System they are divided into strategic and non-strategic trust territories. In the case of the Mandates, the welfare aspect was to be the deciding factor, whilst in the case of the Trusteeship System, it is to be the security aspect. This is a very important distinction between the Mandates System and the Trusteeship System, inasmuch as welfare relates to the population of the territories and security to international security.

Article 76 (a) is supplemented by Article 84, which explains the way in which international peace and security is to be furthered. Whilst Article 76 (a) declares that the furtherance of international peace and security is an objective of the Trusteeship System, Article 84 makes it the positive duty of the administering authority to see that a trust territory under its control plays its part in achieving this aim. For this purpose, the administering authority is permitted to make use of the resources of the trust territory in carrying out the administering authority's obligations towards the Security Council, and at the same time it may use these resources for purposes of local defence and for maintaining law and order within the trust territory. Thus the trust territory is given an active role in the application of enforcement provisions under Chapter VII. However, a limitation is placed on the administering authority's powers over the resources of the trust territory. The forces of the trust territory that may be used are to be volunteer forces, thus ruling out any form of military conscription. In this way, this part of Article 84 could be rendered meaningless through the refusal of the inhabitants of a trust territory to co-operate with the administering authority. However, since the furtherance of international peace and security is the overwhelming objective of the Trusteeship System and of the whole United Nations Organisation,[2] it is arguable that this overrules Article 84, and that therefore the administering authority is justified in taking any measures—including the conscription of forces—in furtherance of international peace and security but in violation of Article 84. The Opinion of the International Court of Justice on *Admission of a State to Membership in the United Nations* (1948), on the other hand, supports the opposite conclusion. In its Advisory Opinion the Court held that an article of the Charter providing special rules for admission to Membership in the United Nations, overruled a general provision which conflicted with these special rules.[3] The

2 Articles 76 (a) and 1 (1).

3 'Article 24, owing to the very general nature of its terms, cannot, in the absence of any provision, affect the special rules for admission which emerge from Article 4' (*I.C.J. Reports 1948*, p. 64).

same reasoning can be applied to prove the supremacy of Article 84 over Articles 1 (1) and 76 (a). It should be pointed out that Article 84 refers only to volunteer *forces*; therefore it is not contrary to this Article for the administering authority to conscript labour for the purpose of providing military facilities for the administering authority, when the obligations of the administering authority towards the Security Council so require.

It is specified in Article 84 that the forces, facilities and assistance from the trust territory can be used only for local defence, apart from their use in carrying out obligations towards the Security Council. Thus the administering Power is not authorised to use such resources for the defence of its own metropolitan territory or for the defence of any part of its colonial empire; the resources of a trust territory may not be used to defend the territory of an adjacent colony of the administering Power. Nor would an administering Power be authorised to use the resources of a trust territory in carrying out its obligations towards an organisation such as the North Atlantic Treaty Organisation (NATO). It would appear that the inclusion of volunteer forces of a trust territory in a local regional army, along the lines of the European army envisaged in the unratified European Defence Community Treaty, is prohibited, since the forces of the trust territory would then be liable to be called upon to serve outside the boundaries of the trust territory for a purpose other than fulfilling the administering authority's obligations towards the Security Council.

When an administering authority makes use of 'volunteer forces, facilities, and assistance from the trust territory in carrying out the obligations towards the Security Council undertaken in this regard by the administering authority,'[4] this use is not restricted to local defence. In this case, volunteer forces from the trust territory might well be called on to serve outside the territory. This might take place either as a result of a special agreement concluded between the administering authority and the Security Council under Article 43,[5] or in furtherance of a

[4] Article 84.

[5] Article 43 (1) reads: 'All Members of the United Nations, in order to contribute to the maintenance of international peace and security, undertake to make available to the Security Council, on its call and in accordance with a special agreement or agreements, armed forces, assistance, and facilities, including rights of passage, necessary for the purpose of maintaining international peace and security.'

decision of the Security Council in which case, under Article 25, 'the Members of the United Nations agree to accept and carry out the decisions of the Security Council in accordance with the present Charter.' In either case the administering authority might be obliged to send the forces of the trust territory overseas, and since this obligation is towards the Security Council, it is in accordance with Article 84. Furthermore, it may be argued that in a situation like the Korean War, the administering authority would be justified in sending volunteer forces from the trust territory to the assistance of a victim of aggression, upon the recommendation of the Security Council.

The Goal of the Trust Territory

Article 76 (b) is concerned with the goal of the trust territories and the way in which the goal is to be achieved. The goal is stated as being 'self-government or independence,' and the inhabitants of the trust territories are to be guided towards this end by political, economic, social, and educational means. In contrast to other non-self-governing territories whose goal is self-government, an alternative of independence is set for trust territories. However, as has been pointed out in an earlier chapter,[6] this was the result of compromise at San Francisco rather than of any premeditated reasoning. Whilst stating that one of the basic objectives of the Trusteeship System is the progressive development towards self-government or independence, this is to take place 'as may be provided by the terms of each trusteeship agreement.' Thus, it appears that a trust agreement could stipulate that the development was to be towards self-government but not independence. So far no trust agreement has omitted or specifically excluded independence as a goal for the territory, but the agreement for Somaliland states that the development shall be towards independence and does not mention self-government. By Chapter XI, however, all non-self-governing territories administered by Members of the United Nations must be guided towards self-government: therefore, self-government must be developed in all trust territories administered by Members, regardless of whether independence is also achieved. Only when a trust territory is administered by a non-Member

[6] See above, Chap. 2, p. 33.

or the Organisation itself[7] is it questionable whether the Charter requires the development of self-government in the territory. This is of practical interest inasmuch as the trust territory of Somaliland was administered by a non-Member until 1955 when Italy was admitted to the United Nations. Thus, until 1955, neither the Charter nor the trust agreement specifically obligated Italy to develop self-government in Somaliland. Two considerations, however, should be taken into account: The achievement of independence would necessarily involve some sort of self-government, if only of an undemocratic nature. Therefore, only if the Charter accords some special meaning to 'self-government'[8] is its omission from a trust agreement of any significance. Secondly, it can be inferred from the Charter that the meaning of 'independence' in Article 76 (b) includes self-government. Since the records of the San Francisco Conference indicate that the possibility of a non-Member administering a trust territory was not anticipated,[9] the provisions of Chapters XI and XII must be read together, and it cannot be presumed that Article 76 (b) was intended to contradict Article 73 (b). It appears that the meaning of the phrase 'self-government or independence' is self-government and independence or self-government alone. If this is so, a non-Member as much as a Member administering authority is obligated to develop self-government in a trust territory, even if the trust agreement refers only to independence.

The 'development towards self-government or independence' in Article 76 (b) is subject to the modification 'as may be appropriate to the particular circumstances of each territory and its peoples and the freely expressed wishes of the peoples concerned.' This brings up the question of what happens if 'self-government or independence' is not the desired goal of the peoples concerned.

According to the Report of the United Nations Visiting Mission to the Trust Territory of the Pacific Islands,[10] the inhabitants of this territory have expressed an overwhelming desire to become American citizens rather than become self-governing or independent. The Visiting Mission merely mentioned this in its Report and did not make any proposals on the subject, and the United States Government has so far

7 This is permitted by Article 81, see below, Chap. 11, pp. 208–213.
8 See above, Chap. 2, p. 21, n. 20.
9 See below, Chap. 11, pp. 206–207.
10 Doc. T/789, August 15, 1950, p. 9.

remained silent on the matter. However, the Visiting Mission's Report is born out by a petition from the House of Council and House of Commissioners of Saipan, stating their desire that all of the Northern Marianas be incorporated into the United States either as a possession or a territory, and that the inhabitants obtain American citizenship.[11] In this case, to insist on the goal of 'self-government or independence' for this trust territory is to deny the principle of self-determination, one of the basic principles of the Charter.[12] The Trusteeship Council adopted a very non-committal resolution which merely noted the wishes of the peoples of the Northern Marianas.[13] It considered that it was inappropriate to make any recommendation as to the possibility of incorporating the Trust Territory into the United States, or as to the acquisition of the nationality and citizenship of the Administering Authority by the inhabitants of the Trust Territory. Of course, the ultimate decision for any such alteration in the status of the Trust Territory would rest with the United States itself. The reticence of the Trusteeship Council's resolution, however, can be explained by the fact that not only does the Charter make no provision for any goal other than self-government or independence, but any other goal would be extremely unsavoury to the majority of the Members of the United Nations. Thus one assumption on which the Trusteeship System is founded, namely that self-government or independence is necessarily the wish of all non-self-governing peoples, has proved in this instance to be false.

The Charter makes no mention of the time within which the objective of self-government or independence is to be achieved, and indeed it would have been impossible to lay down a single time-limit which would accord with the vastly differing stages of development of the trust territories. At San Francisco the Egyptian Delegate suggested that the United Nations should be empowered to declare a trust territory fit for independence and thereon to terminate the trust.[14] This proposal was later dropped. Any specification of a time-limit would therefore have to be inserted into the trust agreements themselves, where it

11 Doc. T/Pet.10/5 of June 12, 1950, p. 2.
12 Article 1 (2).
13 *Official Records of the Trusteeship Council,* Eighth Session, Resolution 317 (VIII).
14 See U.N.C.I.O. *Journal,* June 16, 1945 (*U.N.C.I.O. Docs.,* Vol. 2, p. 145).

could be made to accord with the stage of advancement of each trust territory. With the exception of the trust agreement for Somaliland under Italian administration, no agreement incorporates a specific time-limit or even hints at one. This is a very real shortcoming from the point of view of the anti-colonial Powers in the United Nations. Their continued determination not to lose sight of the goal of self-government or independence, and their continual stress on the latter alternative, has caused a great deal of attention to be focussed on the subject. A resolution passed by the General Assembly at its Third Session included the recommendation that the administering authorities 'take all possible steps to accelerate the progressive development towards self-government or independence of the Trust Territories they administer.'[15] A United Nations Visiting Mission to West Africa in 1949 was directed to observe the progress of the trust territories towards self-government or independence, and the efforts of the administering authorities to achieve this and other objectives of the International Trusteeship System.[16] A similar direction was given to the Visiting Mission to the trust territories in the Pacific in 1950.[17] Up to this point there was no mention of a time-limit.

At its Fourth Session, the General Assembly adopted a resolution containing the main provisions for Italian administration of Somaliland in which an actual time-limit for the attainment of the independence of the territory was specified.[18] Somaliland was to become an independent sovereign State ten years after the approval of a trust agreement by the General Assembly. This resolution stimulated the anti-colonial Powers to further action. If such a backward territory as Somaliland could be considered ready for independence in ten years' time, the question arose whether other territories could not be considered likewise. That same Session, the General Assembly went on to express support of the Trusteeship Council's recommendations to the administering authorities, urging them to take measures to hasten the

[15] *Official Records of the General Assembly,* Third Session, Resolution 226 (III).

[16] *Official Records of the Trusteeship Council,* Fifth Session, Resolution 108 (V).

[17] *Official Records of the Trusteeship Council,* Sixth Session, Resolution 115 (VI).

[18] *Official Records of the General Assembly,* Fourth Session, Resolution 289 (IV) (see *Official Records of the General Assembly,* Fifth Session, Suppl. No. 10).

advancement of the trust territories towards self-government or independence in accordance with objectives laid down in Article 76 (b) of the Charter.[19] The most extensive resolution on the subject was adopted by the General Assembly at its Sixth Session.[20] Whilst pointing out that the progressive development towards self-government or independence was one of the basic objectives of the Trusteeship System, it noted that only in the case of Somaliland had an administering authority submitted information as to the time and manner in which the territory was expected to attain the objective. The General Assembly, therefore, invited the administering authority of each trust territory other than Somaliland, to include in its annual report on its administration, information with respect to the attainment of self-government or independence. This information was to state the measures taken or contemplated to attain this objective in the shortest possible time, the manner in which the particular circumstances of the territory and its people and their freely expressed wishes were being taken into account, the adequacy of the provisions of the existing trust agreement in relation to all the foregoing factors, and the period of time in which it was expected that the trust territory would attain the objective.[21]

At its Fourteenth Session in 1954, the Trusteeship Council adopted the terms of reference for the 1954 Visiting Mission to trust territories in East Africa.[1] These terms directed the Visiting Mission to investigate and report on the steps taken in the three East African trust territories[2] towards the realisation of the objectives of Article 76 (b) of the Charter—the development of the trust territories towards self-government and independence. The Visiting Mission's reports on these territories were considered by the Trusteeship Council at its Fifteenth Session. With regard to Tanganyika, the Visiting Mission suggested that a time-limit could be fixed for the territory to attain self-government within twenty to twenty-five years.[3] On March 4, 1955, the Trusteeship

19 *Official Records of the General Assembly,* Fourth Session, Resolution 320 (IV). 20 *ibid.,* Sixth Session, Resolution 558 (VI).

21 The New Zealand Government recently transmitted to the Trusteeship Council a comprehensive memorandum outlining with dates the steps to be taken towards the achievement of self-government in Western Samoa (Doc. T/1243, April 25, 1956). Cabinet government is envisaged by 1960.

1 *Official Records of the Trusteeship Council,* Fourteenth Session, Resolution 999 (XIV). 2 Somaliland, Ruanda-Urundi, and Tanganyika.

3 See *Report of Visiting Mission on Tanganyika,* Doc. T/1142, pp. 185–

Council gave an oral hearing to an inhabitant of the territory, the spokesman for the *Organisation of the Unofficial Members of the Tanganyika Legislative Council.* This petitioner stated that his Organisation was perturbed at the suggestion regarding the establishment of a time-table for self-government.[4] The problem arises as to whether it is in accordance with the Charter for a time-table to be set for the attainment of self-government by the territory, against the wishes of the inhabitants. Article 76 (b) states that one of the basic objectives of the Trusteeship System is to promote the 'progressive development towards self-government or independence [of the inhabitants of the trust territory] as may be appropriate to the particular circumstances of each territory and its peoples and the freely expressed wishes of the peoples concerned.' The wording of Article 76 (b) implies that it is not only the choice between the alternate goal of 'self-government or independence' that is subject to the 'particular circumstances of each territory' and the wishes of the inhabitants, but also the 'progressive development.' The fixing of a time-table for self-government relates to the 'progressive development,' since this may have the effect of accelerating or retarding the achievement of the goal. Therefore the fixing of this time-limit is a matter which is subject to the 'freely expressed wishes of the inhabitants,' and these wishes must not be ignored by the United Nations.

An example of the way in which primary attention has been focussed on paragraph (b) of the objectives of the Trusteeship System, is to be found in the discussions over permanent trusteeship for the City of Jerusalem. In 1947, the General Assembly passed a resolution on the future of Palestine which recommended the establishment of the City of Jerusalem as a *corpus separatum* to be administered by the United Nations, with the Trusteeship Council designated to discharge the responsibilities of the United Nations.[5] Iraq refused to participate in the Trusteeship Council's discussions on a Statute for the City on the grounds, among others, that *permanent* trusteeship for Jerusalem was illegal

186. The administering authority rejected the Visiting Mission's suggestions, see *Observations of the Administering Authority on the Visiting Mission's Report,* Doc. T/1162, p. 2.

[4] *Official Records of the Trusteeship Council,* Fifteenth Session, 28th Meeting.

[5] *Official Records of the General Assembly,* Second Session, Resolution 181 (II).

inasmuch as trusteeship under the Charter was an intermediary stage leading to self-government.[6] However, the whole idea of a permanent trusteeship for Jerusalem was aimed at furthering international peace and security—also an objective of the Trusteeship System.[7] Iraq was thus holding that the objective of 'development towards self-government or independence' took precedence over the furtherance of international peace and security. The point which Iraq brought out—that permanent trusteeship is not possible under the Charter—renders impossible the exercise of United Nations trusteeship over an area which it is the intention to keep permanently internationalised.

Administrative Unions

The question arises whether 'self-government or independence' is to be achieved by the trust territory as an entity, or whether it may be permitted to unite with an adjacent colonial territory and thus achieve independence or self-government with the colony as a single unit. The fact that the goal of a non-self-governing territory other than a trust territory is not independence but only self-government, has caused the majority of the Members of the United Nations to adopt the line that a trust territory must remain a unit in itself. This results from the distinct preference of anti-colonial Powers for independence as a goal rather than self-government. Thus the whole question of administrative unions—administrative unions between a trust territory and an adjacent non-self-governing territory—has become extremely controversial. The great concern has been to ensure that an administrative union does not develop into a political union in which the trust territory would lose its separate existence and with it its chance of independence. An administrative union was defined by the United Nations Visiting Mission to East Africa in the following way: 'It would be a purely administrative union if it possessed only powers of administration over certain common services, and would be a political union if it possessed full powers of legislation over any or all of the common services.'[8] It is generally conceded that an administra-

6 *Official Records of the Trusteeship Council,* Second Session, 46th Meeting.

7 Article 76 (b).

8 *Report of the Visiting Mission to East Africa on Tanganyika* (Doc. T/218/Add. 1 of November 8, 1948), p. 64.

tive union is beneficial to the inhabitants of a trust territory and the majority of the trust agreements make provision for it.[9]

Administrative unions came into prominence in the General Assembly in 1948. There was general agreement that an administrative union must be in the interests of the inhabitants, must not lead to the loss of the political identity of the trust territory, and should be limited to customs, fiscal and administrative—as distinct from political—matters. The main disagreement centred round the majority opinion that administrative unions should be established only with the prior approval of the Trusteeship Council. The administering authorities argued that the Trusteeship Council's role was one of supervision and that it could review and criticise the policies of the administering authorities only after such policies had been put into effect.[10] An opposing view was that the United Nations had the right to request the administering authority concerned to submit all parts of an administrative union, including territories not under trusteeship, to such supervision by the Trusteeship Council as the latter might consider necessary for the effective discharge of its responsibilities with respect to any trust territory involved in the union.[11] A more extreme view was that of non-trust territory involved in an administrative union with a trust territory should be placed under trusteeship.[12]

After much discussion, the General Assembly endorsed a previous observation of the Trusteeship Council that an administrative union 'must remain strictly administrative in its nature and scope, and . . . must not . . . obstruct the separate development of the Trust Territory . . . as a distinct entity.'[13] It recommended that the Trusteeship Council investigate the whole subject of administrative unions and report back to the

[9] Article 5 in the trust agreements for New Guinea (*United Nations Treaty Series,* Vol. 8, p. 181), Tanganyika (*ibid.,* p. 91), Togoland under United Kingdom administration (*ibid.,* p. 151), Cameroons under United Kingdom administration (*ibid.,* p. 119), and Ruanda-Urundi (*ibid.,* p. 105); Article 4 in the trust agreements for the Cameroons under French administration (*ibid.,* p. 135), and Togoland under French administration (*ibid.,* p. 165).

[10] *Official Records of the General Assembly,* First Part of the Third Session, Fourth Committee, pp. 205–206. See further below, pp. 180–182.

[11] *Official Records of the General Assembly,* First Part of the Third Session, Fourth Committee, Annexes to the Summary Records, pp. 8–9.

[12] *ibid.,* p. 10.

[13] *Official Records of the General Assembly,* Third Session, Resolution 224 (III).

General Assembly, and that the Trusteeship Council request an advisory opinion from the International Court of Justice, whenever appropriate, on the compatibility of such unions with the Charter and the trust agreements.

In 1949, the Trusteeship Council established a Committee on Administrative Unions[14] to examine the problems of such unions and to report thereon to the Trusteeship Council. In the case of the administrative union between the Cameroons under United Kingdom administration and Nigeria, the Committee adopted a very liberal attitude. It noted that although the union represented a complete amalgamation and had the character of a political union, it was not disadvantageous to the trust territory concerned. Under the circumstances it felt that the situation deserved the constant attention of the Trusteeship Council.[15]

In July 1950, the Trusteeship Council decided to establish a Standing Committee on Administrative Unions to undertake regular examinations of administrative unions. Whenever the annual report of a trust territory involved in an administrative union was being examined, the Standing Committee was to report on that union to the Trusteeship Council. In 1952, the Trusteeship Council was asked to prepare a report on administrative unions and their compatibility with the United Nations Charter and the relevant trust agreements.[16] After considering this report, which had been prepared by the Standing Committee,[17] the General Assembly merely asked that the Trusteeship Council continue its study of the problem, and it expressed the hope that the administering authorities would consult the Trusteeship Council before establishing or extending the scope of the unions.[18]

It should be noted that in the case of some of the former Mandates, the goal of 'self-government or independence' represents a complete reversal of policy. Under the League, C Mandates were permitted to be administered as integral parts of the territory of the Mandatories and were never considered candi-

14 *Official Records of the Trusteeship Council,* Fourth Session, Resolution 81 (IV).

15 Doc. T/L. 96 of July 11, 1950, pp. 26–27.

16 *Official Records of the General Assembly,* Sixth Session, Resolution 563 (VI).

17 *Official Records of the General Assembly,* Seventh Session, Suppl. No. 12.

18 *Official Records of the General Assembly,* Seventh Session, Resolution 649 (VII).

dates for self-government or independence. This has been pointed out in the General Assembly by the representative of the Union of South Africa.[19] It is not even certain whether self-government or independence was intended for B Mandates.

The Welfare of the Inhabitants

Article 76 (c) incorporates two principles—the 'respect for human rights' and the 'recognition of the interdependence of the peoples of the world.' The human rights principle as incorporated in this article is mere repetition of what appears in no less than five other places in the Charter. It appears in the Preamble to the Charter where it is the second principle, subordinate only to the maintenance of international peace and security.[20] In Article 1 (3), one of the basic purposes of the United Nations is stated as being the promotion and encouragement of respect for human rights, and this applies as much to the Trusteeship System as to any other part of the Charter, as is indicated in the preamble to Article 76.[1] Article 13, paragraph 1 (b), empowers the General Assembly to initiate studies and make recommendations for the purpose of 'assisting in the realisation of human rights,' and, since the non-strategic trust territories come within the scope of the General Assembly's powers, such studies and recommendations may also cover non-strategic trust territories.[2] Article 55 authorises the United Nations to promote 'universal respect for, and observance of, human rights,' and by Article 56 all Members of the United Nations are pledged 'to take joint and separate action in co-operation with the Organisation for the achievement' of these human rights. Finally, the Economic and Social Council is authorised by Article 62 (2) to make recommendations for the purpose of promoting respect for human rights, and by the terms of Article 62 (3) it may prepare draft conventions for submission to the General Assembly on the subject of human rights. If there is any doubt as to whether this

[19] *Official Records of the General Assembly,* Second Session, Fourth Committee, p. 48.

[20] See second paragraph to the Preamble of the Charter.

[1] 'The basic objectives of the trusteeship system, in accordance with the Purposes of the United Nations laid down in Article 1 of the present Charter, shall be . . .'

[2] For a discussion on whether the General Assembly may make recommendations with regard to strategic trust territories, see below, Chap. 8, pp. 147–148.

function of the Economic and Social Council covers the sphere of trusteeship, the matter is settled by Article 2 of the *Universal Declaration of Human Rights* which was adopted by the General Assembly in 1948.[3] Article 2 reads as follows:

> 'Every one is entitled to all the rights and freedoms set forth in this declaration . . .
>
> 'Furthermore, no distinction shall be made on the basis of the political, jurisdictional or international status of the country or territory to which a person belongs, whether it be independent, trust, non-self-governing or under any other limitation of sovereignty.'

This Declaration was the work of the Economic and Social Council, and in approving it the General Assembly was also acknowledging the competence of the Economic and Social Council to include the inhabitants of trust territories within its studies.

The fact that a special provision on human rights was also included in the Chapter on Trusteeship was probably for purposes of emphasis, since it adds nothing to the other provisions on the subject in the Charter. Throughout the Charter these references to human rights are vague due to the fact that the domestic jurisdiction clause in Article 2 (7) limits the interference within a State. This provision can only be overridden if a violation of human rights threatens international peace and security. If such can be proved to be the case, then the enforcement measures under Chapter VII of the Charter can be brought into operation. In reality, that a violation of human rights threatens international peace and security is not easy to prove, as is evident from the endless unsuccessful attempts that India has made in the General Assembly, to prove that the treatment of people of Indian origin in the Union of South Africa endangers international peace and security.

Although Article 2 (7) may successfully prevent the United Nations taking action to ensure that the human rights provisions of the Charter are put into effect,[4] nevertheless the Members of

[3] The *Universal Declaration of Human Rights* was adopted by the General Assembly on December 10, 1948, at its 183rd Meeting.

[4] Professor Lauterpacht holds that Article 2 (7) does not prevent discussion or the adoption of general or specific recommendations on matters 'within the domestic jurisdiction of any state,' since these do not constitute 'intervention.' In his opinion, 'intervention' is 'a peremptory

the United Nations themselves have a definite legal obligation 'to fulfil in good faith the obligations assumed by them in accordance with the present Charter.'[5] They are therefore legally obliged 'to take joint and separate action in co-operation with the Organisation for the achievement' of 'universal respect for, and observance of human rights and fundamental freedoms for all without distinction as to race, sex, language, or religion.'[6] In the case of the trust territories, this obligation, together with that 'to encourage respect for human rights and for fundamental freedoms for all,' is made specific in the trust agreements, where the administering authorities categorically guarantee fundamental rights to the inhabitants of the trust territories.[7] The supervisory machinery of the Trusteeship System substantially reinforces these obligations, and United Nations intervention in the internal affairs of trust territories is not limited by Article 2 (7). As Professor Lauterpacht says, 'the result . . . is that there is a wider and more explicit measure of international enforcement of—some—human rights and fundamental freedoms of inhabitants of trust territories than in other parts of the world.'[8]

The second part of Article 76 (c) needs no elaboration. The encouragement of the 'recognition of the interdependence of the peoples of the world' is a theme which runs throughout the Charter.

The Interests of Member States

The fourth and last paragraph of Article 76 is concerned with protecting the interests of Members of the United Nations.

demand or an attempt at interference accompanied by enforcement or threat of enforcement in case of non-compliance' (see H. Lauterpacht, *International Law and Human Rights* (1950), p. 168). However, since the only provisions in the Charter providing for enforcement action by the United Nations are in Chap. VII, and since 'the application of enforcement measures under Chap. VII' is specifically stated as not being limited by the domestic jurisdiction clause in Article 2 (7), therefore Professor Lauterpacht's interpretation of intervention renders Article 2 (7) completely meaningless. It means that this Article prohibits 'intervention' in the domestic affairs of any State, and then in the same paragraph excludes everything that constitutes 'intervention' from that restriction. This interpretation is therefore unacceptable inasmuch as it must be presumed that every article of the Charter was intended to have a meaning (see further, *ibid.*, pp. 166–220).

[5] Article 2 (2).

[6] Articles 56 and 55 (c).

[7] See below, Chap. 6.

[8] H. Lauterpacht, *International Law and Human Rights* (1950), p. 161.

Bearing in mind that trading restrictions have long been a source of friction in the international community, the Charter attempts to alleviate this by the inclusion of provisions for the establishment of the open-door in all trust territories.[9] The inclusion of the open-door principle in a general international agreement has precedents in both the League of Nations Covenant and in the General Act of the Conference of Berlin of 1885. All three restrict the open-door territorially: the Trusteeship System to trust territories, the Mandates System to B Mandates, and the Berlin Act to the Conventional Basin of the Congo. Since the B Mandates, with the exception of the Togolands, were already covered by the provisions of the Berlin Act, to a great extent the open-door principle in Article 22 of the Covenant was repetition. Whereas the Covenant only required the open-door to be in operation in B Mandates,[10] the Trusteeship System requires it in all trust territories. In one respect the Berlin Act's provisions were wider than those of the Mandates System or Trusteeship System, in that benefits of the open-door were to be enjoyed by *all* States,[11] whereas in the case of the Mandates and Trusteeship Systems the open-door is applicable only to Members of the League and United Nations respectively. In the Berlin Act, provision was made forbidding the granting of monopolies in the territories concerned,[12] whereas articles authorising monopolies for fiscal and development purposes can be found in both the terms of B Mandates and in the trust agreements. It can be argued that the provisions of the open-door in favour of *all* States, rather than just the Members of the United Nations, is still in operation in those trust territories which were covered by the Berlin Act: the ordinary rules of international law regarding the rights of third parties would guarantee that the rights of non-United Nations Members in the Congo Basin cannot be

[9] The wording of Article 76 (d) is 'to ensure equal treatment in social, economic, and commercial matters for all Members of the United Nations and their nationals.' This means the absence of discrimination in social, economic, and commercial matters. However, the absence of discrimination is the definition of the open-door (see B. Gerig, *The Open-Door and the Mandates System* (1930), p. 167), therefore what Article 76 (d) amounts to is the application of the open-door in social, economic, and commercial matters to all Members of the United Nations.

[10] However, provisions for the open-door were incorporated into the actual terms of the A Mandates also.

[11] See Chapter 1, Article 1 of the Berlin Act of 1885.

[12] See *ibid.*, Article 5.

altered by the provisions of the Charter to which they were not parties.

Article 76 (d) states that the operation of the open-door is not to prejudice the attainment of the objectives of paragraphs (a), (b), and (c) of this article, and that it is subject to the provisions of Article 80. There are thus four possible limitations on the operation of the open-door: security reasons, the welfare of the inhabitants of the trust territory, the attainment of self-government or independence, and the provisions of Article 80—the conservatory clause. Since the operation of the open-door is therefore subject to the welfare of the inhabitants, the United Kingdom's assertion that the open-door had not always operated to the advantage of the inhabitants of the territories concerned has been partly answered.[13] However, a situation might arise in which the open-door would be definitely beneficial to the inhabitants of a trust territory but detrimental to international peace and security, in which case it would seem that the security aspect would take priority, being the first objective of Article 76. Thus in the last analysis the limitations to the open-door principle operate to the advantage of others than the inhabitants—to this extent the fears of the United Kingdom are still well-grounded. This is especially true in the case of a strategic area where, although Article 83 (2) says that the objectives of the Trusteeship System apply to the peoples of strategic areas, the limitations of paragraphs (a), (b), and (c) of Article 76 still apply, and a strategic area would seem to be more subject to security limitations.

The fourth limitation to the open-door is Article 80. This article guarantees the maintenance of existing rights unless and until altered by a trust agreement. Since a trust agreement may alter the rights which United Nations Members enjoy under the Charter, according to Article 80 (1), it would appear that a trust agreement may limit the open-door. But against this argument that a trust agreement may limit the open-door, it can be held that a trust agreement which runs contrary to the objectives in Artitcle 76 must not be approved. Article 80 states that until changed by a trust agreement, the rights of any United

[13] See view of the United Kingdom Delegate at San Francisco, *Summary of Fourth Meeting of Committee II/4*, p. 2 (*U.N.C.I.O. Docs.*, Vol. 10, p. 438).

Nations Member under an existing international instrument may not be altered. Therefore, all Members of the United Nations have to agree to a limitation of the open-door being inserted into a trust agreement. It could be argued with respect to non-strategic territories that approval of the agreement by the General Assembly satisfies this requirement. But in the case of a similar situation in a strategic area this would not be true, since all States are not represented on the Security Council.

The trust agreements for Tanganyika,[14] British administered Togoland,[15] British administered Cameroons,[16] French administered Togoland,[17] French administered Cameroons,[18] Ruanda-Urundi,[19] and Western Samoa,[20] all specifically provide for the open-door. The agreements for New Guinea and Nauru are silent on the matter, but as the Australian Delegate pointed out in the case of the draft agreement for New Guinea, reference was made in the agreement to the obligation to conduct administration in accordance with the Charter and therefore the open-door was binding on the administering authority.[1] The trust agreement for Somaliland under Italian administration, which was concluded in 1950, and which was drawn up by the Trusteeship Council, made specific reference to the operation of the open-door.[2] This was in line with the whole agreement which was extremely detailed, due to the fact that Italy was a Non-Member of the United Nations and therefore it was considered that the trust agreement should incorporate all the provisions by which Members of the United Nations were bound under the Charter. The only agreement which rejects the open-door is that for the Pacific Islands under United States administration, which instead guarantees most-favoured nation treatment.

When it is recalled that at San Francisco it was the United States which insisted that the provisions of the Charter should include the guaranteeing of equality of economic and commercial

[14] Article 9 (*United Nations Treaty Series,* Vol. 8, p. 91).
[15] Article 9 (*ibid.,* p. 151).
[16] Article 9 (*ibid.,* p. 119).
[17] Article 8 (*ibid.,* p. 165).
[18] Article 8 (*ibid.,* p. 135).
[19] Article 8 (*ibid.,* p. 105).
[20] Article 4 (*ibid.,* p. 71).
[1] *Official Records of the General Assembly,* Second Part of the First Session, Fourth Committee, Part 2, Sub-Committee, 1, p. 19.
[2] Article 15 (*Official Records of the General Assembly,* Fifth Session, Suppl. No. 10).

opportunity to all Members of the United Nations in the trust territories,[3] it is strange to find that the only trust agreement which specifically rejects this is the agreement for the Pacific Islands under United States administration. This agreement states that 'the Administering Authority . . . shall accord to nationals of each Member of the United Nations and to companies and associations organised in conformity with the laws of such Member, treatment in the Trust Territory no less favourable than that accorded therein to nationals, companies and associations of *any other United Nation except the Administering Authority*.'[4] Thus, instead of equality of treatment, the United States was proposing to grant most-favoured-nation treatment, and thus pursue a policy to which she herself had objected in the past when it had been applied to colonial territories of other Powers.[5] This interpretation of equality of treatment, however, is not without precedent in the history of the United States. It was used in a controversy with Great Britain over the question of the Panama Canal tolls. In this case, the Hays-Pauncefote Treaty of 1901 stipulated that 'all nations' using the future Panama Canal should pay the same tolls. In 1912, the United States Congress passed an Act specifically exempting American coastwise shipping from paying any tolls, and legal arguments

[3] See Summary Reports of the meetings of Committee II/4 at San Francisco (*U.N.C.I.O. Docs.*, Vol. 10).

[4] Italics added. Article 9 of the Trust Agreement (*United Nations Treaty Series*, Vol. 8, p. 190 *et seq.*). In the *Case Concerning the Rights of Nationals of the United States of America in Morocco* (1952), the International Court of Justice decided with regard to the French Protectorate of Morocco, that the Protector was not exempt from being treated as a *tertium comparationis* in the operation of the standard of equality of treatment in the Protectorate (see *I.C.J. Reports 1952*, p. 176 at p. 185).

[5] The United States objected to the omission of the 'open door' in the C Mandates, with the result that these Mandates were confirmed by the League without the assent of the United States (see Royal Institute of International Affairs, *The Colonial Problem* (1937), p. 94). It should be pointed out, however, that the United States implicitly acquiesced in Japan's according only most-favoured-nation treatment with regard to commerce, navigation and customs duties in the Pacific Islands C Mandate (see Q. Wright, *Mandates Under the League of Nations* (1930), p. 452, n. 57).

The United States also objected to France, under a decree of December 3, 1948, claiming a preferential position with regard to the restrictions on foreign imports into the French Protectorate of Morocco (see *I.C.J. Reports 1950, Pleadings*, p. 15 *et seq. Case Concerning the Rights of Nationals of the United States of America in Morocco.* See further, B. Cheng, *Rights of United States Nationals in the French Zone of Morocco* [*International and Comparative Law Quarterly*, Vol. 2, July 1953, p. 354 *et seq.*]).

were put forward to the effect that 'all nations' meant 'all other nations.' Great Britain protested against this interpretation. The Act was finally repealed a few years later after a great deal of persuasion from President Wilson.

During the discussions in the Security Council which preceded the approval of the trust agreement for the Pacific Islands, it was again the United States and the United Kingdom which were in disagreement over the question of 'equal treatment . . . for all Members of the United Nations.' The United Kingdom proposed the deletion of the phrase 'except the Administering Authority' from the draft agreement, arguing that it was contrary to the provisions of the Charter. The United States Delegate gave two reasons for rejecting this British proposal: he said that the open-door provision was subject to the provision that it must not prejudice the attainment of the objectives enumerated in Article 76 (a), (b), and (c); and further, he pointed out that Article 83 (2) merely provided that 'the basic objectives set forth in Article 76 shall be applicable to the people of each strategic area' and that there was no mention of their being applied to other people.[6] In reply to this last point it can be said that since the objectives enumerated in Article 76 apply to the Trusteeship System generally, they apply to all trust territories unless there is a provision in the Charter exempting them. As to the first point put forward by the United States Delegate, the question is who is competent to decide whether the application of the open-door in a trust territory is prejudicial to the objectives in Article 76 (a), (b), and (c). Further, it might be asked if it is possible to determine whether or not the application of the open-door in a particular trust territory prejudices the other objectives of the Trusteeship System, without its having actually been tried out in the territory. The trust agreement for the Pacific Islands was finally approved with the controversial phrase left in, not because its legality had been established, but because it was realised that if approval were not given the United States might withdraw the agreement altogether and not submit the territory to trusteeship[7]—a fact which was responsible for the approval of many imperfections in the various trust agreements.

[6] *Official Records of the Security Council,* Second Year, No. 31, pp. 663–665.

[7] The United States Delegate to the Security Council mentioned that his country might be forced to do this (see *Official Records of the Security Council,* Second Year, No. 31, p. 665).

A further obligation in Article 76 (d) is to ensure equal treatment for the nationals of all Members of the United Nations in the administration of justice. This provision has been generally agreed to and even the trust agreement for the Pacific Islands states that 'the Administering Authority shall ensure equal treatment to the Members of the United Nations and their nationals in the administration of justice.'

PART THREE

THE TRUST AGREEMENTS

CHAPTER 5

THE SUBMISSION OF A TERRITORY TO TRUSTEESHIP

It is provided in several articles of the Charter that a territory is to be brought under the Trusteeship System by means of a trust agreement. According to Article 75, the Trusteeship System was to be established for the purpose of administering and supervising such territories 'as may be placed thereunder by subsequent individual agreements.' Similarly, Article 77 (1) states that the System is to apply to such territories 'as may be placed thereunder by means of trusteeship agreements.' Article 77 (2) goes on to say that 'it will be a matter for subsequent agreement as to which territories . . . will be brought under the trusteeship system and upon what terms.' At the same time, it is provided by Article 80 (1) that existing rights are to be upheld in the trust territories 'except as may be agreed upon in individual trusteeship agreements . . . placing each territory under the trusteeship system, and until such agreements have been concluded.' While it is quite definitely laid down that a territory is to be brought under the System by means of an agreement, the nature of this agreement is far from clear.

The Nature of the Agreement

The agreement referred to in Article 75 appears to be between the United Nations and some other party or parties. The agreement referred to in Article 77 (2) is an agreement specifying the territories to which the System is to apply, and outlining the terms under which they are to be brought under the System. There is no indication that the United Nations is to be a party to this agreement nor that it is the same agreement as the one placing a territory under trusteeship. Indeed, it is not even stated that an individual agreement for each territory is envisaged—it could be a single agreement specifying all the territories which are to be brought under the System and fixing the terms upon which this is to take place.

Article 79 states that 'the terms of trusteeship . . . shall be agreed upon by the states directly concerned . . . and shall be approved as provided for in Articles 83 and 85'—by the Security Council or the General Assembly. This suggests that there are two agreements: one between the 'States directly concerned,' and the other between the United Nations and, presumably, the future administering authority—the latter must be included in order that it may be bound by the terms of the agreement. In the first agreement, the 'States directly concerned' act as a drafting conference, framing the agreement which is to be submitted to the Organisation and the administering authority for approval.

According to Article 81, 'the trusteeship agreement shall in each case include the terms under which the trust territory will be administered,' thus distinguishing between the 'agreement' and the 'terms.' When this article is read in conjunction with Article 79, it can be interpreted as stating that the explicit terms of the agreement shall be concluded by the 'States directly concerned,' but that the actual agreement is to be concluded between the future administering authority and the General Assembly, or Security Council, acting for the Organisation. The distinction here is similar to that between the articles of a treaty and the treaty itself. However, since it is the terms of trusteeship drawn up by the 'States directly concerned' that the General Assembly or Security Council is to approve, no alterations to these terms may be made by the General Assembly or Security Council without the consent of the 'States directly concerned.' In this way the 'States directly concerned' become more than an ordinary drafting conference drawing up terms which the parties to the treaty may accept or reject at will; they themselves conclude an agreement, and this agreement forms the contents of a second agreement between the administering authority and the General Assembly (or Security Council). The position of the General Assembly is somewhat analogous to that of a State which is faced with the opportunity of ratifying a treaty the terms of which have already been fixed by signature: it can only approve or disapprove the agreement, but it has no authority to alter the terms in any way unless the unanimous assent of the other parties to the agreement (the 'States directly concerned') is obtained.[1]

1 See Articles 14, 15, and 16 of the Draft Convention on the Law of Treaties prepared under the auspices of the Faculty of the Harvard Law

In the case where the United Nations is designated as the administering authority, the question arises as to the parties to the actual agreement, since there cannot be an agreement between the Organisation (as administering authority) and itself (the Organisation as the supervisory authority).[2] In the case of the draft Statute for Jerusalem formulated by the Trusteeship Council in 1948, the Trusteeship Council was to undertake the administrative duties of the United Nations, and therefore presumably the agreement was intended to be one between the Trusteeship Council as administering authority, and the General Assembly who would approve the agreement.[3]

During the discussions in the Security Council on the draft trusteeship agreement for the Pacific Islands, the United States Delegate asserted that the draft trusteeship agreement was in the nature of a bilateral contract between the United States and the Organisation—in this case the Security Council.[4] However, Article 83 (1) states that 'all functions of the United Nations relating to strategic areas, including the approval of the terms of the trusteeship agreements and of their alteration or amendment, shall be exercised by the Security Council,' which means that there must be an agreement before the Organisation is brought in, for it is only brought in to approve an agreement which has already been drawn up. Article 79 definitely envisages two distinct processes: the agreement between the 'States directly concerned,' and the approval by the Security Council or General Assembly, as the case may be. Without the first stage there is no agreement for the Organisation to approve. In only one case has there been any agreement between the 'States directly concerned'—in the case of the trust territory of Nauru—and this is not the kind of agreement anticipated in Article 79. The agreement for Nauru states that 'the Administering Authority

School (29 *American Journal of International Law* (1935), Supplement, p. 870 *et seq.*). For a different view, see the Advisory Opinion of the International Court on *Reservations to the Convention on Genocide* (1951), which maintained that alterations (reservations) to a treaty by a new party may be permissible in certain circumstances: 'it is the compatibility of a reservation with the object and purpose of the Convention that must furnish the criterion for the attitude of a State in making the reservation on accession . . .' (*I.C.J. Reports 1951*, p. 24).

2 See further below, Chap. 11, p. 335 *et seq.*

3 *Official Records of the Trusteeship Council,* Second Session, Third Part, Annex, p. 6, Article 3.

4 *Official Records of the Security Council,* Second Year, No. 23, p. 476.

will be responsible for the peace, order, good government and the defence of the Territory, and for this purpose, in pursuance of *an Agreement made by the Governments of Australia, New Zealand and the United Kingdom,* the Government of Australia will on behalf of the Administering Authority and except and until otherwise agreed by the Governments of Australia, New Zealand and the United Kingdom continue to exercise full powers of legislation, administration and jurisdiction in and over the Territory.'[5] This, however, is really an administrative agreement whereby the three Powers agree which one shall act for them; it is not the agreement on the terms of trusteeship to which Article 79 refers.

Since the trust agreement is not binding until approved by the Organisation, the United Nations can be said to be a party to it. However, the power to approve is contingent upon an agreement having been made between the 'States directly concerned.'[6] Thus, the question arises as to the identity of these 'States directly concerned.'

The 'States Directly Concerned'

According to Article 79, the 'States directly concerned' include the 'mandatory power in the case of territories held under mandate by a Member of the United Nations.' Thus, according to this article, it is obligatory to include the Mandatory Power only if it is a Member of the United Nations—a point brought up by the United Kingdom Delegate during the discussion on the trust agreement for the Pacific Islands.[7] Thus, the exclusion of Japan from the Security Council's discussions was in conformity with Article 79. It is difficult, however, to see how a Mandatory could be considered *not* to be a 'State directly concerned' regardless of whether or not it is a Member of the United Nations, and Article 79 certainly does not prohibit a non-Member Mandatory being considered a 'State directly concerned'—it merely does not insist on it. In general, the 'States directly concerned' may be either Members or non-Members, since it is only specified that they be 'States.' But beyond this, the Charter gives very little help as to the identity of these mysterious States.

5 Article 4 (*United Nations Treaty Series,* Vol. 10, p. 3). Italics added.
6 Articles 83 (1) and 85 (1).
7 *Official Records of the Security Council,* Second Year, 116th Meeting, p. 464.

The Soviet Union was continually attempting to get the 'States directly concerned' defined, both at San Francisco[8] and later.[9] So there was no question of the drafters of the Charter being unaware of the uncertainty and ambiguity of the phrase. The Soviet Delegate to the General Assembly expressed the opinion that the problem should be solved by the United Nations defining the phrase.[10] The United Nations, however, showed no inclination to do so.

From the provision in Article 79 that 'the terms of trusteeship, including their alteration or amendment, shall be agreed upon by the *states* directly concerned,'[11] the question arises as to whether two or more States must be involved in this process to justify the use of the plural 'States.' This problem is similar to the one raised by Professor Kelsen, who questions whether the violation of more than one principle of the Charter is necessary to justify expulsion from the United Nations, since Article 6 speaks of the violation of 'principles.' Professor Kelsen considers that this must be decided by the organs of the United Nations which have to apply Article 6.[12] Adapting this opinion to the question of the 'States directly concerned' gives the duty of interpreting the use of 'States' in Article 79 to the organs of the United Nations which approve the trust agreements—namely, the Security Council and General Assembly. It might be argued that the plural 'States' was used to conform with paragraph 1 (b) of Article 77, which provides that the Trusteeship System shall apply to 'territories which may be detached from enemy states as a result of the Second World War.' In this case it might refer to an agreement which would be required between the victorious Powers to whom the territories were surrendered. The San Francisco proceedings throw no light on this point. However, Article 79 speaks of the terms of trusteeship being 'agreed upon by the states directly concerned, *including* the mandatory power in the case of territories held under mandate by a Member of the

[8] See *Summary Report of Fourth Meeting of Committee II/4* (*U.N.C.I.O. Docs.*, Vol. 10, p. 441).

[9] See *Official Records of the General Assembly*, Second Part of the First Session, 62nd Plenary Meeting, pp. 1281–1283. See also *The Question of the 'States Directly Concerned,'* Memorandum prepared by the U.N. Secretariat (Doc. A/C.4/36, October 16, 1946).

[10] See *Official Records of the General Assembly*, Second Part of the First Session, 62nd Plenary Meeting, p. 1281.

[11] Italics added.

[12] See H. Kelsen, *The Law of the United Nations* (1951), pp. 710–711.

United Nations,'[13] clearly envisaging at least one other State besides the Mandatory, unless 'including the mandatory power' was inserted to make it compulsory for a Mandatory to be considered a 'State directly concerned.' One thing that is certain is that the inhabitants of the territory in question have no right to take part in the drawing up of the terms of trusteeship, since this is reserved to States.

The lack of definition of the 'States directly concerned' leaves the phrase open to many different interpretations. The Soviet Union held that all Members of the Security Council were 'States directly concerned.'[14] In the case of the former Mandates, the United States claimed that she was a 'State directly concerned' inasmuch as she was one of the Principal Allied and Associated Powers to whom Germany had ceded the territories in 1919.[15] A similar line of reasoning might be used, in the case of territories detached from the enemy in 1945, to include all the Powers to whom these territories were surrendered among the 'States directly concerned.'[16] It could be argued that, since all trust territories are under United Nations supervision, all Members of the United Nations can claim to be directly concerned in the case of every trust agreement.

According to Article 80 (1), the rights of 'any States or any peoples or the terms of existing international instruments to which Members of the United Nations may respectively be parties' cannot be altered by Chapter XII (the International Trusteeship System), except as may be agreed upon in individual trust agreements. Thus any State having a commercial treaty effective in a proposed trust territory might well argue that it is a 'State directly concerned,' unless the rights under the commercial treaty are to be maintained in the trust agreement. Similarly, substantial investment by a State or its nationals in such a territory may impel the State to consider itself 'directly concerned.' Recognition by the United Nations of the right of such a State to be 'directly concerned' would provide reasonable assurance of security to potential investors in areas which might conceivably

13 Italics added.
14 *Official Records of the General Assembly,* First Part of the First Session, Fourth Committee, Sub-Committee 1, p. 174.
15 See United States: Department of State, *Bulletin,* February 3, 1946, and December 1, 1946.
16 This argument was valid for the Pacific Islands and Somaliland.

become future trust territories. This is an important practical consideration in view of the intense need for foreign investment in backward areas.[17]

Whilst the identity of the 'States directly concerned' was not revealed at San Francisco, there is no indication in the San Francisco proceedings as to who is to identify them subsequently.[18] When the question arose in the General Assembly in 1946, there seemed to be general agreement that this could not be done by the State submitting the agreement alone. Speaking for the United Kingdom, Mr. Ivor Thomas said that he 'agreed with the representatives of the United States and the Soviet Union that the 'States directly concerned' in each case could not be determined solely by the Member submitting the draft agreement, and that the right to be a State directly concerned was open to both large and small States.'[19] Whether, in practice, any other party besides the 'Member submitting the draft agreement' did actually determine the 'States directly concerned' can best be ascertained by examining the cases of the territories placed under trusteeship.

The draft trust agreement for Ruanda-Urundi was submitted by Belgium to the United Kingdom whom it considered to be a 'State directly concerned,' and whose approval the Belgian Delegate later informed the General Assembly had been obtained. The draft agreement was presented also to the United States, the Soviet Union, China and France, for information only.[20] France presented the draft trust agreements for Togoland and the Cameroons under French administration for approval to the United Kingdom, whom it considered to be a 'State directly concerned,' and to the other permanent members of the Security Council and the other Member administering an African mandate for information purposes.[1] The United Kingdom did not

[17] The deterrent effect of uncertainty regarding the future of a territory on potential investors has been pointed out in an interesting Report by a Study Group of Members of the Royal Institute of International Affairs on *The Colonial Problem* (1937), pp. 94–95.

[18] That this lack of definition of the 'States directly concerned' was intentional is obvious from the records of the Executive Committee of the United Nations. See *Report of the Executive Committee to the Preparatory Commission of the United Nations* (Doc. PC/EX/113/Rev.1, November 12, 1945), p. 66, par. 8.

[19] *Official Records of the General Assembly,* Second Part of the First Session, Fourth Committee, Sub-Committee 1, p. 178.

[20] *Official Records of the General Assembly,* Second Part of the First Session, Fourth Committee, p. 195.

[1] *ibid.*

even inform the United Nations as to whom it considered directly concerned in respect of the draft agreements which it was drawing up; it merely stated that it was negotiating with 'other Members of the United Nations.'[2] In actual fact, the United Kingdom Government sent the drafts of the agreements for Togoland and the Cameroons to France and the Union of South Africa as 'States directly concerned,' and to the United States, the Soviet Union and China for information only; the draft agreement for Tanganyika was sent to the Governments of Belgium and the Union of South Africa as 'States directly concerned,' then also to the United States, the Soviet Union and China for information.[3] In the case of the draft agreement for New Guinea, the Australian Government published the terms and then proceeded to discuss them with the United Kingdom, France, New Zealand and the United States.[4] The terms were not drawn up by the 'States directly concerned,' since they were published before such States were consulted, although the States with whom Australia discussed the terms did have the opportunity to submit amendments to the agreement subsequently. Referring to the draft agreement for Western Samoa, the New Zealand Delegate, Sir Carl Berendsen, informed the General Assembly that 'in the light of difficulty of interpreting Article 79, which was badly drafted, the New Zealand Government, in order to expedite the establishment of the Trusteeship Council, had proceeded pragmatically in the matter of the 'States directly concerned' without thereby prejudicing the rights of any States. Consultations had been held with the United States, the United Kingdom, Australia and France, who were considered to be 'States directly concerned.' If New Zealand's interpretation of this difficult clause was wrong, the Committee and the General Assembly could rectify the matter.'[5] In practice, New Zealand seems to have been the only State that recognised that any one besides herself had the right to specify the 'States directly concerned,' although this was not brought up until after she had obtained the approval of the States that she had identified as directly

[2] *ibid.*

[3] Hansard, *Parliamentary Debates*, House of Commons, Vol. 418, col. 150 (January 23, 1946).

[4] *Official Records of the General Assembly*, Second Part of the First Session, Joint Committee, Part 1, Annex 12.

[5] *Official Records of the General Assembly*, Second Part of the First Session, Fourth Committee, Sub-Committee 1, p. 5.

concerned. In the case of Nauru, an agreement was made between the joint administering authority of the United Kingdom, Australia and New Zealand, to the effect that Australia should be entrusted with the actual administration on behalf of all three of them; the terms were then drawn up, but there was no recognition of any 'States directly concerned' outside the three mentioned, and these were stated to be the joint administering authority.[6] With regard to the Pacific Islands, the United States took the line that Article 79 provided only that 'all interested parties have a chance to be heard,' and in practice this seems to have been the attitude adopted by all the States presenting draft trust agreements. When it came to placing Somaliland under trusteeship, there seems to have been a complete deviation from the Charter provisions. The terms of trusteeship were not agreed upon by 'States directly concerned,' but were drawn up by a drafting committee appointed by the Trusteeship Council and subsequently adopted by the Council; then they were approved by the General Assembly. The whole process took place within the Organisation, and the administering Power, Italy, who must obviously be considered a 'State directly concerned,' was not even permitted a vote in the drafting committee which drew up the terms of trusteeship.

Thus, in spite of the assertion of the United Kingdom Delegate that 'the "States directly concerned" in each case could not be determined solely by the Member submitting the draft agreement' that is in fact what did occur, and the Organisation, in approving the trust agreements, acquiesced in the practice. This can be explained by the anxiety of the General Assembly to conclude the trust agreements as quickly as possible so that the Trusteeship Council could be established, and also by the fears of Members that States submitting the agreements might withdraw them altogether if their actions were subjected to criticism—as was indeed threatened by the United States with regard to the Pacific Islands.[7]

The Soviet Union maintained that the trust agreements were illegal, and that therefore the Trusteeship Council was not established legally (since the establishment of the Trusteeship Council was contingent upon the conclusion of trust agreements); as a

[6] See further below, Chap. 11, pp. 204–205.

[7] *Official Records of the Security Council,* Second Year, No. 31, p. 615.

result the Soviet Union refused to participate in the work of the Trusteeship Council until April 1948. The Soviet Delegate told the General Assembly that 'it could not be said that the draft trusteeship agreements which had been submitted were consistent with the Charter, since the provisions of the Charter that the States directly concerned must agree to the trusteeship agreement had not been fulfilled, because the phrase "States directly concerned" had not yet been defined.'[8] Mr. Ryckmans, the Belgian Delegate, expressed the view that 'if the fifty-four United Nations agreed to accept the trusteeship agreements, there could be no question that all the States directly concerned had given their consent'[9]; presumably he was referring to the approval of the agreements by the General Assembly. Several points arise with regard to this statement. The trust agreements do not have to be approved by a unanimous vote of the General Assembly, and therefore a State which considered itself directly concerned could be outvoted in the General Assembly. If Mr. Ryckmans meant that this approval by the General Assembly established that the General Assembly itself had played its part in deciding on the identity of the 'States directly concerned,' that is another matter. But this is not the same thing as each of the fifty-four Members deciding the question, unless this can be deduced from the fact that the Members of the United Nations have agreed to regard a two-thirds vote of the General Assembly as authoritative. Furthermore, it does not take care of any non-Members who might consider themselves directly concerned, unless Article 2 (6) can be invoked to cover this point.[10] Nor does Mr. Ryckmans' view accord with the Charter since the

[8] *Official Records of the General Assembly,* Second Part of the First Session, Fourth Committee, Sub-Committee 1, p. 182.

[9] *ibid.*

[10] Article 2 (6) reads as follows: 'The Organisation shall ensure that states which are not members of the United Nations act in accordance with these Principles [the Principles of the United Nations] so far as may be necessary for the maintenance of international peace and security.' See also Advisory Opinion of the International Court of Justice on *Reparation for Injuries Suffered in the Service of the United Nations* (1949) (*I.C.J. Reports 1949,* p. 174) on the position of a non-Member State as regards the United Nations Organisation: '. . . the Court's opinion is that fifty States, representing the vast majority of the members of the international community, had the power, in conformity with international law, to bring into being an entity possessing objective international personality, and not merely personality recognised by them alone, together with capacity to bring international claims' (*ibid.,* p. 185).

fifty-four United Nations, as Members of the General Assembly, only *approve* the trust agreements, whereas under Article 79 the 'States directly concerned' are required to agree upon the actual terms. If their agreement meant just that they were to *approve* the terms of trusteeship, then the insertion in Article 79 that 'the terms of trusteeship . . . shall be agreed upon by the states directly concerned' is superfluous, since in any case they were involved in the approval stage in the case of non-strategic areas, by the fact of being Members of the General Assembly.

The Trusteeship System was thus brought into being without the question of the 'States directly concerned' having been settled. In shelving the problem as they did, the delegates were merely postponing to a later date a matter which was bound to recur when any of the trust agreements came up for alteration.

The Right to Place a Territory under the System

Only in the case of category (c) of the territories enumerated in Article 77 (1) as being eligible for trusteeship, is there reference to who shall place a territory under the Trusteeship System. Here it is provided that territories shall be placed under the System by 'States responsible for their administration.' Nothing is said about such States being Members of the United Nations, so that presumably it is open to non-Members to place their dependencies under trusteeship should they be so inclined. The requirements are merely that the entity so doing should be a State, and that such State must be responsible for the administration of the territory concerned. It should be noted that Article 77 does not require the State submitting a territory to trusteeship to possess the legal title to the territory, it is merely necessary for the State to be responsible for the territory's administration. However, the ordinary rules of international law require that a State must possess title to a territory before it is entitled to dispose of it.[11]

The Charter gives no indication as to who may place either a former mandate, or an ex-enemy territory, under the Trustee-

11 As Dr. Schwarzenberger has pointed out (*International Law* (1949), Vol. 1, p. 143), the maxim *Nemo potest plus juris transferre ad alium quam ipse habet* is part of international law. This received authoritative confirmation from the Permanent Court of Arbitration in the Case of the *Island of Palmas* (1928) (P.C.A. 19) (see 2 Scott, *Hague Court Reports*, p. 84 *et seq.*).

ship System; it leaves the impression that any one may do so. There is no specification that it must be done by a State, which leaves open the possibility of the United Nations Organisation or some other international body placing a territory under trusteeship. In the case of a mandate, there is no requirement in the Charter that it should be placed under trusteeship by the Mandatory.[12] However, the consent of the Mandatory must be obtained, since the territory can only be brought under the System by means of a trust agreement which must be agreed upon by the 'States directly concerned'; and whoever this phrase does or does not include, it certainly includes the Mandatory.[13]

A resolution adopted by the General Assembly on February 9, 1946, invited all States administering territories under mandate to negotiate trust agreements in conjunction with the 'States directly concerned' with a view to placing the mandates under the Trusteeship System.[14] It did not direct its invitation at the Mandatory Powers but at the States administering the mandates. This was probably due to the General Assembly's desire to include the United States in the invitation, inasmuch as the former Japanese mandate was then under United States administration. In spite of the resolution, however, the right of the United States to submit the Japanese mandate to trusteeship raises many serious doubts.

The United States based its right to place the Japanese mandate under trusteeship on the resolution of the General Assembly, and on the presumption that Japan had forfeited her mandate. 'In utter disregard of the mandate, Japan used the territories for aggressive warfare, in violation of the law of nations. . . . This, under international law, was a criminal act; it was an essential violation of the trust, and by it Japan forfeited the right and capacity to be the mandatory of the islands.'[15] This was the

[12] The United States presented a draft trust agreement for Palestine to the General Assembly in 1948, although she was not the Mandatory for Palestine nor was she responsible for its administration (see Doc. A/C.1/277 of 1948).

[13] See above, p. 80.

[14] *Official Records of the General Assembly,* First Part of the First Session, Resolution 9 (I).

[15] *Official Records of the Security Council,* Second Year, No. 23, p. 472. Japan's criminality in this respect was established by the Tokyo Tribunal in its Judgment. One of the principal points on which the Prosecution relied in support of its charge of Crimes Against Peace was that, in her

explanation given to the Security Council by the United States Delegate, who further held that Japan had accepted this forfeiture by signing the Instrument of Surrender.[16] The first question that arises is whether the surrender of the mandate by Japan could take effect before the Peace Treaty between her and the Allies came into force. Two of the Allied Powers who signed the Instrument of Surrender, Australia and the United Kingdom, held that the surrender of the mandate was contingent upon the entry into force of the Peace Treaty. Sir Alexander Cadogan expressed the view of the United Kingdom in the following way: 'Although this means that the United States carries out the functions of government in the islands, the fact remains that the mandatory power is *de jure* Japan and that this situation cannot, strictly speaking, be changed except by means of provisions in the final peace treaty.'[17]

This view is generally upheld by international law, as was pointed out by the Permanent Court of International Justice in its Advisory Opinion on the *German Settlers in Poland* (1923): 'The cession and occupation of the German territories was left to be effected by the coming into force of the Treaty of Peace.'[18] The Australian Delegate to the Security Council suggested that the trust agreement for the Pacific Islands should come into force 'on the date on which the interim or final treaty of Peace between Japan and the Allied Powers, victorious in war against Japan, becomes binding on Japan.'[19] This suggestion was not accepted by the Security Council, and the trust agreement was approved and came into operation on July 18, 1947, over four years before the entry into force of the Peace Treaty with Japan. The

General Preparation for war, 'Japan continually and progressively fortified the islands for which she held a mandate from the League of Nations' (Appendix A, Section 5 (c). See *International Military Tribunal for the Far East, Judgment* (1948) mimeographed records), Annexes, p. 69).

16 *Official Records of the Security Council,* Second Year, No. 20, p. 413. Under the Instrument of Surrender (Royal Institute of International Affairs: *Survey of International Affairs 1939–1946: The Far East 1942–1946* (1955), p. 498), Japan accepted the provisions set forth in the Potsdam declaration which stated that 'the terms of the Cairo declaration shall be carried out' (*ibid.,* p. 493). According to the Cairo declaration, Japan was to 'be stripped of all the islands in the Pacific which she has seized or occupied since the beginning of the first world war in 1914' (*ibid.,* p. 491), which included the Mandated Islands.

17 *Official Records of the Security Council,* Second Year, No. 23, p. 464.

18 B. 6, p. 28 (See 1 Hudson, *World Court Reports,* p. 208 *et seq.*).

19 *Official Records of the Security Council,* Second Year, No. 26, p. 521.

creation of this trust territory rested on a very controversial legal basis and was an example of convenience overruling legality. It was generally agreed that this territory should eventually come under the administration of the United States, and not even those States who questioned the legality of the method adopted were prepared to obstruct it. This was plainly put into words by Sir Alexander Cadogan: 'If, however, the majority of my colleagues wish to proceed in the sense requested by the United States representative, then, in deference to their views and to the desire of the United States Government to have at once what all concerned are agreed upon it should have eventually, I shall not oppose such a course.' [20]

Perhaps the most fundamental question to be answered concerning the Japanese mandate is whether Japan had the *right* to surrender it. If the answer is in the affirmative this would seem to imply that Japan possessed sovereignty over the territory, since international law does not sanction a State disposing of a territory to which it does not have legal title. The history of the mandate gives little ground for attributing sovereignty over it to Japan. The territory which later comprised the Japanese mandate was surrendered by Germany to the Principal Allied and Associated Powers by Article 119 of the Treaty of Versailles (1919). These Powers in turn did not surrender sovereignty to Japan,[1] they either retained it or passed it on to the League of Nations. The Allied Supreme Council, in May 1919, allocated the territory to Japan to be administered *on behalf of* the League.[2] Japan remained legally accountable to the League even after she withdrew from the Organisation, a fact which she herself acknowledged by continuing to submit reports on the mandate. This in itself indicates that not even Japan herself considered that she possessed sovereignty over the mandate. The only thing Japan was entitled to surrender was the right to

[20] *Official Records of the Security Council,* Second Year, No. 23, p. 464.

[1] In the Advisory Opinion on the *International Status of South-West Africa* (1950), the International Court of Justice said that 'the terms of this Mandate [Mandate for South-West Africa], as well as the provisions of Article 22 of the Covenant and the principles embodied therein, show that the creation of this new international institution did not involve any cession of territory or transfer of sovereignty to the Union of South Africa' (*I.C.J. Reports 1950*, p. 132). This is equally true with regard to Japan and her mandate.

[2] See preamble to the Mandate Treaty (U.N. Doc. A/70, *Terms of League of Nations Mandates*).

administer the mandate, so long as others possessing rights in the situation acquiesced, and so long as the League requirements were satisfied. Article 7 of this Treaty states that the consent of the League Council is required for any alteration in the terms of the Treaty.[3] At the time at which the mandate was surrendered by Japan, the League was still in existence; Japan should therefore have consulted the League and obtained the Council's consent to the transfer of administration.[4] To transfer the mandate without such consent was clearly illegal. Thus even had Japan possessed sovereignty over the mandate, she did not have the right to transfer administration to another Power in violation of her treaty obligations to the League.

Another theory with regard to the sovereignty over the mandates is that it rested in the Principal Allied and Associated Powers. Even if this theory is upheld it still does not legalise the placing of the former Japanese mandate under trusteeship in 1947. According to this theory, each of the Principal Allied and Associated Powers of 1919 had rights under the mandate. Two of these Powers became enemy States during the Second World War—Italy and Japan. The United States, supported by Poland and France, held that Japan had forfeited any rights that she might have in the mandates through waging an aggressive war in violation of the Briand-Kellog Pact.[5] But this was never decided upon by the League of Nations, and therefore it would seem that the only way that this could be established legally was through the renunciation of such rights by Japan and Italy themselves. In the Peace Treaty with Italy, Italy specifi-

[3] Article 1 of the Mandate designated the Emperor of Japan as the Mandatory, and Article 2 stated that administration would be exercised by the Mandatory. Thus the transfer of administration from the Emperor is an alteration in the terms of the Mandate, requiring the consent of the League Council.

[4] The Japanese Instrument of Surrender came into force on September 2, 1945, the League wound up on April 18, 1946.

[5] The Charter of the International Military Tribunal for the Far East empowered the Tribunal to try Far Eastern war criminals for Crimes against Peace (Section 2, Article 5 (a). See *International Military Tribunal for the Far East, Judgment* (1948) (mimeographed records), Annexes, p. 19 *et seq.*), which was stated to include waging of a war of aggression or a war in violation of treaties. The Treaties mentioned specifically in the Appendix to the Charter as having been violated included the Briand-Kellog Pact (Appendix B, pars. 33–34. See *ibid.*, pp. 97–98). However, nowhere in the Tribunal's Judgment was it stated that Japan had forfeited her rights in the Mandates by her criminal acts.

cally renounced all rights, titles and claims under the Mandate System.[6] Japan did not legally do the same until the Peace Treaty came into force in 1951[7]—*after* the territory became a trust territory, since the terms of the Instrument of Surrender were left to be put into effect by the Peace Treaty.[8]

A third theory of sovereignty with regard to the mandates is that it rested in the League, and it is on this assumption that the best case can be made to establish the legality of the United States' placing of the Japanese mandate under trusteeship. If the sovereignty of the territory rested in the League, since there was no transfer to the United Nations, the sovereignty can be said to have died with the League. Thus the mandate became *terra nullius* and the title then passed to the Power in actual occupation of the territory. This was not the former Mandatory Japan but the United States, since the League wound up seven months *after* the United States took over control of the mandate. On this basis it could be held that the United States had a perfect right to submit the territory to trusteeship, or to annex it or dispose of it in some other way. But any legal title that the United States did have to place the former mandate under trusteeship, arose not from the surrender of Japan, but from the assumption that the League was the sovereign of the mandate, that the mandate lapsed upon the death of the League, and thereupon from the United States' occupation of the territory. However, this interpretation is not supported by the International Court of Justice which, in its Advisory Opinion on the *International Status of South-West Africa,* rejected the South African contention that the mandate had lapsed.[9]

The Role of the United Nations

The main role of the United Nations in the bringing of a territory under trusteeship is its approval of the terms of the trust agreement, drawn up by the 'States directly concerned.' By this means, the United Nations, acting through the General

[6] See Article 40 of the Peace Treaty with Italy (Cmd. 7481 [1948] p. 20).

[7] By Article 2 (d) of the Treaty of Peace with Japan, 'Japan renounces all right, title and claim in connection with the League of Nations Mandates System, and accepts the action of the United Nations Security Council of April 2, 1947, extending the trusteeship system to the Pacific Islands formerly under mandate to Japan' (Cmd. 8392 [1951]).

[8] See text to n. 18, above.

[9] *I.C.J. Reports 1950*, p. 132.

Assembly or Security Council, plays an essential part in the conclusion of the agreement, since without its approval the agreement cannot enter into force. The Charter provides that this function of the Organisation is to be exercised by the Security Council in the case of trust agreements for strategic areas, and by the General Assembly for all other trust agreements.[10] At this stage, the trust agreement takes on the character of a treaty between the Organisation and the administering authority, since the latter's approval is necessary for the terms of the agreement to become binding upon it. In practice, this approval by the administering authority has been implied rather than specifically stated, since, with one exception, the future administering authority has itself presented the final agreement to the Organisation for approval. It seems to be a valid assumption that if such administering authority had not approved the agreement, it would not have presented it to the General Assembly or Security Council. Therefore, with two exceptions, the trust agreements entered into force upon the approval by the United Nations.[11] In the case of Somaliland, the situation was somewhat different. The administering authority, Italy, had taken no real part in the drawing up of the trust agreement and of its presentation to the General Assembly; therefore the agreement specified that ratification by Italy was required before the agreement could enter into force.[12] The only other agreement which did not automatically enter into force upon the approval of the United Nations, was that for the Pacific Islands under the United States administration. This agreement incorporated the provision that it would come into force 'when approved by the Security Council of the United Nations and by the Government of the United States after due constitutional process.'[13] However, this was due entirely to United States domestic requirements.

The United Nations is not entirely confined to the approval

[10] Articles 83 (1) and 85.

[11] Article 15 of the trust agreements for Togoland (*United Nations Treaty Series*, Vol. 8, p. 165) and the Cameroons (*ibid.*, p. 105) under French administration, specifying that the agreements would enter into force as soon as they had received the approval of the General Assembly, was superfluous.

[12] Article 23 of the agreement for Somaliland under Italian administration (see *Official Records of the General Assembly*, Fifth Session, Suppl. No. 10, p. 8).

[13] *United Nations Treaty Series*, Vol. 8, p. 190, Article 16.

stage of bringing a territory under trusteeship. Although the initiative for placing a territory under trusteeship must come from the State or States responsible for the territory and entitled to dispose of it—since the Charter presupposes the existence of a trust agreement before the United Nations is brought in to approve it—the role of the Organisation is not altogether passive in these early stages. Article 10 of the Charter authorises the General Assembly to make recommendations to Members on any matter within the scope of the Charter, which of course includes trusteeship. This authorisation was made use of in the case of South-West Africa, when the General Assembly recommended that the Government of the Union of South Africa present a trust agreement for the territory of South-West Africa.[14]

[14] *Official Records of the General Assembly,* Second Part of the First Session, Resolution 65 (I).

CHAPTER 6

CONTENTS OF THE TRUST AGREEMENTS

IN the previous chapter it was pointed out that there are in fact two agreements involved in the process of bringing a territory under trusteeship. The important one, however, is the agreement which is approved by the United Nations, and it is this agreement that is referred to as the trust agreement in this study, unless otherwise stated.

The trust agreement provides the legal basis for the supervision of a trust territory by the United Nations and for its administration by the administering authority. It confers powers of administration on the administering authority designated in the agreement, and bestows supervisory powers on the Organisation. Thus, the trust agreement is the basic law for the application of the United Nations Trusteeship System to any particular territory. This suggests that the trust agreement must be superior to any other international instrument. However, Article 103 of the Charter establishes that, so far as concerns the Members of the United Nations, the provisions of the Charter take precedence over any other international instrument. Therefore the provisions of the Charter, especially those in Chapters XII and XIII, are superior to the provisions of the trust agreements for territories administered by Members of the United Nations; and since the admission of Italy to Membership in 1955, all trust territories have been administered by Members. From a strictly legal point of view, the provisions of the trust agreements are operative only to the extent that they are in conformity with the Charter. A trust agreement must not seek to negate the provisions of the Charter but should be concerned with implementing them, for example, by providing ways in which the United Nations' supervisory powers may be most effectively put into operation in the particular territory in question.[1]

[1] In the case of the trust agreement for Tanganyika (*United Nations Treaty Series,* Vol. 8, p. 91), Article 16 requires that the administering authority send a special representative to be present in the Trusteeship Council during the examination of the annual report on Tanganyika. This provision is thus helping towards a realistic examination of the report by providing an authority from the territory to answer any queries

In General

Since the Charter is superior to any other international instrument, a trust agreement must not forbid the exercise of supervision by the United Nations in the manner laid down in Article 87 of the Charter. By means of this article, the General Assembly and Trusteeship Council are authorised to consider reports, accept and examine petitions, and provide for periodic visits to the trust territories at times agreed upon with the administering authority. Paragraph (d) of Article 87 states that the General Assembly and the Trusteeship Council may 'take these and other actions in conformity with the terms of the trusteeship agreements.' This clause has been held to qualify the application of paragraphs (a), (b) and (c) by permitting them to be effected only so long as the trust agreement allows for it,[2] and indeed the proceedings at San Francisco[3] give good reason for this view. However, since the essence of United Nations trusteeship is administration by an administering authority and supervision by the United Nations, and since Article 87 (a), (b) and (c) provides the way in which this supervision is to be exercised, the above interpretation of paragraph (d) is not in conformity with the Charter provisions on trusteeship when taken as a whole. The only interpretation of paragraph (d) which makes sense of Chapters XII and XIII of the Charter, is that the actions in paragraphs (a), (b) and (c) are necessarily in accordance with the trust agreements, but that 'these and other actions' are to be exercised by either the General Assembly and the Trusteeship Council or by the Security Council and the Trusteeship Council, depending on whether or not the territory is designated as strategic, and which will be determined in 'conformity with the terms of the trusteeship agreements.' At the same time, the actual details of the means by which paragraphs (a), (b) and (c) and 'other actions' are to be implemented will be laid down in the trust agreement.

If there is any mention in a trust agreement of the territory being placed under the United Nations Trusteeship System, then the provisions of Chapters XII and XIII of the Charter automati-

that may arise. This is based on Rule 74 of the Trusteeship Council's Rules of Procedure which permits, but does not require, such a course of action by an administering authority (see *Rules of Procedure of the Trusteeship Council*, Doc. T/1/Rev.3, p. 12).

2 See H. Kelsen, *The Law of the United Nations* (1951), p. 613, n. 4.

3 *U.N.C.I.O. Docs.*, Vol. 10, p. 679 *et seq.*

cally apply, since they comprise the only system of United Nations Trusteeship which the Charter supplies. There is no need for there to be any mention of Chapters XII and XIII or for any of the provisions therein to be incorporated into the trust agreement in order for them to become operative in the territory concerned. However, Article 81 of the Charter does require that the terms of trusteeship be included in the trust agreement.

Article 81 states that a trust agreement must include the terms under which a territory is to be administered. The question arises as to whether the terms of trusteeship need be specifically stated in full in the agreement, or whether this requirement of Article 81 is complied with if the agreement includes provision to the effect that administration is to be in accordance with the Charter. Obviously it was intended when the Charter was drafted that a trust territory should be administered in accordance with the Charter, therefore, presumably Article 81 is referring to any terms *additional* to those in the Charter under which the territory is to be governed. Such additional terms might take the form of the trust territory being required to achieve independence in a stated period of time as is the case with the trust agreement for Somaliland.

Article 81 further requires that the contents of the trust agreement include the designation of the administering authority, which is to be the authority exercising the administration of the trust territory. If the actual exercise of administration is delegated by one authority to another, the latter must be named in the trust agreement and becomes the actual administering authority according to the way in which the term is used in the Charter.[4] If the administering authority designated in the agreement delegates the exercise of administration to another authority, then the trust agreement must be altered to allow for the designation of the latter authority as the administering authority of the territory.

Article 77 (1) provides that a trust agreement is to be the means by which a territory is placed under trusteeship, thus clearly establishing that the Trusteeship System does not automatically apply to any territory.

[4] Thus, Nauru is administered by a single administering authority which is Australia, although the trust agreement incorrectly designates a joint administering authority of Australia, New Zealand and the United Kingdom. See further below, Chap. 11, pp. 204–205.

If the territory concerned is to become a strategic trust territory, or if an area within it is to be strategic, this must be stated in the terms of the trust agreement itself[5]; otherwise the presumption is that the territory is an ordinary trust territory falling under the authority of the General Assembly. The reason for this requirement in Article 82 is that by Article 83 the trust agreement for a strategic area must be approved by the Security Council rather than by the General Assembly, and all subsequent functions of the United Nations must be exercised by the Security Council. It is not very clear from Article 83 what happens if a trust agreement designates only a portion of the territory as a strategic area. The Security Council is authorised and required to exercise the functions of the United Nations, including the approval of the terms of the trust agreement, only for an area designated as strategic. Similarly, Article 85 (1) requires the General Assembly to approve the terms of the trust agreement for every area *not* designated as strategic. In the case where a trust agreement designates only a portion of the territory as strategic, the functions of the General Assembly and the Security Council with regard to the approval of the agreements overlap. Therefore, it appears that such an agreement must be approved by both the General Assembly and the Security Council. This might be done by the trust agreement being divided into two parts: one relating to the strategic area and the other relating to the rest of the territory. Each part would then come under the respective competent United Nations organ. Such an arrangement would prevent the General Assembly and Security Council overstepping their powers with regard to the trust agreement.

A further provision which it would seem to be necessary to insert in the trust agreement, although the Charter does not require this, is a specification as to the territory to be placed under trusteeship.

The Charter envisages that trust agreements will fall into two broad categories—strategic and non-strategic. But a third category appeared in practice—that of an agreement designating a non-Member of the United Nations as the administering authority. Theoretically this is possible whether the territory in question is a strategic or non-strategic trust, but the only example to date is that of a non-strategic trust territory adminis-

[5] Article 82.

tered by a non-Member. Since a non-Member is not bound by the provisions of the Charter, such a trust agreement is necessarily far more detailed than the others to allow for the inclusion therein of provisions by which a Member is automatically bound by virtue of such Membership. The provisions of the trust agreements in each of the three categories mentioned require examination to the extent to which they reflect, go beyond, or tend to contravene the provisions of the Charter on trusteeship as laid down in Chapters XII and XIII.

Non-Strategic Territories Administered by Members

There are at present ten trust agreements for non-strategic territories under the administration of United Nations Members,[6] but inasmuch as the agreement for Somaliland is considered separately,[7] only the remaining nine are dealt with here. In each of these cases a single Member is the administering authority and the administering authority a former Mandatory of the territory under the Mandate System of the League of Nations. The preambles to all these agreements make reference to the fact that the administering authorities originally acquired jurisdiction over the territories in the form of mandates from the League of Nations, and the first article of each agreement is devoted to delimiting the territory to which the agreement refers.[8]

Provisions Reflecting Chapters XII and XIII

Designation of Administering Authority.—In accordance with the provisions of Article 81 of the Charter, each of the trust agreements includes the designation of the administering authority, although in the case of Nauru this is incorrectly stated.[9]

[6] These territories are as follows: New Guinea under Australian administration, Nauru under Australian administration, Ruanda-Urundi under Belgian administration, the Cameroons under French administration, Togoland under French administration, Western Samoa under New Zealand administration, the Cameroons under United Kingdom administration, Togoland under United Kingdom administration, Tanganyika under United Kingdom administration, and Somaliland under Italian administration.

[7] See below, p. 111 *et seq.*

[8] The trust agreements for Tanganyika (*United Nations Treaty Series,* Vol. 8, p. 91), the Cameroons (*ibid.,* p. 119) and Togoland (*ibid.,* p. 151) under the United Kingdom are identical; likewise the agreements for the Cameroons (*ibid.,* p. 135) and Togoland (*ibid.,* p. 165) under French administration are identical; therefore reference will be made only to the agreements for Tanganyika and the French Cameroons, the others mentioned above being considered included in such references.

[9] See below, pp. 107–108.

Administration in accordance with the Charter

The agreements for Nauru and New Guinea[10] include the provision that the administering authority undertakes to administer the trust territory in accordance with the Charter, whilst the agreement for the French administered Cameroons provides that the administering authority shall exercise the duties of trusteeship as defined in the Charter.[11] The other agreements do not include such a general provision except for that in respect of Western Samoa[12] in which case the text of Chapters XII and XIII of the Charter is annexed to the agreement. The absence of similar provisions in the other agreements does not imply that the territories need not necessarily be administered in accordance with the Charter, since all Members of the United Nations are bound by the Charter provisions regardless of whether the trust agreements specifically state this.

Application of Article 76

In each case, the agreement states that the administering authority is to administer the territory in such a manner as to achieve the basic objectives of Article 76. The agreement for the French administered Cameroons uses less compulsive wording, substituting the obligation to 'promote the basic objectives' in place of to 'achieve the basic objectives.'[13] Further details concerning the achievement of the objectives of Article 76 (b) are to be found in the agreements. All the agreements incorporate further provisions on the political advancement of the inhabitants which is to be achieved through assuring them a progressively increasing share in the administrative services, legislative bodies and the government of the territories. With the exception of that for Nauru, all the agreements specifically provide that educational advancement shall be effected in the territory. In the case of the French administered Cameroons, the economic and social progress of the inhabitants is separately assured.[14] In the agreements for Tanganyika, Ruanda-Urundi, and the French administered Cameroons[15] there are detailed

10 Article 3 (*United Nations Treaty Series,* Vol. 10, p. 3), and Article 3 (*ibid.,* Vol. 8, p. 181) respectively.
11 Article 2.
12 *United Nations Treaty Series,* Vol. 8, p. 71.
13 Article 2.
14 Article 7.
15 Article 9, Article 9 (*United Nations Treaty Series,* Vol. 8, p. 105) and Article 8 respectively.

articles guaranteeing the 'open-door,'[16] subject to its not prejudicing the attainment of Article 76 (a), (b) and (c). The same is guaranteed in the agreement for Western Samoa through the reproduction of the text of Article 76 (d) in this case.

Contribution of the territory to international peace and security

The trust agreements reflect the importance attached by the drafters of the Charter to the furtherance of international peace and security as the primary aim of the International Trusteeship System. To this end, all the agreements incorporate provisions to implement Article 84 of the Charter. In the case of Nauru and New Guinea,[17] this is limited to requiring the administering authority to take all desirable measures for the defence of the territory and the maintenance of international peace and security; in the other agreements detailed provision is made for the voluntary recruitment of native troops and for the establishment of bases and fortifications in the territory. The omission of these last provisions in the agreements for Nauru and New Guinea is a reflection of their very backward stage of development, as compared with the African trust territories. It is not anticipated that Nauru and New Guinea could provide much assistance to the Security Council in any enforcement action it might take; likewise, in the event of an armed attack against one of these territories, the administering authority can expect to have to shoulder the main burden of the defence of the territory.

Supervision by the United Nations

All of the agreements make special reference to the obligation of the administering authority to collaborate with the United Nations in the discharge of its supervisory functions under Articles 87 and 88. In the majority of cases this duty is specified as being to co-operate with the General Assembly and the Trusteeship Council in the exercise of these functions, but for some reason, in the agreements for Nauru, New Guinea and Western Samoa,[18] reference is made only to co-operation with the Trusteeship Council. Since Article 87 assigns the United

16 For further discussion on the 'open-door,' see above, Chap. 4, p. 68 *et seq.*
17 Article 7 in both agreements.
18 Articles 5 (1) 8 (1) and 14 respectively.

Nations' supervisory functions over trust territories to the General Assembly and 'under its authority, the Trusteeship Council,' it is not clear why these three agreements referred to the Trusteeship Council only. Although in practice, the Trusteeship Council rather than the General Assembly has come to exercise the functions stated in Article 87, it does so only under the authority of the General Assembly, and the right of the General Assembly itself to exercise this role remains. Since the administering authorities for Nauru, New Guinea and Western Samoa are all bound by Article 87 of the Charter by virtue of their membership in the Organisation, they are obliged to co-operate with the General Assembly as well as the Trusteeship Council, in spite of the omission in the trust agreements.

Certain of the agreements make further reference to the specific functions of the United Nations authorised by Article 87. Those for Tanganyika, Ruanda-Urundi, the French administered Cameroons and Western Samoa[19] state that the administering authority is to make an annual report to the United Nations on the basis of the Trusteeship Council's Questionnaire. In the cases of Tanganyika, Ruanda-Urundi and the French administered Cameroons, the obligation to facilitate periodic visits by the United Nations to the trust territories is written into the agreements. The agreement for the French Administered Cameroons is the most complete of all to the extent that, in addition to incorporating the administering authority's obligations with regard to the annual reports and visiting missions, it also provides that the administering authority shall appoint a representative to take part in the General Assembly's or Trusteeship Council's examination of the petitions concerning the territory. This fulfils the requirement of Article 87 (b) that petitions be examined in consultation with the administering authority concerned.

Alteration of the agreement

The question of the alteration of the trust agreements is given consideration in the agreements for Western Samoa, Tanganyika, Ruanda-Urundi and the French administered Cameroons,[20] which merely state that they shall not be altered

[19] Articles 3, 3, 2, and 14 respectively.
[20] Articles 15, 18, 18, and 12 respectively.

except as provided in the Charter. These provisions add nothing to the requirements for alteration provided in Chapter XII.

Role of the administering authority

Each of the agreements incorporates an elaboration of the role of the administering authority. Full powers of legislation, administration and jurisdiction are accorded to the administering authorities, subject to the provisions of the Charter and the trust agreements.

Provisions going beyond Chapters XII and XIII

There are various provisions in the trust agreements which, whilst they are not in contradiction with the provisions of the international Trusteeship System, go beyond the requirements of Chapters XII and XIII. Such provisions fall into two groups: those which accord additional rights or duties to the administering authority, and those which guarantee additional rights to the inhabitants of the trust territory. The former group of provisions cover a wide variety of subjects, whilst the latter are concerned with land policy and human rights.

Application of international conventions

In each of the agreements, the administering authority concerned undertakes to apply appropriate international conventions to the trust territory. In each case a qualifying phrase is used, either to the effect that such conventions should be appropriate to the territory or that they should be in the interests of the inhabitants—both of which allow for discretionary powers to be exercised by the administering authority. The agreements for Nauru and New Guinea [1] leave no doubt about the use of this discretion, stating that the conventions should be appropriate to the territory 'in the opinion of the administering authority.' The conventions to be applied are not restricted to United Nations conventions except in the agreement for the French administered Cameroons.[2] In the agreement for Ruanda-Urundi, appropriate recommendations are also to be applied to the territory.[3] In the case of the French administered Cameroons, Tanganyika and Western Samoa [4] these recommendations are

[1] Article 6 in both agreements.
[2] Article 6.
[3] Article 7.
[4] Articles 6, 7, and 7 respectively.

to be restricted to those of the United Nations and the specialised agencies, whilst they are restricted to recommendations of the specialised agencies alone in the case of New Guinea and Nauru.[5]

Co-operation of the territory in regional organisations

The agreements for Western Samoa, Ruanda-Urundi, Tanganyika and the French administered Cameroons[6] all provide for the co-operation of the trust territories in regional or specialised international organisations not inconsistent with the spirit of the Charter. In each case, the initiative for such co-operation is to come from the administering authority rather than the inhabitants of the trust territory.

Reference of disputes to the International Court

The agreements for Western Samoa, Tanganyika, Ruanda-Urundi and the French administered Cameroons[7] provide that disputes concerning the agreements between the administering authority and another Member of the United Nations, which cannot be settled by 'negotiation or other means,'[8] shall be referred to the International Court. This provision affects only the administering authority, since it cannot be held to bind another Member which may be a party to such a dispute without this Member's consent. Whether the International Court could claim competence to judge such a dispute would depend entirely upon whether the Member party to the dispute agreed to submit it to the Court. What this provision in the agreement establishes is that the consent of the administering authority has been obtained in advance.

It is only disputes which cannot be settled by 'negotiation or other means' which, according to the trust agreements, are to be submitted to the International Court. Thus the Court assumes jurisdiction only in the last resort. This question was dealt with by the Permanent Court of International Justice with regard to the mandate for Palestine, and since the Mandate Treaty for Palestine provided for the submission of disputes

[5] Article 6 in both agreements.
[6] Articles 13, 15, 15, and 14 respectively.
[7] Articles 16, 19, 19, and 13 respectively.
[8] This reads by 'negotiation or similar means' in the agreement for Western Samoa.

which could not 'be settled by negotiation'[9] to the Permanent Court, an analogy can be drawn from this case and applied to the trust territories. It appears from this case of the *Readaptation of the Mavrommatis Jerusalem Concession* (Jurisdiction) (1927), that the jurisdiction of the Court lay only in exceptional cases.[10]

Administrative unions

Provision for the administering authority to constitute the trust territory into an administrative union or federation with another non-self-governing territory under its control, is contained in the agreements for Tanganyika, Ruanda-Urundi, the French administered Cameroons and New Guinea.[11] This provision has caused much concern to non-administering Members of the United Nations, who fear that such a union or federation would tend to obscure the separate identity of the trust territory and delay its achievement of independence. In no case is the administering authority given unqualified authorisation to constitute a trust territory into an administrative union; it is subject to such a course being in conformity with the objectives of the Trusteeship System. There is no indication as to who is competent to decide whether an administrative union is in conformity with the objectives of the Charter, and in practice this has caused much disagreement. Numerous attempts have been made in the United Nations to establish that an administrative union should only be established with the prior permission of the Trusteeship Council,[12] thus attempting to give the power of deciding on the compatibility of an administrative union with the objectives of the Charter to the Trusteeship Council. What was definitely decided, however, was that an administrative union must remain entirely administrative in character and scope and that it must not obstruct the separate development of the trust territory as a distinct entity.[13]

[9] Article 26 (see *Terms of League of Nations Mandates,* republished by the United Nations (1946), No. 3).
[10] Permanent Court of International Justice, *Collection of Judgments,* Series A, No. 11.
[11] Articles 5, 5, 4, and 5 respectively.
[12] See further above, Chap. 4, pp. 64–66.
[13] *Official Records of the General Assembly,* Third Session, Resolution 224 (III).

Contents of annual reports

In the agreements for Tanganyika, Ruanda-Urundi and the French administered Cameroons,[14] it is stated that the annual report by the administering authority shall include information concerning the measures taken to give effect to suggestions and recommendations of the General Assembly and Trusteeship Council. When the Trusteeship Council's Provisional Questionnaire was adopted on April 25, 1947, one of the questions included in it required just such information as the agreements above had included.[15]

Designation of strategic area

The right of the administering authority to propose the designation of the whole or part of the trust territory as a strategic area at a future date, is authorised in the agreements for Tanganyika, Ruanda-Urundi and the French administered Cameroons.[16] The only way in which such a proposal by the administering authority could be effected is through an alteration in the trust agreement itself,[17] since Article 82 of the Charter requires that a strategic area be designated in the trust agreement.

Alienation of native land

All the trust agreements forbid the creation or transference of rights over native land or natural resources in favour of a non-native, except with the prior permission of the competent public authority. Thus the alienation of native land in favour of white settlers is possible only in so far as it is in accordance with the policy of the administering authority.

Human rights

In all of the agreements, freedom of speech, the press, assembly, religion and petition is guaranteed. This is an advance over Article 76 (c) of the Charter by means of which the administering authority is required only to 'encourage respect for' human rights and fundamental freedoms. However, in each agreement there is an escape clause added, which, although the wording may

14 Articles 16, 16, and 2 respectively.
15 Question 246 (Doc. T/44).
16 Articles 17, 17, and 11 respectively.
17 See below, Chap. 7, for a discussion on the alteration of a trust agreement.

vary, is in each case similar in effect. In the case of the Tanganyika agreement, the freedoms guaranteed are 'subject only to the requirements of public order.'[18] In effect, this clause is wide enough to permit the administering authority to suppress these freedoms in the case of any substantial opinions against the administering authority being expressed by the inhabitants. The reason for the suppression of the freedoms could be that the expression of such opinions tended to rouse the inhabitants, and thus was a threat to public order.

In the case of Western Samoa,[19] free entry of missionaries of any nationality is guaranteed; this provision is similar to Article 11 of the Convention on the Revision of the Berlin and Brussels Acts, concluded in 1919 at St. Germain-en-Laye.[20] In the agreements for Tanganyika, Ruanda-Urundi and the French administered Cameroons,[1] the free entry of missionaries is restricted to those of the nationality of a Member of the United Nations. The most detailed concern with the welfare of the inhabitants is found in the agreement for Western Samoa.[2] In this agreement, the slave-trade and slavery as well as forced labour are forbidden, the traffic in arms and ammunition is to be controlled, and there is to be control over the importation, manufacture and distribution of intoxicating beverages. It is appropriate that it should be in a Pacific trust agreement that such provisions are found, since they reflect the provisions on these matters embodied in the Conventions of St. Germain-en-Laye of 1919, which Conventions are applicable only to African territories

Provisions tending to contravene Chapters XII and XIII

Designation of administering authority.—In the agreement for Nauru, Australia, New Zealand and the United Kingdom are designated as the joint administering authority,[3] although it is further stated that the actual administration is to be exercised by Australia.[4] This is not in accordance with the Charter which provides that the trust agreement 'will designate the authority

[18] Article 14 of the agreement.
[19] Article 9.
[20] M. O. Hudson, *International Legislation*, Vol. 1, pp. 344–352.
[1] Articles 13, 13, and 10 respectively.
[2] Article 6.
[3] Article 2.
[4] Article 4.

which will exercise the administration of the trust territory. Such authority, hereinafter called the administering authority . . .'[5] The Chapter has accorded a particular meaning to the term 'administering authority': it is to be the title of the authority which exercises the actual administration of the territory. Therefore in the case of Nauru this is Australia, and not a joint administering authority of Australia, New Zealand and the United Kingdom, as the agreement asserts.[6]

Powers of administration

The most extensive powers given to an administering authority for the purpose of administration are found in the agreement for New Guinea,[7] where the administering authority is permitted to administer the territory 'as if it were an integral part of Australia.' This is not specifically provided for in the Charter although it is not prohibited. It follows the line permitted in the case of C Mandates under the League of Nations which, by Article 22 (6), were permitted to be administered 'as integral portions' of the territory of the Mandatory. Similar provision is made in the agreement for the French administered Cameroons for the territory to be administered as an integral part of French territory, subject to the provisions of the Charter and the trust agreement.[8] Here power is accorded to the administering authority which it did not receive as the Mandatory for the French administered Cameroons. This power to administer New Guinea and the French administered Cameroons as integral portions of the territory of the administering authority can be reconciled with Chapters XII and XIII of the Charter only so long as it does not retard the development of the territory towards self-government or independence.

A similar problem is raised by the provisions in the agreements for Tanganyika, the French administered Cameroons, New Guinea and Ruanda-Urundi for the establishment of an administrative union between the trust territory in question and an adjacent non-self-governing territory under the control of the administering authority.[9] Even if a trust territory's administra-

[5] Article 81 of the Charter.
[6] See further below, Chap. 11, pp. 204–205.
[7] Article 4.
[8] Article 4.
[9] See above, p. 105.

tion as an integral portion of the territory of the administering authority, or its entrance into an administrative union, is not permitted to contravene the objectives of Article 76 of the Charter, such administration may well prevent full compliance with the submission of annual reports on the trust territory. The Trusteeship Council's Questionnaire requires details and statistics which it might be impossible to supply for the trust territory alone, if the territory is administered in conjunction with another. To the extent that this is the case, the provisions in the trust agreements permitting administration of a trust territory as an integral part of the administering authority's territory, or allowing the formation of administrative unions, run contrary to the Charter.

Establishment of monopolies

Article 76 (d) of the Charter establishes that the open-door is to be applied in trust territories to all Members of the United Nations and their nationals.[10] If this is strictly applied, it prevents the administering authority from setting up such essential monopolies as a fiscal system. However, a modifying clause is found in Article 76 (d), which is to the effect that the maintenance of the open-door shall be subject to this not prejudicing the attainment of the other objectives of the Trusteeship System.[11] If the administering authority were to be denied the right to establish essential administrative monopolies in a territory, this would obviously retard the progress of the territory towards self-government or independence, and therefore it cannot be held that Article 76 (d) prohibits the establishment of such essential administrative monopolies.

[10] See above, Chap. 4, p. 69, n. 9.

[11] In the official French edition of the Charter, the punctuating of Article 76 (d) is different from that of the official English text. The English text reads as follows: 'to ensure equal treatment in social, economic, and commercial matters for all Members of the United Nations and their nationals, and also equal treatment for the latter in the administration of justice, without prejudice to the attainment of the foregoing objectives and subject to the provisions of Article 80.' Thus both the 'equal treatment in social, economic, and commercial matters' and the 'equal treatment . . . in the administration of justice' are subject to the 'foregoing objectives' and to Article 80. However, in the official French text, a semi-colon is substituted for the comma after 'and their nationals' ('*assurer l'égalité de traitement dans la domaine social, économique et commercial à tous les Membres de l'Organisation et à leurs ressortissants; . . .*'). Therefore in this text, it is only '*l'égalité de traitement dans l'administration de la justice*' that is subject to '*la réalisation des fins énoncées ci-dessus*' and to Article 80.

The trust agreements for Tanganyika, Ruanda-Urundi and the French administered Cameroons [12] all incorporate provisions permitting the administering authority to establish monopolies. In the cases of Ruanda-Urundi and Tanganyika, the administering authority is permitted to establish fiscal monopolies and such other monopolies for the economic advancement of the territory as are in the interests of the inhabitants. In the selection of agencies to carry out these economic monopolies, no discrimination is to be exercised on the grounds of nationality, except where the Government (*i.e.*, the administering authority) controls the agency. This does not necessarily conform to the Charter provision of Article 76 (d), since it is conceivable that the establishment of a certain economic monopoly might be in the interests of the inhabitants of the trust territory, but that it would not be any *more* in their interests to have the monopoly operated by the administering authority than by any other Member of the United Nations. In according itself this preferential treatment in the trust agreement, the administering authority is providing the basis for a possible violation of Article 76 (d). In the case of the French administered Cameroons, there is no clause specifically granting preferential treatment to the administering authority, but provision is made for the establishment of such public enterprises or joint undertakings 'as appear to the Administering Authority to be in the interests of the economic advancement of the inhabitants of the Territory.' [13] In this instance, the administering authority is according to itself the sole right to judge whether the open-door would be prejudicial to the economic advancement of the territory—a right which Article 76 does not authorise.

Limitations to the open-door

Both the agreements for Tanganyika and for Ruanda-Urundi [14] provide that equality of treatment cannot be claimed by any Member of the United Nations unless such Member grants most-favoured-nation treatment to the inhabitants, companies and associations of the trust territory. Although this provision is of obvious benefit to the inhabitants, Article 76 (d) of the

[12] Articles 10, 10, and 9 respectively.
[13] Article 9 (3).
[14] Article 11 in both agreements.

Charter does not permit such a limitation on the operation of the open-door, unless it can be established that this provision is necessary for the attainment of one of the objectives in Article 76 (a), (b) and (c).

Non-Strategic Territory Administered by a Non-Member

Inasmuch as the agreement for Somaliland was drawn up for a territory to be administered by a non-Member, this agreement is considered separately from those for the other non-strategic territories. Only in this context of non-Member administration can the provisions of the agreement be fully understood. Furthermore, there exists the possibility of a non-Member, such as Switzerland, being requested to undertake trusteeship administration at some future date; from this point of view, the agreement for Somaliland provides an interesting pattern. The following analysis of the agreement for Somaliland is undertaken primarily in the light of the situation existing up to the admission of Italy to the United Nations in December 1955, the ways in which Italy's Membership effects the provisions of the agreement being noted in the relevant places.

When the Charter provisions on trusteeship were drafted, it was not anticipated that a non-Member would be designated as the administering authority for a trust territory, although the possibility of an administering authority ceasing to be a Member of the United Nations but continuing to administer a trust territory was considered. The United States and United Kingdom Delegations were asked to prepare a Joint Statement to be annexed to the Report of the Rapporteur of Committee II/4 of the San Francisco Conference.[15] The most important opinion emerging from the Report was that termination of United Nations Membership did not in itself necessitate the transfer of a trust territory from administration by the State withdrawing from the Organisation. This, and the fact that Article 81 of the Charter did not specify that an administering authority must be a Member, laid the foundation for the designation of non-Member Italy as the administering authority for Somaliland.

In considering the contents of the trust agreement for Somali-

[15] See *Report of the Rapporteur of Committee II/4*, p. 14 (*U.N.C.I.O. Docs.*, Vol. 10, p. 620). See further above, Chap. 2, pp. 32–33.

land under Italian administration,[16] it is necessary to bear in mind several points that distinguish this agreement from all others: when the agreement was drafted, Italy was not a Member of the United Nations and would therefore be bound by the provisions of the Charter only insofar as they were incorporated into the trust agreement; as a non-Member, Italy could not become a Member of the Trusteeship Council; the trust agreement for Somaliland was drafted by the United Nations itself rather than by the prospective administering authority; Italy did not administer the territory in the period immediately prior to its designation as the administering authority; the territory was placed under Italian administration to be administered as a trust territory for a fixed period of time only; Italy had the option of accepting or rejecting the trust agreement only, and was therefore placed in a position similar to that of the United Nations with respect to the other trust agreements.

Provisions reflecting Chapters XII and XIII

Designation of administering authority.—In accordance with Article 81 of the Charter, the administering authority is designated in the agreement.[17] This is stated as being the Government of Italy, in accordance with the Charter provisions on International Trusteeship as stated in Chapters XII and XIII.[18] Chapter XI which applies to all non-self-governing territories administered by Members of the United Nations, including the trust territories, did not apply to Somaliland, since Italy did not undertake to administer it in accordance with Chapter XI. The fact that Chapter XI did not apply to Somaliland is probably in part responsible for the extremely detailed provisions on social and welfare conditions in the Agreement and its Annex. Since only by means of its undertakings in the trust agreement did Italy become bound by the Charter provisions on trusteeship, this provision that administration is to be in accordance with the Trusteeship Chapters of the Charter assumes an importance far beyond its compliance with Article 81 of the Charter. Now, however, Italy is bound by Chapters XI, XII and XIII by reason of her Membership in the United Nations.

16 For text of the trust agreement, see *Official Records of the General Assembly*, Fifth Session, Suppl. No. 10.

17 Article 2.

18 Article 3.

Application of Article 76 (b)

In Articles 3 and 4 of the Agreement, the administering authority undertakes to advance the territory politically, economically, socially and educationally.[19] This is set out in a detailed and specific manner in which obligations assumed by the administering authority go far beyond the requirements of Article 76 (b).

Application of Article 76 (d)

The maintenance of the open-door in the trust territory and the granting of equal treatment in the administration of justice to the nationals of Members of the United Nations is assured by Article 15 of the Agreement. So long as the administering authority was not a Member of the United Nations, the requirement of equality of treatment as set forth in Article 76 (d) of the Charter permitted preferential treatment to the administering authority and its nationals. As a result of this, the administering authority guarantees equality of treatment to 'all states Members of the United Nations and their nationals and for its own nationals.' Whilst ruling out any preferential treatment for Italian nationals, this provision did not prevent the Italian Government claiming preferential treatment—a claim which would not have been in conflict with the wording of Article 76 (d). This loophole has now been closed by the admission of Italy to Membership in the Organisation. In conformity with Article 76 (d), the open-door is made conditional to the over-riding objectives of Article 76 (a), (b) and (c).

Contribution of the territory to international peace and security

In accordance with Article 76 (a) and 84 of the Charter, the Agreement contains provision for the defence of the territory and for the maintenance of international peace and security.[20] For these purposes, volunteer defence forces may be raised and installations established in the territory. One aspect of Article 84 is inapplicable. Under this article an administering authority is permitted to employ local forces and facilities from the trust territory to carry out its obligations towards the Security Council. However, a non-Member has incurred no obligations towards

19 Article 3 (1), (2), (3), and Article 4.
20 Article 6.

the Security Council and therefore has no need of the facilities and forces of the trust territory for this purpose.[1]

Supervision by the United Nations

The administering authority undertakes to co-operate fully with the General Assembly and Trusteeship Council in the exercise of their supervisory functions under Articles 87 and 88 of the Charter.[2] The administering authority specifically undertakes to render annual reports on the basis of the Trusteeship Council's Questionnaire, to facilitate periodic visits to the trust territory, and to designate a representative to be present at sessions of the Trusteeship Council at which reports and petitions relating to Somaliland are under consideration. This last provision was especially important in that it provided both the authority for, and imposed the obligation upon, Italy to designate a representative to the Trusteeship Council. As a non-Member, Italy would not normally have been represented on the Trusteeship Council; this would have prevented the examination of petitions by the United Nations in consultation with the administering authority, as required by Article 87.

Alteration of the agreement

The administering authority is authorised to propose, at any future date, the alteration or amendment of the trust agreement.[3] Such alteration or amendment may only be effected through the means prescribed in Articles 79 and 85 of the Charter.

Role of the administering authority

Full powers of legislation, administration and jurisdiction are accorded to the administering authority, subject to the provisions of the Charter, the trust agreement and the Annex to the trust agreement.[4] Presumably the provisions of the Charter referred to were those in Chapters XII and XIII, since Italy was not bound by any others. Italian laws may be applied to the territory so long as they are not incompatible with the achievement of independence.

1 For a further discussion of the obligations towards the Security Council to which Article 84 refers, see below, Chap. 11, p. 216.
2 Article 5.
3 Article 21.
4 Article 7.

Provisions going beyond Chapters XII and XIII

Many of the provisions appearing in the trust agreement go beyond anything required by Chapters XII and XIII of the Charter, and the agreement is far more detailed than any of the other trust agreements. The social and welfare aspects receive detailed attention in the agreement and more than compensate for the fact that the provisions of Chapter XI were not applicable to the territory. The administering authority itself is subject to more restrictions and duties by means of the agreement than is any other administering authority, partly because the agreement was drafted by the United Nations and also to compensate for the fact that Italy was not a Member of the United Nations.

Political advancement

Whilst Article 76 (b) of the Charter allows for the development of a trust territory towards self-government *or* independence as may be appropriate to the territory, no such choice of alternatives is permitted for Somaliland. The goal of the trust territory is specifically stated to be 'independence' within ten years.[5]

Economic advancement

The administering authority is required to promote not only the economic advancement of the territory but also its self-sufficiency.[6] This is in view of the territory's being destined for independence within a fixed period of time. Thus measures which may promote the economic advancement of the territory but tie it to the administering authority's metropolitan territory must not be permitted, since these do not promote the self-sufficiency of the territory.

Social advancement

The way in which social advancement is to be achieved is set out in detail[7]; it prohibits or controls many of the matters which were the subject of previous international conventions. These include the control of traffic in arms and ammunition,[8]

[5] Article 3 (1).
[6] Article 3 (2).
[7] Article 3 (3).
[8] *Convention on Control of Trade in Arms and Ammunition,* signed at St. Germain-en-Laye, 1919 (see M. O. Hudson, *International Legislation,* Vol. 1, p. 323 *et seq.*).

control of the liquor traffic,[9] prohibition of slavery and slave-trading,[10] and control of dangerous drugs.[11] In addition, the health of the inhabitants of the territory is to be advanced by the development of adequate health and hospital services, forced labour is prohibited except in time of public emergency when adequate remuneration and protection for the workers must be assured, and existing international conventions on prostitution are to be applied.

Educational advancement

Educational advancement is to be conducted with due respect for the indigenous culture and religion. Elementary education is to be free, and secondary and vocational training to be provided. Teaching about the United Nations, the basic objectives of the Trusteeship System, and the Universal Declaration of Human Rights is required.[12]

Alienation of land

No alienation of land or resources in favour of non-indigenous persons or companies controlled by such persons is permitted, except with the permission of the Territorial Council.[13]

Human rights

Freedom of speech, press, religion, assembly and petition is guaranteed to the inhabitants in the same way as in the other agreements.[14]

Annex of constitutional principles

A unique feature of the Trust Agreement for Somaliland is the Declaration of Constitutional Principles which is annexed to it. This provides the basis for the Constitution of the territory and is in effect a bill of rights for the inhabitants of Somaliland.

9 *Convention on the Liquor Traffic in Africa,* signed at St. Germain-en-Laye, 1919 (*ibid.*, p. 352).

10 *Convention on the Revision of the Berlin and Brussels Acts,* signed at St. Germain-en-Laye, 1919, Article 2 (*ibid.*, pp. 344–352).

11 *Convention for Limiting the Manufacture and Regulating the Distribution of Narcotic Drugs,* 1931 (see League of Nations Doc. C.287.M.125. 1934).

12 Article 4. This provision is in line with General Assembly Resolution 324 (IV), which is applicable to all trust territories.

13 Article 14.

14 Article 20.

It vests the sovereignty of the territory in the peoplé, and requires the administering authority to establish a representative legislaure and an independent judiciary. At the same time civil liberties are guaranteed to the inhabitants of the territory, and the administering authority accepts the Universal Declaration of Human Rights as a standard of achievement for the territory.

Application of international conventions

The administering authority undertakes to maintain in force any international agreements which are in operation in the territory, and to apply any recommendations and conventions of the United Nations and specialised agencies that are in the interests of the inhabitants and in conformity with the objectives of Article 76 of the Charter, the Trust Agreement and the provisions of General Assembly Resolution 289 (IV).[15] This provision is similar to those appearing in all the non-strategic trust agreements.

Co-operation with the specialised agencies

As in the case of Western Samoa, Tanganyika, Ruanda-Urundi and the French administered Cameroons, provision is made in the Agreement for Somaliland to co-operate in regional and specialised international organisations. Somaliland is also to co-operate with the specialised agencies.[16]

Reference of disputes to the International Court

As in the case of Western Samoa, Tanganyika, Ruanda-Urundi and the French administered Cameroons, the administering authority for Somaliland agrees to submit to the International Court all disputes with Members of the United Nations concerning the agreement, if they cannot be settled by negotiation.[17]

Contents of Annual Report

Following the pattern established in the agreements for Tanganyika, Ruanda-Urundi and the French administered

15 Article 12. This Resolution laid down the basic principles for the administration of Somaliland by Italy, the transfer of administration from the United Kingdom to Italy, and requested the Trusteeship Council to negotiate a draft trust agreement with Italy for submission to the General Assembly.

16 Article 13.

17 Article 22.

Cameroons, the Agreement for Somaliland provides that information concerning measures taken to give effect to the suggestions and recommendations of the General Assembly and Trusteeship Council, shall be included in the administering authority's annual report on the territory. In addition, the first annual report on Somaliland was to include a report on the position in Somaliland of property of nationals, associations and companies of the Members of the United Nations.[18]

Exercise of administration

The administration of the territory is to be exercised by the administering authority not only in accordance with Chapters XII and XIII of the Charter and the Trust Agreement, but also in conformity with Resolution 289 (IV) of the General Assembly[19] and with the Declaration of Constitutional Principles annexed to the Trust Agreement.[20]

The Advisory Council

Unlike the administering authorities of the other trust territories, the administering authority for Somaliland is assisted in its role by an Advisory Council.[1] This Advisory Council is composed of Colombia, Egypt and the Philippines,[2] whose advice on certain matters Italy is required to seek, and who must be kept fully informed of the political, economic, social and educational advancement of the territory, including relevant legislation.[3] The Advisory Council enjoys full diplomatic privileges and immunities and has free access to any information sources necessary for the performance of its duties.[4] Members of the Advisory Council who are not also Members of the Trusteeship Council, are entitled to participate without vote in the debates of the Trusteeship Council on questions specifically concerning Somaliland. They are also permitted, either individually or collectively, to make written or oral statements to the Trusteeship Council.[5] The existence of this Advisory Council serves two purposes: it provides some means of United Nations control over the exercise of administration in the trust territory; and it also gives a chance

18 Article 18.
19 See above, p. 117, n. 15.
20 Article 3.
1 Article 2.
2 *ibid.*
3 Article 8.
4 Articles 9 and 10.
5 Article 11.

to non-administering Members of the United Nations to obtain an inside view of the administration of a trust territory, and to exercise more influence therein than is possible in the case of any other trust territory.

Termination of the agreement

In conformity with General Assembly Resolution 289 (IV), provision is inserted into the agreement for its termination ten years after its entry into force,[6] at which time the territory is to become an independent State. At least eighteen months prior to this, the administering authority is required to submit to the Trusteeship Council a plan for the transfer of governmental functions to the independent Government of the territory.[7] These provisions are very important in that they represent the only case in which a definite date has been set for the achievement of independence by a trust territory. Furthermore, the Somaliland agreement is the only one requiring the achievement of independence by the territory—the others permit the alternative of self-government. Finally, the establishment of a specific date for the independence of all trust territories is something the non-administering Powers in the United Nations have been attempting to achieve by resolutions.[8]

Provisions tending to contravene Chapters XII and XIII

The provisions in the Agreement for Somaliland which tend to contravene the trusteeship provisions of the Charter consist of the authorisation to establish monopolies,[9] and the limitation on the open-door assuring the benefits of it only to such Members as grant most-favoured-nation treatment to the inhabitants, companies and associations of Somaliland.[10] Both these matters are dealt with in the same manner as in the Agreement for Tanganyika.[10a]

Strategic Territory

A strategic trust territory differs from other trust territories in that all the functions of the United Nations with regard to it are

6 Article 3.
7 Article 25.
8 *e.g.*, General Assembly Resolution 558 (VI) of 1951. See further above, Chap. 4, p. 59 *et seq.*
9 Article 16 (b) and (c).
10 Article 17.
10a See above, pp. 109–111.

exercised by the Security Council. From this fact, it might appear that the concept meant strategic from the point of view of the security of the United Nations as a whole. However, strategic trusteeship was an American concept, and it was devised as a compromise between the non-annexation principle of the Atlantic Charter and the security requirements of the United States. Since a strategic trust territory comes under the supervision of the Security Council, and since the five permanent members of that body possess a permanent veto in it, strategic trusteeship provides an ideal arrangement for any of the five permanent members who wish to place territories under the Trusteeship System. The only State so far to take advantage of this strategic trusteeship is the United States, who placed the former Japanese Mandated Islands under trusteeship as a strategic territory.[11]

Provisions reflecting Chapters XII and XIII

Designation of administering authority.—The United States of America is designated as the administering authority in accordance with Article 81 of the Charter.[12]

Administration in accordance with the Charter

The administering authority undertakes to administer the territory in accordance with the Charter,[13] which it is compelled to do by reason of Membership in the United Nations.

Application of Article 76

As with all the other trust agreements, the agreement for the Pacific Islands specifies that the objectives of Article 76 of the

[11] For text of trust agreement, see *United Nations Treaty Series,* Vol. 8, p. 190. As to the possibility of additional territories being designated as strategic trust territories in the future, it is interesting to note the following provision in the Peace Treaty with Japan (1951): 'Japan will concur in any proposal of the United States to the United Nations to place under its trusteeship system, with the United States as the sole administering authority' certain specified Pacific Islands, including the Ryukyu and Bonin groups (Article 3, see Cmd. [8392] 1951). Considering the strategic position of these islands and the fact that they have been under the control of the U.S. Department of the Army since their capture from Japan, it is unlikely that the U.S. Government had anything other than strategic trusteeship in mind when this provision was inserted into the Peace Treaty.

[12] Article 2.

[13] Article 4.

Charter are to be applied to the trust territory.[14] Details of the political, economic, social, and educational development of the territory are included in the agreement.[15] The social development of the territory is to be furthered through the control of traffic in arms and ammunition and in dangerous drugs and alcohol; thus the substance of the 1919 St. Germain-en-Laye Conventions becomes applicable to the territory.[16] In the case of political advancement, the Agreement originally required this to be towards self-government only. However, the United States accepted a Soviet proposal to insert 'or independence' into the Agreement.[17]

Contribution of the Territory to International Peace and Security

The administering authority is authorised to take measures to implement Article 84 of the Charter.[18]

Designation of strategic area

As required by Article 82 of the Charter, the designation of the territory as strategic is included in the terms of the Trust Agreement.[19]

Alteration of Agreement

The Agreement may not be altered without the consent of the administering authority.[20] This provision is superfluous since the agreement of the administering authority is required in any case by international law. Furthermore, Article 79 of the Charter requires the agreement of the 'States directly concerned' to any alteration, and the administering Power is obviously a 'State directly concerned.' The Soviet Union proposed in the Security Council that this provision of the Trust Agreement be altered to read as follows: 'the terms of the present agreement may be altered, supplemented or terminated by decision of the Security Council.'[1] The United States was

14 Article 4.
15 Article 6.
16 See Conventions mentioned in n. 8–11 above, pp. 115–116.
17 *Official Records of the Security Council,* Second Year, No. 31, 124th Meeting (April 2, 1947), p. 644.
18 Article 5.
19 Article 1.
20 Article 15.
1 *Official Records of the Security Council,* Second Year, No. 20, 113th Meeting (February 26, 1947), p. 415.

unwilling to accept this proposal, which in theory would have amounted to the administering authority having given its consent in advance to any alteration. However, in practice by the use of the veto, the United States would have been able to prevent the Security Council making a decision to alter, supplement or terminate the Agreement.

Role of administering authority

The administering authority is accorded full powers of administration, legislation and jurisdiction over the territory.[2] Originally, the Agreement included the provision that the territory might be administered 'as an integral part of the United States.' This had been permitted when the territory was a C Mandate under Japanese administration, but it is not provided for in the Charter. Upon the suggestion of the Soviet Union, the United States agreed to delete this provision.[3]

Provisions going beyond Chapters XII and XIII

Application of international conventions.—The administering authority undertakes to apply to the territory, such provisions of international conventions and recommendations as may be appropriate and conducive to the achievement of the basic objectives of the System.[4] Such conventions and recommendations are not limited to those of the United Nations.

Co-operation of the territory in regional organisations

There is provision in the Agreement for the co-operation of the territory in regional commissions or specialised international bodies.[5]

Administrative unions

The administering authority is authorised to constitute the territory into an administrative union or federation with other territories under the control of the administering authority, so long as this is not inconsistent with the basic objectives of the Trusteeship System or the Trust Agreement.[6]

[2] Article 3.
[3] *Official Records of the Security Council,* Second Year, No. 23, 116th Meeting (March 7, 1947), pp. 472–473.
[4] Article 14.
[5] Article 10.
[6] Article 9.

Human rights

As with the other trust agreements, fundamental human rights are guaranteed to the inhabitants, including freedom of speech, press, assembly, and religion, with the addition of freedom of migration and movement.[7]

Status of inhabitants

The administering authority is required to provide the status of citizenship of the trust territory to the inhabitants, and to afford them diplomatic and consular protection when outside the territory.[8]

Security

Greater powers for the implementation of Article 84 of the Charter are granted to the administering authority for the Pacific Islands than to any other administering authority. In addition to the means specified in Article 84 itself, the administering authority is permitted to establish naval, military and air bases and to erect fortifications in the territory, and to station and employ armed forces there.[9]

Provisions tending to contravene Chapters XII and XIII

The open-door.—Whereas Article 76 (d) requires the application of the open-door to the trust territories, the Agreement for the Pacific Islands permits preferential treatment to the administering authority.[10] Furthermore, it expressly denies open-door rights to the aircraft of any State other than the administering authority, permitting such aircraft to fly in and out of the territory only after specific agreements have been concluded between the administering authority and the State whose nationality the aircraft possesses.[11]

7 Article 7.
8 Article 11.
9 Article 5.
10 Article 8. See above, Chap. 4, pp. 71–73.
11 However, the same is probably true in the case of every other trust territory, although it is not specifically stated in the trust agreements. The *Chicago Convention on Civil Aviation* (Cmd. 6614–1945) forbids both foreign military and civil aircraft flying over the territory of a contracting State without prior authorisation (see Articles 3 (c) and 6 [Cmd. 6614, pp. 33–34]), and 'for the purpose of this Convention the territory of a State shall be deemed to be the land areas and territorial waters adjacent thereto under the sovereignty, suzerainty, protection or

Supervision by the United Nations

By Article 83, all functions of the United Nations with respect to strategic trust territories are to be exercised by the Security Council. This obviously was intended to include supervision of the territory, since otherwise an essential element of trusteeship is missing. However, the Trust Agreement for the Pacific Islands authorises the administering authority to limit the application of supervision by the United Nations, in the case of any areas which the administering authority may specify as closed for security reasons.[12] This is clearly in conflict with the Charter since it allows the administering authority to prevent any supervision over the territory if it so desires.

mandate of such State' (Article 2, see *ibid.*, p. 33). This provision covers trust territories, and since all the administering authorities are signatories to the Chicago Convention, the flying of foreign aircraft over a trust territory is subject to prior authorisation by the administering authority in every case.

[12] Article 13.

Chapter 7

ALTERATION OR TERMINATION OF A TRUST AGREEMENT

The general rules of international law with regard to the alteration of an agreement require that the consent of all the contracting parties must be obtained, unless some other method is specified in the agreement itself. None of the trust agreements is very enlightening on the question of alteration. Some, for example, the agreement for New Guinea, contain no mention of alteration. The agreement for the Pacific Islands under United States administration states that 'the terms of the present Agreement shall not be altered, amended or terminated without the consent of the Administering Authority,'[1] which is superfluous anyway, since the United States as a contracting party would have to agree to any alteration under the ordinary rules of international law. However, the inclusion of this provision in the agreement was intended to prevent future arguments concerning the supremacy of the Security Council and the subordination of the administering authority in the trust territory. Other trust agreements, such as those for Togoland[2] and the Cameroons[3] under United Kingdom administration, provide that the terms of the agreement shall not be altered or amended except as provided for in Articles 79, and 83 or 85 of the Charter.

Under Article 79 of the Charter, the procedure for the alteration of the terms of trusteeship is the same as that for its conclusion: namely, that the terms of trusteeship 'shall be agreed upon by the states directly concerned, including the [former] mandatory power in the case of territories [formerly] held under mandate by a Member of the United Nations, and shall be approved as provided for in Articles 83 and 85.' As pointed out in a previous chapter,[4] there are two agreements in reality, and, as in the case of conclusion, any alteration must be agreed upon by the 'States directly concerned' and must be followed by the approval of the

1 Article 15 (*United Nations Treaty Series,* Vol. 8, p. 190).
2 *ibid.*, p. 151.
3 *United Nations Treaty Series,* Vol. 8, p. 119.
4 See above, Chapter 5, p. 77 *et seq.*

General Assembly (or Security Council in the case of a strategic area) and the administering Power.

The question arises as to whether the 'States directly concerned' in the alteration of a trust agreement are necessarily the same States as were concerned in its conclusion. To comply with the general rules of international law, all the States which took part in the conclusion of the agreement must take part in its alteration.[5] Professor Kelsen argues that it is possible to interpret Article 79 of the Charter to mean that the Security Council or General Assembly may approve an agreement which provides for alteration without the consent of the 'States directly concerned.'[6] However, as has been pointed out in a previous chapter,[7] the trust agreements must not seek to negate the provisions of the Charter.

The question arises as to whether some additional States may claim to be directly concerned in the alteration of a trust agreement, although they were not recognised as such in the conclusion of the agreement. A Report of the Fourth Committee of the General Assembly stated that there had been 'no specification by the General Assembly of "States directly concerned" in relation to the proposed Trust Territories. Accordingly, the General Assembly in approving the terms of Trusteeship does not prejudge the question of what States are or are not "directly concerned" within the meaning of Article 79. It recognises that no State has waived or prejudiced its right hereafter to claim to be such a "State directly concerned" in relation to approval of subsequently proposed Trusteeship agreements and any alteration or amendment of those now approved, and that the procedure to be followed in the future with reference to such matters may be subject to later determination.'[8] Two points arise with respect to this statement: Firstly, in stating that the General Assembly had not specified the 'States directly concerned,' a competence was being attributed to the General Assembly which

[5] See Separate Opinion of Judge Schuecking in the *Oscar Chinn Case* (1934): '. . . no convention can acquire valid existence that is contracted in disregard of the rule forbidding a limited group of signatories of the Act to modify its terms' (P.C.I.J. Series A/B, No. 63. See 3 Hudson, *World Court Reports*, p. 480).

[6] See Hans Kelsen, *The Law of the United Nations* (1951), pp. 653–656.

[7] See above, Chap. 6, p. 95.

[8] *Official Records of the General Assembly,* Second Part of the First Session, Fourth Committee, Part 1, p. 302, Annex 22a.

it did not possess. Article 85 gives the General Assembly the authority to *approve* the trust agreements and only to proceed with other functions *once the agreements are in force;* therefore it did not have the power to interpret this phrase since its authority only started with the approval of agreements which had already been drawn up by the 'States directly concerned.' Secondly, Article 79 provides that the terms of trusteeship 'shall be *agreed* upon by the States directly concerned,'[9] in other words that the trust agreements have to be concluded by the 'States directly concerned' who must take part in the actual procedure of drawing up the agreement. From this it can be argued that a trust agreement is not valid without the participation in its conclusion of the 'States directly concerned,'[10] and therefore if its validity is to be upheld States cannot subsequently claim to fall into the category of 'States directly concerned.' However, an exception would have to be made in the case of a State which subsequently became directly concerned in the trust territory through the development of an intensive fishing interest in the territorial waters of the territory or in some other similar way.

There were attempts at San Francisco and later in the United Nations itself, to establish more rigid provisions as regards the alteration of a trust agreement. The Egyptian Delegate at San Francisco proposed that provisions be inserted into the Charter for the transfer of a trust territory to another administering authority 'whenever there is any violation of the terms of the trusteeship arrangements by the administering authority, or when the administering power has ceased to be a member of the United Nations, or has been suspended from membership.'[11] This was not received too well by the Conference, and Egypt subsequently withdrew the proposal. In furtherance of this, however, a joint statement by the Delegates of the United Kingdom and the United States was included in the *Report of the Rapporteur of Committee II/4*. This statement expressed the opinion that such events as Egypt envisaged would not of neces-

9 Italics added.

10 The Soviet Union maintained that since the 'States directly concerned' had never been identified, they had *not* taken part in the conclusion of the trust agreements, and consequently the agreements were invalid (see *Official Records of the General Assembly,* Second Part of the First Session, 62nd Plenary Meeting, pp. 1282–1283).

11 *Summary Report of the Fourteenth Meeting of Committee II/4* (*U.N.C.I.O. Docs.,* Vol. 10, p. 547).

sity require the transfer of a trust territory to another administering Power, and that in any case the matter could 'only be decided upon at the time and in the light of all relevant circumstances.'[12]

A Soviet proposal, adopted by Sub-Committee I of the Fourth Committee of the General Assembly during the Second Part of the First Session, recommended the insertion into the texts of the trust agreements a provision that the agreement should 'remain in force for a period of ...... years and thereafter . . . be reviewed and modified according to the degree of attainment of the purposes set forth in Article 76 of the Charter of the United Nations.'[13] This was violently objected to by the prospective administering Powers and it did not find its way into any of the agreements. The attitude of these Powers was expressed by the Belgian Delegate, Mr. Ryckmans, who said that 'the principle of periodic revision, with periods determined in the agreements . . . was contrary to the Charter. According to Article 79 of the Charter, the procedure for revision of trusteeship agreements was clearly the same as for the negotiation of the original agreements.'[14] This statement is not absolutely correct, since there is not necessarily a contradiction between the Charter provisions for the alteration of an agreement and the principle of periodic revision as stated in the Soviet proposal. There is nothing in the Charter which forbids the insertion of a clause in a trust agreement providing for the periodic revision of the agreement. The subsequent modification of the agreement 'according to the degree of attainment of the purposes set forth in Article 76' would merely have to be agreed upon by the 'States directly concerned' and approved by the administering authority and the Organisation, in order to reconcile it with the Charter. Without the agreement of all these parties, no modification of the trust agreement could take place, and therefore the proposed administering Powers had little reason to be concerned.

A far more controversial proposal on the subject of the altera-

[12] *Report of the Rapporteur of Committee II/4,* Annex C, p. 14 (*U.N.C.I.O. Docs.,* Vol. 10, p. 620). Japan continued to hold her mandate after she withdrew from the League (see further below, Chap. 11, pp. 206–207).

[13] *Official Records of the General Assembly,* Second Part of the First Session, Fourth Committee, Sub-Committee 1, Annex 4 (a), p. 236.

[14] *Official Records of the General Assembly,* Second Part of the First Session, Fourth Committee, Sub-Committee 1, p. 92.

tion of an agreement was suggested by the Soviet Delegate to the Security Council for insertion into the agreement for the Pacific Islands. He proposed that Article 15 of the agreement should read as follows: 'The terms of the present agreement may be altered, supplemented or terminated by decision of the Security Council.'[15] By general international law there would be nothing to prevent the inclusion of such a provision, since all the parties concerned in the conclusion of the agreement would have to consent to the provision in order for it to be incorporated into the agreement; there is nothing to prevent the parties to an agreement agreeing in advance to an alteration in a manner which does not include their participation. In so doing, the parties would be surrendering their own rights which they are certainly entitled to do. However, whilst such a provision as the Soviet Delegate proposed might be considered compatible with general international law, it is doubtful whether it could be held compatible with the Charter itself. Article 79 is quite specific in providing the same method for altering an agreement as is employed in its conclusion; there is no provision for the revision method of Article 79 to be over-ruled by the terms of the trust agreement. It would appear that a trust agreement which contains a provision running contrary to the provisions of the Charter itself should not be approved by the Organisation. If it is approved, strictly speaking, the illegal article should be held inoperative under the terms of Article 103 of the Charter, which provides that the obligations of Members under the Charter prevail over their obligations under any other international instrument in the event of a conflict. The obligation of parties to a trust agreement to take part in its alteration under Article 79, takes precedence over their obligation to allow this to be waived under an article of the trust agreement itself. Thus, whilst it might be held that additional requirements for alteration of a trust agreement may be inserted into the agreement and upheld, these requirements must not attempt to get round the method provided in the Charter itself. On the other hand, it might be argued that it cannot have been the intention of the framers of the Charter that its provisions should be so inflexible as to preclude any *de facto* revision in the light of changing

15 *Official Records of the Security Council,* Second Year, 113th Meeting, p. 415.

circumstances. This argument is given added weight where the parties concerned, such as the States directly concerned under Article 79, waive their rights resulting from a strict interpretation of the Charter.

CONDITIONS FOR ALTERATION

Before an alteration of a trust agreement may take place there are certain conditions which must be satisfied, the most important of which would seem to be that the alteration must not in any way prejudice the achievements of the aims of the System as set out in Article 76 of the Charter. At the same time, the consent of all the contracting parties to the agreement must be obtained before the alteration can take place. An alteration to an agreement which permitted the annexation of the territory by the administering Power (or by any other State), before self-government has been achieved, would be contrary to the Charter, since it would be detrimental to the achievement by the inhabitants of the territory of self-government or independence. Since Article 76 (b) provides no alternative other than development towards self-government or independence, should the inhabitants of a trust territory desire annexation by the administering Power or any other similar arrangement, the territory must first achieve self-government or independence before the separate status of the territory is liquidated. This is necessary if the strict wording of the Charter is to be complied with.

The most likely types of alteration to a trust agreement are the designation of an ordinary trust territory as a strategic area, and the change of administering authority. In the former case, this change is provided for in the terms of some of the trust agreements and the possibility for it exists in the case of all the trust territories. However, such a change in the character of a trust territory from a non-strategic to a strategic territory must not be detrimental to 'international peace and security.' This may appear to be an anachronism inasmuch as the idea of strategic trusts is based on the maintenance of peace and security, but in practice it is the strategic interests of the administering authority, rather than of the international community, which have been the decisive factors in designating the only strategic trusteeship as such.[16] The problem of deciding whether a change from a

[16] See United States, Senate: *Hearings before the Committee on Foreign Relations on the Charter of the United Nations* (1945), (U.S. Government Printing Office, Washington, D.C., p. 314 *et seq.*).

non-strategic to a strategic status by a trust territory was detrimental to international peace and security, would necessarily fall on all the parties to the trust agreement—the States directly concerned who were involved in the initial agreement on the terms of trusteeship, and the administering authority and the General Assembly who concluded the final trust agreement—plus the Security Council. It would appear that both the General Assembly and the Security Council would have to signify their approval to a change of this kind in the status of a trust territory: the General Assembly would be concerned since, as a party to the original agreement, it must take part in its alteration, and the Security Council would be called in since its approval to the terms of the agreement is necessary in the case of all strategic areas.

In the case of a change in the administering authority of a trust territory, the agreement of both the new and the old administering authority would be required. The old administering authority must be brought in as a contracting party to the original agreement, and the new administering authority must agree to the terms of the amended agreement before it can be considered bound by them. The chief aim of the Trusteeship System which would be likely to be prejudiced by the change of administering authorities is that of the goal of 'self-government or independence.' It is unlikely that both the new and the old administering authorities would have identical ideas as to how the goal could be best achieved, and the very change in administration would require a new group of administrative officers in the territory who would not have had experience with the particular problems of the inhabitants. This would be further complicated if the language of the new administering authority were different from that of the former. The matter is not merely hypothetical inasmuch as it is involved in a question which has been before the United Nations since 1947, originally known as the Ewe Problem and more recently the Togoland Unification Problem.

The Ewe Problem arose from demands for the unification under one administration, of the Ewe people divided between French-administered Togoland, British-administered Togoland, and an adjacent section of the Gold Coast Colony. Concurrent demands were received from the inhabitants of the two Togolands for unification under a single administration of the two trust territories as a whole. Inasmuch as the Ewe demands involved the union of trust territories with territory subject only to the limited provisions of Chapter XI of the Charter, they did not come within the sphere of the Trusteeship System and were not seriously considered by any organ of the United Nations. Furthermore, in its Special Report to the Trusteeship Council in February 1950, the United Nations Mission to West Africa indicated that the union of the two Togolands was the prevalent desire of the inhabitants.[17] Such a union, it should be noted, would involve a change of administration for at least one of the territories.

In 1954 a new aspect was added to what had by then become the Togoland Unification Problem. Under the terms of the trust agreement (Article 5), British-administered Togoland is administered as an integral part of the Gold Coast. The Gold Coast, however, has a target date of 1956 set for self-government, after which it will no longer be possible to administer Togoland under the present agreement. In 1954, the United Kingdom decided to place the problem of the future of British-administered Togoland before the United Nations,[18] after which it was considered by both the Trusteeship Council and the General Assembly. Two alternatives exist for British-administered Togoland: integration with a self-governing Gold Coast as suggested by the United Kingdom,[19] or continuation under trusteeship. Inasmuch as the United Kingdom has expressed unwillingness to continue the administration of Togoland after the achievement of self-government by the Gold Coast,[20] the alternatives are either termination of the trusteeship status and thus of the agreement, or the designation of a new administering authority and thus an alteration to the agreement. These two alternatives were put to the inhabitants of British-administered Togoland in a plebiscite conducted under United Nations supervision in the Spring of 1956, the results of which showed an overwhelming preference for integration with the Gold Coast.[21]

17 *Official Records of the Trusteeship Council,* Seventh Session, Suppl. No. 2 (Doc. T/789), p. 82, par. 103.

18 See written answer by the Colonial Secretary on June 22, 1954, to a question in the House of Commons (Hansard, *Parliamentary Debates,* 529 H.C., cols. 9–10).

19 See Doc. A/2660 of June 21, 1954.

20 See statement to this effect by the Governor of the Gold Coast, Sir Charles Arden-Clarke (*The Times,* October 7, 1955, p. 7, col. 7).

21 *The Times,* May 12, 1956, p. 6, col. 4. The results of the plebisite will be considered by the General Assembly at its eleventh session before further action is taken.

The Initiative for Alteration

Chapter XII of the Charter indicates that the initiative for the alteration of a trust agreement must come from the 'States directly concerned' since Article 79 gives the General Assembly power only to *approve* the alteration. It is relevant to take note of the report approved by the General Assembly's Fourth Committee, to the effect that the General Assembly should instruct the Trusteeship Council, 'if it is of the opinion that, in the light of changing circumstances and practical experience, some alteration or amendment of any such Trusteeship Agreement would promote the more rapid achievement of the basic objectives of the Trusteeship System, to submit such proposed alteration or amendment to the Administering Authority so that, if agreed on pursuant to Article 79, such alteration or amendment may then be submitted to the General Assembly for approval.'[1] There seems to be no basis in the Charter for the General Assembly to empower the Trusteeship Council to make such recommendations to an administering authority. However, by Article 10, the General Assembly itself 'may make recommendations to the Members of the United Nations' on any question within the scope of the Charter. It is interesting to note that the General Assembly is empowered to make recommendations only to Members, and therefore the article could not be invoked in the case of a non-Member administering State, unless Article 2 (6) can be interpreted to give such authority to the General Assembly.[2] This was obviously foreseen when non-Member Italy was designated as an administering authority, as the trust agreement for Somaliland specifically asserts the right of both the Trusteeship Council and the administering authority to propose the alteration or amendment of the agreement.[3] Since the admission of Italy to Membership in the United Nations, the General Assembly too has acquired the right to propose alterations to the agreement for Somaliland.

[1] Report of Sub-Committee 1, Doc. A/C.4/69 (*Official Records of the General Assembly,* Second Part of the First Session, Fourth Committee, Part I (Annex 22), p. 300).

[2] This empowers the Organisation to ensure that non-Members act in accordance with the principles of the Charter so far as may be necessary for the maintenance of international peace and security.

[3] Article 21 (see *Official Records of the General Assembly,* Fifth Session, Suppl. No. 10, p. 8).

Termination of an Agreement

A special form of alteration of a trust agreement is termination, for which additional conditions apply. There is no mention in the Charter of termination of an agreement; but in view of the inherently temporary nature of the trusteeship status, and considering that the goal of each trust territory is 'self-government or independence,' it would be absurd to suppose that the drafters of the Charter did not intend the agreements to be terminated. It would be more reasonable to assume that they saw the problem in the wider context of alteration, and considered that the same rules would apply for termination. In any case, as Judge Read pointed out in his Separate Opinion on the *International Status of South-West Africa* (1950), 'any legal position, or system of legal relationships, can be brought to an end by the consent of all persons having legal rights and interests which might be affected by their termination.'[4] Nevertheless, the matter was raised at San Francisco. Egypt, favouring the insertion of provision into the Charter for the termination of the trust agreements, proposed 'that in all trust territories, within its competence, the General Assembly shall have the power to terminate the status of trusteeship, and declare the territory to be fit for full independence, either at the instance of the administering authority, or upon the recommendation of any member of the Assembly.'[5] In opposition to this proposal, it was held that termination without the consent of the administering authority would be contrary to the voluntary basis of the System, although some of the agreements themselves might contain provisions for termination through independence. In general it was held that provisions for termination were unnecessary.

Of the trust agreements, only that for Somaliland contains any special provision for termination. By Article 24, the agreement is to be terminated ten years after the date of its approval by the General Assembly, and thereupon Somaliland is to become an independent sovereign State. Thus the agreement will automatically terminate at the end of ten years due to the 'expiration of the period of time for which the treaty was concluded.'[6]

[4] *I.C.J. Reports 1950,* p. 167.

[5] *Summary Report of the Fourteenth Meeting of Committee II/4,* p. 5 (*U.N.C.I.O. Docs.,* Vol. 10, p. 547).

[6] Hackworth, *A Digest of International Law,* Vol. 5, p. 297. See also L. Oppenheim (ed. Lauterpacht), *International Law,* Vol. 1 (Seventh

Not even the method specified in Article 79 will be required, since the termination of this treaty after ten years, which was the intention of the parties to it, cannot be considered an alteration of its terms.[7] Indeed the alteration would take place if the treaty is *not* terminated, due to the fact that the territory is not considered ready for independence or for any other reason, since to prolong the treaty requires an alteration in its terms by lengthening the period for which it is to run.

Conditions for Termination

Since the goal of the Trusteeship System is 'self-government or independence,' it would seem that a trust agreement must be terminated when that stage of development has been reached by the inhabitants of the territory. The question arises as to who is to decide whether this goal has been attained by any particular trust territory. To comply with Article 79 of the Charter, this must be decided upon by the General Assembly (or Security Council in the case of strategic areas), the administering authority and the 'States directly concerned,' since termination is a form of alteration. It is here that difficulty may be anticipated. Whilst the attitudes of the administering Powers have in general

Edition), p. 841, 'all such treaties as are concluded for a certain period of time only, expire with the expiration of such time, unless they are renewed, or prolonged for another period'; Sir Arnold McNair, *La Terminaison et la Dissolution des Traités* (Académie de Droit International, *Recueil des Cours,* 1928, Vol. 2, p. 465); Article 33 of the Draft Convention on the Law of Treaties prepared under the auspices of the Harvard Law School Faculty, reads as follows: 'Subject to any provision concerning its renewal or continuance contained in the treaty or agreed upon by the parties, a treaty concluded for a fixed period of time is terminated by the expiration of that period' (29 *American Journal of International Law,* 1935, Supplement, p. 1168).

7 Support for the automatic termination of a treaty on the grounds that such was the intention of the parties was given by the International Court of Justice in 1952. In the *Case Concerning the Rights of Nationals of the United States of America in Morocco* (1952), before the International Court, the United States contended that she acquired in French Morocco, jurisdiction in all cases in which a United States citizen or protégé was defendant, through the operation of the most-favoured-nation clause in the U.S.-Moroccan Treaty of 1836. Due to the fact that the last State to enjoy such rights under treaty, Great Britain, specifically renounced them in 1937, the Court rejected the U.S. contention: 'According to this view, rights or privileges which a country was entitled to invoke by virtue of a most-favoured-nation clause, and which were in existence at the date of its coming into force, would be incorporated permanently by reference and enjoyed and exercised even after the abrogation of the treaty provisions from which they had been derived . . . this contention is inconsistent with the intentions of the parties now in question' (*I.C.J. Reports 1952,* p. 191).

been to consider self-government within their own imperial systems as a worthy achievement for any trust territory under their charge,[8] the tendency in the General Assembly has been to stress 'independence' and almost ignore the alternative of 'self-government.' Fear of the trust territory in question being subsequently absorbed into the colonial empire of the administering Power will be likely to make the General Assembly very wary of consenting to the termination of trusteeship until it is quite certain that the territory is sufficiently independent to stand by itself.

Apart from the assumption that the achievement of 'self-government or independence' is a satisfactory reason for terminating a trust agreement, there are no other guides either in the Charter or the agreements as to when an agreement should be terminated. Nor are there any guiding rules to help in deciding whether the goal of the System has been reached. A useful precedent from the practice of the Mandates System might well be followed in the United Nations. In 1931, the Council of the League of Nations approved an opinion of the Permanent Mandates Commission entitled *General Conditions Which Must be Fulfilled before the Mandates Régime Can be Brought to an End in Respect of a Country Placed under that Régime.*[9] Already, the General Assembly has approved a list of factors to help in deciding whether a non-self-governing territory has achieved the goal of Chapter XI.[10] There seems to be no reason why the General Assembly could not produce a similar guide for the Trusteeship System, and although it would not be binding on the parties to the trust agreements it would nevertheless have strong persuasive effect. This should be undertaken before the question of terminating a particular trust agreement comes before the Organisation, since any such study should be free from the special prejudices which might arise in the case of the termination of a particular agreement.

8 The trust territories under French administration form part of the French Union, whilst those under British administration are closely allied to neighbouring British colonial territories. It is interesting to note that in British thinking, self-government is a stage *towards* independence and must necessarily be reached *before* independence.

9 League of Nations, *The Mandates System–Origins–Principles–Application* (1945), pp. 118–120.

10 *Official Records of the General Assembly,* Eighth Session, Resolution 742 (VIII). See below, Chap. 12.

DETERMINATION OF THE 'STATES DIRECTLY CONCERNED'

As has been shown in the case of the approval of the trust agreements, the most troublesome problem facing the United Nations with regard to these agreements has been that of identifying the 'States directly concerned.'[11] Since the issue is likely to recur again and again, there is a pressing need to get the 'States directly concerned' defined. Considering that the Members of the United Nations were unable to agree upon the identity of these States during the conclusion of the trust agreements, it seems unlikely that they will do any better in sanctioning an alteration which will not require the same urgency as the conclusion. There are several reasons why the question is likely to continue to face the United Nations.

In the first place, all territories are intended ultimately to achieve self-government or independence which in itself involves an alteration of the trust agreements to allow their termination. If the Trusteeship System is to have any meaning, its goal of self-government or independence for every trust territory cannot be allowed to be jeopardised by mere formalistic quibbling.[12]

In the second place, it is not only in the case of the termination of a trust agreement that the problem of the 'States directly concerned' is likely to arise; other problems may appear which will require the alteration of an agreement. One of the possible solutions to the Togoland Unification Problem involves the alteration of a trust agreement.[13]

Finally, there are other events which could give rise to a very pressing need for the alteration of an agreement, and which must be prepared for in advance. Should the identity of an administering Power disappear through its absorption into another State, or through the voluntary surrender of its sovereignty become absorbed into a federal structure, such as a European federation, the trust agreements for territories under the administering Power's control would have to be altered to allow for the designation of the new administering authority. This would be necessary even if the new administering authority should be the larger entity into which the administering Power had been absorbed, since the administering Power is men-

[11] See above, Chap. 5, p. 80 *et seq.*

[12] For a discussion on the meaning of 'self-government or independence,' see above, Chap. 4, pp. 57–58.

[13] See above, pp. 131–132 *et seq.*

tioned by name in all the trust agreements and this name would need to be altered. This alteration is required by the provisions of Article 79 of the Charter, although under general international law the rules governing State succession might apply automatically.[14]

Having recognised the need to get the 'States directly concerned' defined, the problem remains as to how this is to be done.[15] The ambiguity of the phrase might be solved by applying to some organ for an interpretation. Three such organs immediately come to mind: the Trusteeship Council, the General Assembly, and the International Court of Justice.

In considering the claim of the Trusteeship Council, it is relevant to note a statement included in the Report of the Rapporteur of Committee IV/2 at the San Francisco Conference. This reads as follows: 'In the course of the operation from day to day of the various organs of the Organisation, it is inevitable that each organ will interpret such parts of the Charter as are applicable to its particular functions.'[16] However, in the case of the Trusteeship Council, this provision breaks down for the following reason: Article 79 provides that the 'States directly concerned' shall agree upon the terms of trusteeship. The Trusteeship Council, however, only came into being after the agreements had been drawn up and approved, since Article 86 based the composition of the Council upon how many and which Members submitted trust agreements. Therefore at the time

[14] The succession of States to international treaties (which is what the trust agreements are) was upheld by the Permanent Court of International Justice in its Judgment on the *Free Zones of Upper Savoy and District of Gex* (1932): 'The concord of wills thus represented by the Manifesto confers on the delimination of the zone of Saint-Gingolph the character of a treaty stipulation which France must respect as Sardinia's successor in the sovereignty over the territory in question' (P.C.I.J. Series A/B, No. 46, see 2 Hudson, *World Court Reports*, pp. 545–546). See also the Dissenting Opinion of Judge Caloyanni in the *Readaptation of the Mavrommatis Jerusalem Concessions* (1927): 'We are therefore in point of fact concerned with the execution of the international obligations which the Palestine administration was bound to respect by maintaining the concessions obtained by M. Mavrommatis from the State to which the British Government succeeded as succession State and at the same time as Mandatory' (P.C.I.J. Series A, No. 11, see 2 Hudson, *World Court Reports*, pp. 131–132).

[15] For a discussion of the problem of interpreting the Charter, see Pollux, *The Interpretation of the Charter* (23 *British Year Book of International Law*, 1946, pp. 54–82).

[16] *Report of the Rapporteur of Committee IV/2*, Doc. 933 (*U.N.C.I.O. Docs.*, Vol. 13, p. 709).

when the 'States directly concerned' first aroused controversy, the Trusteeship Council did not exist, and so it cannot be the competent organ to interpret the phrase.

To say that the General Assembly is the competent organ is to establish a hierarchy within the Organisation itself which is clearly ruled out by Article 7 (1) of the Charter.[17] Only if the Charter specifically authorises the General Assembly to assume powers with regard to another organ can such competence be said to exist. But, since, apart from the approval of the terms of trusteeship, by Article 85 (1) the General Assembly's competence with regard to trusteeship only begins once the agreements are in force, therefore the General Assembly cannot be the appropriate body. It is doubtful whether the General Assembly's power to make recommendations on any question within the scope of the Charter, as provided in Article 10, extends to the interpretation of an article of the Charter.

At San Francisco, it was stated in Committee IV/2 that 'it would always be open to the General Assembly or to the Security Council, in appropriate circumstances, to ask the International Court of Justice for an advisory opinion concerning the meaning of a provision of the Charter.'[18] The Charter itself, in Article 96 (1), provides that the General Assembly may ask the International Court of Justice 'to give an advisory opinion on any legal question.' Likewise, the General Assembly, in a resolution adopted at its Second Session, authorised 'the Trusteeship Council to request advisory opinions of the International Court of Justice on legal questions arising within the scope of the activities of the Council.'[19] If the question of the interpretation of the 'States directly concerned' were to be referred to it, what would the Court's reasoning be? If the text of an article of a treaty is not clear, the usual practice of international lawyers is to consult the preparatory records in order to ascertain 'the intention of the parties' at the time at which the treaty was con-

[17] Article 7 (1) establishes the General Assembly and the Trusteeship Council among the six principal organs of the Organisation. They are thus of equal status, although, since the Trusteeship Council is required to report to the General Assembly, the General Assembly may be considered as *primus inter pares*.

[18] *U.N.C.I.O. Docs.*, Vol. 13, p. 709.

[19] *Official Records of the General Assembly*, Second Session, Resolution 171 (II).

cluded.[20] Since the proceedings at San Francisco leave the issue open, it has been argued that the International Court is not competent to interpret the phrase since it would involve the *making* of international law.[1] However, as was stated in the Advisory Opinion of the International Court on *Admission of a State to Membership in the United Nations* (1948)[2]: 'According to Article 96 of the Charter and Article 65 of the Statute [of the Court], the Court may give an advisory opinion on any legal question . . .'; and 'nowhere is any provision to be found forbidding the Court, "the principal judicial organ of the United Nations," to exercise in regard to Article 4 of the Charter, a multilateral treaty, an interpretative function which falls within the normal exercise of its judicial powers.'[3] Article 79 could well be substituted for Article 4 in this instance.

The only other way to obtain an interpretation would be to set up an *ad hoc* Committee of Jurists for this purpose. If an authoritative interpretation were required, however, it would be necessary to 'embody the interpretation in an amendment to the Charter,' as stated by Committee IV/2 at San Francisco.[4]

The importance of clearing up the uncertainty of the meaning of the 'States directly concerned' cannot be over-emphasised. That the trust territories should be prevented from attaining their final aim of 'self-government or independence' through inability on the part of United Nations Members to agree on the identity of the 'States directly concerned' would be farcical; the history of the placing of the territories under trusteeship has, however, shown that such is not impossible. An interpretation of the phrase 'States directly concerned' would go a long way towards preventing this.

20 See G. Schwarzenberger, *International Law* (1949), Vol. 1, p. 208 *et seq.*

1 Professor Lauterpacht argues that the duty of the Court is to make the treaty work, even where the use of an ambiguous phrase in a treaty is due to the absence of an effective common intention by the parties at the time the treaty was concluded. The Court must nevertheless assume a common intention and arrive at this by taking into account the purpose of the treaty as a whole (see H. Lauterpacht, *Restrictive Interpretation and the Principle of Effectiveness in the Interpretation of Treaties* (26 *British Yearbook of International Law*, 1949, p. 48 *et seq.*).

2 *I.C.J. Reports 1948*, p. 57 *et seq.*

3 *I.C.J. Reports 1948*, p. 61.

4 *U.N.C.I.O. Docs.*, Vol. 13, p. 709.

PART FOUR

MACHINERY OF SUPERVISION

CHAPTER 8

ORGANS OF THE UNITED NATIONS CONCERNED WITH TRUSTEESHIP

THE functioning of the International Trusteeship System implies two elements—supervision and administration.[1] The supervisory aspect is undertaken by the United Nations itself through the General Assembly, the Security Council and the Trusteeship Council, whilst the administration of the trust territories is exercised by administering authorities.[2] This chapter is concerned with the Organisation in its supervisory capacity under the Trusteeship System. This involves two main considerations: the determination of these supervisory functions, and the part played by the various United Nations organs in their exercise.

The United Nations derives its functions with respect to trusteeship from the Charter and from the terms of the individual trust agreements. Whilst a trust agreement cannot legally be allowed to limit the trusteeship functions accorded to the United Nations by the Charter,[3] it may allocate additional functions to the Organisation. In approving a trust agreement the Organisation is consenting to undertake any additional functions which the agreement may accord to it. However, a trust agreement may only impose supervisory functions on the Organisation with respect to the particular trust territory to which the agreement refers; the general trusteeship functions of the United Nations are derived from the Charter. According to Article 81 of the Charter, the functions of the United Nations must be included in the terms of the trust agreement, since it is stated that the agreement is to include 'the terms under which the trust territory will be administered.' These terms relate to both the obligations which the administering authority undertakes and the supervisory functions which the United Nations is to exercise over the administration of the territory. Since administration and supervision

[1] Article 75 of the Charter states that the United Nations is to establish an international trusteeship system for 'the administration and supervision of such territories as may be placed thereunder.'

[2] See below, Chap. 11.

[3] See above, Chap. 6, p. 95.

are the essential elements of United Nations trusteeship, both of these must be included in the terms of trusteeship. But if the agreement says that the territory is to be administered in accordance with the Charter provisions on trusteeship, or if the agreement merely mentions that the territory in question is a United Nations trust territory,[4] then the provision of Article 81 is complied with and the functions of the United Nations defined in the Charter automatically follow. So long as some reference to the Charter provisions on trusteeship is made, then it is only the functions of the United Nations other than those specified in the Charter which must be written into the trust agreement; by Article 87 (d) such additional functions are clearly authorised to be undertaken by the Organisation, so long as they are included in the terms of the agreement.[5]

The general functions of the United Nations with respect to trusteeship are laid down in Articles 83, 85, 87 and 88 of the Charter. These articles impose on the Organisation the duty to approve the terms of trusteeship for the territories to be placed under the System,[6] including their alteration or amendment, to exercise supervision over the administration of the territories, and to formulate a questionnaire on the basis of which the administering authorities shall make an annual report to the Organisation. Four organs of the United Nations are specifically mentioned in the Charter with respect to the exercise of trusteeship functions: the General Assembly, the Security Council, the Trusteeship Council, and the Economic and Social Council.

The General Assembly

Article 85 allocates all functions of the United Nations with regard to non-strategic areas to the General Assembly, and in this it is to be assisted by the Trusteeship Council. The General Assembly is obligated to make use of this assistance by the compulsive wording of Article 85 (2), which provides that the

[4] All the trust agreements mention that the territories in question are to be United Nations trust territories. See further above, Chap. 6.

[5] See below Appendix 1 for text of Article 87 (d).

[6] This gives the Organisation the power, and indeed the duty, to ensure that the trust agreements are in accordance with the Charter. If an agreement is not in accordance with the Charter, then the Organisation should refuse to approve it. Approval implies that in the opinion of the Organisation, the agreement is in conformity with the provisions of the Charter.

Trusteeship Council '*shall* assist the General Assembly in carrying out these functions.'[7] It is true that the obligation is actually placed on the Trusteeship Council by the wording of this article. But if the General Assembly does not make use of the Trusteeship Council's assistance, then the Trusteeship Council is unable to comply with the provisions of Article 85 (2). Since it must be presumed that the Trusteeship Council is bound to comply with the provision of articles of the Charter, the General Assembly must enable it to do so in this instance. It is not stated in what manner the Trusteeship Council is to assist the General Assembly, and therefore this obligation upon the General Assembly does not prevent it dealing with the administering authorities directly. Article 85 (2) does not require the General Assembly to approach the administering authorities through the medium of the Trusteeship Council.

Article 85 does not elaborate upon the functions which the General Assembly is to exercise as regards non-strategic areas beyond stating that these include the approval of the terms of the trust agreements and of their alteration or amendment. However, the main function of the United Nations with regard to trusteeship is the supervision of the trust territories, and Article 87 suggests ways in which this supervision may be exercised. The specific ways mentioned are through the consideration of annual reports submitted by the administering authorities, the acceptance of petitions and their examination in consultation with the administering authority concerned, and the dispatch of periodic visiting missions to the trust territories at times agreed upon with the administering authority.[8] Other methods of supervision are authorised so long as they are in conformity with the terms of the trust agreements.[9]

Article 87 authorises the General Assembly only to *consider* reports; it does not provide for any further action after the consideration. However, by Article 10 of the Charter, the General Assembly is entitled to 'make recommendations to the Members of the United Nations' on 'any questions or any matters within the scope of the present Charter or relating to the powers or functions of any organs provided for in the present

[7] Italics added.
[8] Article 87, paragraphs (a), (b) and (c).
[9] Article 87 (d).

10

Charter.' Reports from the administering authorities are certainly within the scope of the Charter, and therefore the General Assembly is authorised to make recommendations to the administering authorities in furtherance of its consideration of these reports. Likewise, the General Assembly may make recommendations to a Member administering authority with respect to petitions concerning the territory under its administration, or as a result of the report of a United Nations Visiting Mission to the territory.

The General Assembly may also make *general* recommendations on trusteeship matters to the administering authorities, but since this power is based on Article 10 the recommendations are limited to Members. This is interesting in view of the fact that the administering authority of a trust territory need not be a Member of the United Nations,[10] and in practice, one territory, Somaliland, was under non-Member administration until 1955. Although the trust agreement for Somaliland under Italian administration refers to recommendations of the General Assembly,[11] the Charter itself does not authorise the General Assembly to make such recommendations to a non-Member, except under Article 11 (2).[12] This latter article limits the recommendations to non-Members to questions involving the maintenance of international peace and security which have been brought before the General Assembly by a Member, the Security Council, or a non-Member. Furthermore, under the provisions of this article, only to a 'State concerned' in such a question is the General Assembly empowered to make a recommendation. This does not cover general recommendations by the General Assembly to a non-Member on such questions as education or the status of women in the trust territory; therefore, the General

10 It may be a non-Member or the Organisation, see below, p. 206 *et seq.*

11 Article 5 (1) of the trust agreement for Somaliland provides that the Administering Authority undertakes '. . . to include in this report i.e. the annual report) information relating to the measures taken to give effect to the suggestions and recommendations of the General Assembly and of the Trusteeship Council' (*Official Records of the General Assembly,* Fifth Session, Suppl. No. 10, p. 6).

12 'The General Assembly may discuss any questions relating to the maintenance of international peace and security brought before it by any Member of the United Nations, or by the Security Council, or by a state which is not a Member of the United Nations in accordance with Article 35, paragraph 2, and, except as provided in Article 12, may make recommendations with regard to any such questions to the state or states concerned or to the Security Council or to both.'

Assembly was not authorised to make such recommendations to Italy until she became a Member. It would appear from the records of the Trusteeship Council[13] and of the Committee for Italian Somaliland[14] that the question of the authority of the General Assembly to make recommendations to Italy, as mentioned in Article 5 (1) of the trust agreement, was not discussed at all.

Whilst Article 85 authorises the General Assembly to undertake trusteeship functions only with regard to non-strategic trust territories, the question arises whether Article 10 permits the General Assembly to concern itself with strategic areas or territories. The General Assembly is authorised to 'discuss any questions or any matters within the scope of the present Charter' and to make recommendations to Members or to the Security Council, and strategic trust territories are certainly within the scope of the Charter. However, Article 83 (1) allocates all functions of the United Nations for strategic areas to the Security Council, and Article 16 authorises the General Assembly to exercise only such trusteeship functions as are assigned to it under Chapters XII and XIII. The question is whether Articles 83 and 16, when read together, limit the authority which the General Assembly enjoys under Article 10. But even if the effect of Articles 16 and 83 is to prevent the General Assembly from *exercising the functions* of the United Nations with regard to strategic trust territories, this does not rule out the possibility of the General Assembly *discussing* matters affecting the strategic trust territories which are certainly 'within the scope of the present Charter.'

It must also be considered whether the General Assembly may make recommendations to the Members of the United Nations or to the Security Council on matters affecting the strategic trust territories, since this authority is limited only by Article 12 of the Charter. Article 12 states that 'while the Security Council is exercising in respect of any dispute or situation the functions assigned to it in the present Charter, the General Assembly shall not make any recommendations with regard to that dispute or situation unless the Security Council so requests.'

13 See *Official Records of the Trusteeship Council,* Sixth Session, p. 6 *et seq.*

14 Doc. T/449, January 19, 1950.

Thus if the Security Council requests the General Assembly to make recommendations on the matter of strategic trusteeship, the General Assembly is authorised to do so. It is necessary to consider whether the 'situation' referred to in Article 12 covers strategic trusteeship generally, or whether it refers to the specific trusteeship functions of the Security Council authorised by Articles 24 (2) and 83. If it refers only to the specific trusteeship functions of the Security Council authorised by the Charter, then the General Assembly is not prevented from making recommendations on other matters concerning strategic trust territories. The wording of Article 12 would seem to justify this interpretation. Furthermore, since Article 12 forbids the General Assembly to make recommendations only *whilst* the Security Council is exercising its functions, it can be contended that the General Assembly may make recommendations on strategic trusteeship matters at any other time.

The question of the General Assembly's concern with strategic trust territories arises in the case of a trust territory of which only a portion is designated as a strategic area. It would appear that both the General Assembly and Security Council must approve the terms of trusteeship for such a territory, unless two separate agreements are concluded for it. This follows from Articles 85 (1) and 83 (1) of the Charter which require the General Assembly to approve the terms of trusteeship for all non-strategic areas, and the Security Council to do likewise for all strategic areas. A similar problem follows with respect to the exercise of United Nations supervision over the trust territory. Unless the administering authority were to submit two separate annual reports on the trust territory, then the General Assembly and Security Council would be exercising concurrent consideration of a single report. In this way the General Assembly would be exercising supervision over both strategic and non-strategic areas, as would the Security Council.[15] The same would be true in the case of petitions concerning the trust territory as a whole.

The General Assembly is required by Article 18 (2) to elect

15 A possible solution would be for the report to indicate that the portion concerning the strategic area was for the Security Council to consider. However, the general section of the report giving a general over-all picture of the economic and social conditions of the territory would still be subject to the scrutiny of both the Security Council and the General Assembly, unless these matters were to be duplicated in the section on the strategic area.

the non-permanent members of the Trusteeship Council in accordance with the provisions of Article 86, paragraph 1 (c). This function is particularly mentioned as being an important question which requires the two-thirds majority vote of the General Assembly. According to the provisions of Article 86, paragraph 1 (c), these non-permanent members of the Trusteeship Council are to be elected for three-year terms and are eligible for immediate re-election.

Article 22 of the Charter permits the General Assembly to establish such subsidiary organs as it deems necessary for the performance of its functions. Under the provisions of this article, six main committees have been established to deal with the matters on the agenda of the General Assembly, while other committees have been established to deal with specific matters. These committees operate under the authority of the General Assembly and exercise only such powers as the General Assembly assigns to them. Their function is to consider such items as the General Assembly may refer to them and they may not introduce new items into their deliberations.[16] The General Assembly's Rules of Procedure deal quite extensively with this matter of subsidiary organs and specify that one of the Main Committees of the General Assembly is to be a Trusteeship Committee.[17] The Trusteeship Committee also deals with matters concerning the non-self-governing territories referred to in Chapter XI of the Charter. Since the Trusteeship Committee operates only as a subsidiary organ of the General Assembly, all recommendations of the Committee are subject to approval by the General Assembly meeting in plenary session before they become official General Assembly recommendations. The function of the Committee is not to replace the General Assembly, but to discuss such matters on the General Assembly's agenda as are assigned to it before they are dealt with by the General Assembly itself. In this way minor issues may be eliminated in advance by the Committee. The Trusteeship Committee itself may also appoint sub-committees to assist it.

The Trusteeship Committee is identical in composition with the General Assembly, in that all Members of the United Nations

16 Rule 99 of the General Assembly's Rules of Procedure (U.N. Doc. A/520/Rev. 3 of June 1, 1954, p. 18).

17 Rule 101 (*ibid.*). This is the General Assembly's Fourth Committee.

are represented. For this reason, it might be assumed that the General Assembly would automatically adopt any recommendations proposed by the Committee. However, whereas the Committee votes by simple majority,[18] the General Assembly itself is required to vote by a two-thirds majority on all matters relating to the operation of the Trusteeship System.[19] Thus recommendations which receive the bare number of votes required in the Trusteeship Committee generally fail to achieve the required two-thirds in the General Assembly.

The Security Council

Article 83 (1) of the Charter allocates all functions of the United Nations with regard to strategic trust territories to the Security Council. This is specified as including the approval of the terms of the trust agreements and of their alteration or amendment. The Security Council itself derives the authority to carry out these trusteeship functions from Article 24 (2), which states that the specific powers granted to the Security Council for this purpose are laid down in Chapter XII of the Charter. It is interesting to note that Article 24 does not refer to Chapter XIII which introduces annual reports, petitions and visiting missions into the Trusteeship System. Nor does Article 83 refer to these methods of supervision. The question is whether Article 83 (3), in referring to the Security Council's performance of 'those functions of the United Nations under the trusteeship system relating to political, economic, social and educational matters in the strategic areas' is to be understood as including the methods of supervision stated in Article 87.[20] Two factors point to an affirmative answer to this question. Firstly, the only means of exercising supervision over a trust territory which are given in the Charter are those stated in Article 87, and Article 75 clearly establishes that supervision is an essential element of United Nations Trusteeship. Secondly, Article 24 (2) refers to 'the specific powers granted to the Security Council' in Chapter XII. Unless Article 83 (3) is to be understood as including the supervisory means laid down in Article 87, the powers granted to the Security Council in Chapter XII are anything but specific.

18 Rule 126.
19 Article 18 (2) of the Charter.
20 *i.e.*, annual reports, petitions and visits.

In the only strategic trust agreement which has so far been approved—that for the Pacific Islands under United States administration—it has been specifically stated that the provisions of Article 87 of the Charter are applicable to the territory.[1] At first, this appears to confer powers on the General Assembly to put into practice the system of annual reports, petitions and visits with regard to the strategic trust territory, since Article 87 refers only to the General Assembly, and to the Trusteeship Council acting under the General Assembly's authority. However, Article 83 (1) says that 'all functions of the United Nations relating to strategic areas . . . shall be exercised by the Security Council' which requires the substitution of the Security Council for the General Assembly with respect to Article 87. What has happened in practice is that the Security Council has been substituted for the General Assembly in the carrying out of the supervisory functions of Article 87. Thus the administering authority of the Pacific Islands makes its annual report to the Security Council, and the Trusteeship Council, after examining it, has reported thereon to the Security Council instead of the General Assembly. In fact the Trusteeship Council exercises all its functions with regard to the Pacific Islands under the authority of the Security Council, reporting back to the Security Council in the same way as it does to the General Assembly for non-strategic trust territories.[2]

The Trusteeship Council

The only supervisory function allocated to the Trusteeship Council absolutely is the formulation of a questionnaire to provide the basis for the annual reports of the administering authorities to the General Assembly.[3] All the other supervisory functions are accorded primarily to the General Assembly, and to the Trusteeship Council only *under the authority* of the General Assembly. On the surface, it appears that even the formulation of the Questionnaire, whilst it is to be undertaken entirely by the Trusteeship Council, is done under the authority of the General Assembly, since Article 85 (2) states that the Trusteeship Council shall operate 'under the authority

1 Article 13 of the Trust Agreement for the Pacific Islands (*United Nations Treaty Series,* Vol. 8, 1947, p. 190 *et seq.*).

2 See further below, pp. 155–158.

3 Article 88.

of the General Assembly' in carrying out the United Nations' functions of trusteeship. However, since the General Assembly is itself not authorised to formulate the Questionnaire, it cannot authorise the Trusteeship Council to do so. Therefore, for the exercise of this function, the Trusteeship Council gets its authority not from the General Assembly but directly from the Charter. The Charter appears to accord two contradictory positions to the Trusteeship Council: by Article 7 (1) it is established as a principal organ of the United Nations along with the General Assembly and the Security Council; yet in the exercise of all its supervisory functions, with the exception of the formulation of the Questionnaire, it operates under the authority of the General Assembly or Security Council.

The functions relating to trusteeship which the Trusteeship Council may exercise under the authority of the General Assembly include the consideration of annual reports, the acceptance and examination of petitions, and the dispatch of visiting missions to the trust territories at times agreed upon with the administering authority. Once the Trusteeship System was established, these functions were assigned initially to the Trusteeship Council which would submit a report on its discharge of these functions to each session of the General Assembly. In this way the General Assembly supervises the Trusteeship Council in the exercise of its functions under Article 87. In addition, Rule 104 of the Trusteeship Council's Rules of Procedure[4] authorises the Trusteeship Council to submit recommendations to the General Assembly with respect to the trust agreements. In the exercise of this function, the Trusteeship Council acts as an advisory body, although there is no obligation on the General Assembly to accept the Trusteeship Council's recommendations.

The Trusteeship Council and the General Assembly

Whilst the Trusteeship Council exercises its trusteeship functions under the authority of the General Assembly, the determination of the exact position of the Trusteeship Council with regard to the General Assembly is not clear. Professor Kelsen says that the Trusteeship Council is intended to be the 'auxiliary organ' of the General Assembly and Security Council, and that 'it does not have more authority in trusteeship matters than these two

[4] U.N. Doc. T/1/Rev. 3, p. 17.

organs which it has to assist.'[5] This is not quite true of the Trusteeship Council as regards its relationship with the General Assembly, for Article 88 confers the function of formulating the Questionnaire upon the Trusteeship Council alone. It is true that Article 85 confers upon the General Assembly the functions of the United Nations regarding trust agreements for non-strategic territories, but this does not include the formulation of the Questionnaire when this function is specifically accorded to another organ. Moreover, Article 85 does not confer *all* functions of the United Nations for non-strategic trust agreements upon the General Assembly, as does Article 83 in the case of the Security Council and strategic agreements. Article 85 merely mentions 'the functions of the United Nations with regard to trusteeship agreements for all areas not designated as strategic,' whereas Article 83 authorises the Security Council to exercise '*all* functions of the United Nations relating to strategic areas.'[6] Moreover, in the case of the General Assembly, it is doubtful whether 'the functions of the United Nations with regard to trusteeship *agreements*' include all functions with regard to the trust *territories*. Surely the formulation of a questionnaire is not a function with regard to the trust *agreements*. It is only with regard to the trust agreements and the functions under Article 87 that the Trusteeship Council is placed as the 'auxiliary' of the General Assembly, not with regard to the Questionnaire under Article 88.

In 1950, China and the Philippine Republic introduced a proposal in the Trusteeship Council[7] to the effect that the Trusteeship Council should recommend to the administering authorities that the flag of the United Nations be flown in all trust territories.[8] This proposal was in pursuance of a General Assembly resolution which requested the Trusteeship Council to recommend to the administering authorities that this be put into

5 H. Kelsen, *The Law of the United Nations* (1951), p. 689.

6 Italics added.

7 U.N. Doc. T/L.9 (see *Official Records of the Trusteeship Council*, Sixth Session, p. 607).

8 This was opposed by Australia, New Zealand, France, Belgium and the United Kingdom, who argued that the proposal was based on a misconception of the respective functions of the United Nations and the administering authority. Ultimate authority in the territories, they argued, rested with the administering authorities (*Official Records of the Trusteeship Council*, Sixth Session, pp. 608–609).

effect.[9] The Delegate of the Philippines argued that if the Trusteeship Council did not adopt his country's proposal, it was not showing proper respect for the General Assembly. Thus the question arises as to whether the Trusteeship Council is bound to accept the recommendations of the General Assembly. As has been stated by a member of the Trusteeship Department of the United Nations Secretariat, 'the constitutional difficulty quite clearly lies in the fact that the members of the Trusteeship Council have an unquestioned right to vote as they see fit and cannot be compelled to vote otherwise merely because another body of the United Nations issues instructions to the Council.'[10]

The Charter allocates trusteeship functions for non-strategic trust territories to the General Assembly,[11] whilst the Trusteeship Council is to act as the agent and assistant of the General Assembly in carrying out these functions.[12] If the Trusteeship Council does not accept the recommendations of the General Assembly, it is not assisting the General Assembly with these functions, and is therefore not exercising the role assigned to it in the Charter. On the other hand, the General Assembly, in the resolution mentioned above, only *requested* the Trusteeship Council to recommend to the administering authorities that the United Nations flag be flown in the trust territories. If the interpretation put forward by the Delegate of the Philippines is accepted, then the General Assembly's *request* amounts to an order, and nowhere in the Charter is such an extensive power given to the General Assembly.[13] In fact, the Trusteeship Council did not adopt

9 *Official Records of the General Assembly,* Fourth Session, Resolution 325 (IV). The resolution requested the Trusteeship Council to recommend to the administering authorities concerned that the flag of the United Nations be flown over all trust territories side by side with the flag of the administering authority concerned and with the territorial flag if such existed.

10 H. A. Wieschhoff, *Trusteeship and Non-Self-Governing Territories (Annual Review of United Nations Affairs,* 1953, pp. 49–60 at p. 53).

11 Article 85 (1).

12 Article 85 (2).

13 See, however, the view of Judge Lauterpacht in his Separate Opinion on *South-West Africa–Voting Procedure,* Advisory Opinion of June 7, 1955 (*I.C.J. Reports 1955,* p. 67 *et seq.* at p. 118), to the effect that the General Assembly resolutions 'are often, in form and substance, directives addressed to the organs of the United Nations such as the Trusteeship Council . . . as such they are endowed with legal validity and effect.' See also F. B. Sloan, *The Binding Force of a Recommendation of the General Assembly of the United Nations* (23 *British Yearbook of International Law,* 1948, pp. 1–33 at p. 5): 'Thus resolutions addressed to the . . . Trusteeship Council . . . create binding obligations.'

the draft resolution and was therefore not accepting the recommendation of the General Assembly.[14] However, reconsidering the matter at its next session, the Trusteeship Council did accept the recommendation of the General Assembly with the proviso that the administering authorities be allowed any latitude necessary to handle any practical administrative difficulties arising therefrom.[15]

The Trusteeship Council and the Security Council

The Trusteeship Council assists the Security Council in the exercise of trusteeship functions for strategic areas, 'subject to the provisions of the trusteeship agreements and without prejudice to security considerations.'[16] Whereas the Charter specifies the functions which the Trusteeship Council may exercise under the General Assembly's authority for non-strategic areas, the same is not true with regard to strategic areas.[17] Two questions arise in this respect: whether the Trusteeship Council may formulate a questionnaire for territories within the competence of the Security Council, and whether the Trusteeship Council may assist the Security Council to carry out the supervisory functions stated in Article 87. The fundamental issue behind the two questions is whether Article 83 (1), in attributing all the functions of the United Nations relating to strategic areas to the Security Council, is to be interpreted as automatically substituting the Security Council for the General Assembly in Articles 87 and 88.

Since Article 83 (3) uses the compulsive wording 'the Security Council *shall* . . . avail itself of the assistance of the Trusteeship Council,'[18] therefore the Security Council is not permitted to by-pass the Trusteeship Council and reserve all the trusteeship functions to itself, unless the provisions of the trusteeship agreement or security considerations permit this.[19] However, the

14 The voting on the draft resolution was a tie, and therefore, in accordance with Rule 38 of the Trusteeship Council's Rules of Procedure, the proposal was defeated (see *Official Records of the Trusteeship Council*, Sixth Session, p. 613).

15 *Official Records of the Trusteeship Council*, Seventh Session, p. 613.

16 Article 83 (3).

17 Article 83 (3) says that the Security Council shall 'avail itself of the assistance of the Trusteeship Council to perform those functions of the United Nations under the trusteeship system relating to political, economic, social, and educational matters in the strategic areas.'

18 Italics added.

19 See Article 83 (3).

Security Council is permitted to avail itself of the assistance of the Trusteeship Council *only* in the case of functions 'under the trusteeship system relating to political, economic, social, and educational matters in the strategic areas.' This does not include functions regarding the trust agreement such as alteration, amendment or termination. Thus the role of the Trusteeship Council with regard to the Security Council is more limited than it is with regard to the General Assembly, inasmuch as there is no authority for the Trusteeship Council to assist the Security Council with matters affecting the trust agreements.

The relationship of the Trusteeship Council to the Security Council was considered at some length by both these organs themselves. The majority group in the Trusteeship Council asserted that the Trusteeship Council fulfilled the same functions as regards strategic areas as it did for non-strategic areas, the difference being only that in one case the Trusteeship Council reported to the Security Council and in the other case to the General Assembly.[20] This ignores the question of functions regarding the trust agreement, which has just been discussed.

The Trusteeship Council established a special committee to examine the problem of the relationship between itself and the Security Council,[1] and the Security Council referred the matter to its Committee of Experts.[2] This Committee of Experts drew up a draft resolution which the Trusteeship Council was asked to consider and report its views back to the Security Council.[3] This draft resolution would request the Trusteeship Council to perform for the strategic trust territory the functions outlined in Articles 87 and 88 of the Charter; to transmit a questionnaire for the strategic territory to the Security Council; to examine and report to the Security Council on all reports and petitions received in respect of strategic areas; and to submit to the

[20] *Official Records of the Trusteeship Council,* Second Session, First Part, pp. 581–587. See especially the opinion of Mr. Ryckmans, the Belgian Delegate: 'To my mind the Charter is quite clear. There is only one Trusteeship System. The Trusteeship Council's functions with regard to strategic and non-strategic areas are the same, except that in one case it reports to the General Assembly and in the other to the Security Council' (pp. 585–586).

[1] *Official Records of the Trusteeship Council,* Second Session, Resolution 10 (II).

[2] *Official Records of the Security Council,* Second Year, No. 104, p. 2763; and Doc. S/599 (*ibid.,* pp. 2753–2754).

[3] Doc. S/642 (*Official Records of the Security Council,* Fourth Year, No. 18, p. 617).

Security Council its reports and recommendations on political, economic, social, and educational matters affecting strategic areas. The Security Council subsequently adopted this draft resolution.

The draft resolution calls for comment. The functions outlined in Article 87 of the Charter do fall within the 'political, economic, social, and educational matters' concerning which the Security Council is authorised to avail itself of the assistance of the Trusteeship Council; the same is true with regard to Article 88. However, authority to avail itself of the Trusteeship Council's assistance does not mean authority to hand over the functions to the Trusteeship Council entirely. The Trusteeship Council would be doing much more than assisting the Security Council; it would be actually *exercising* the functions. The case is different from that under Article 87 where the Trusteeship Council operates under the 'authority' of the General Assembly. For if the General Assembly authorises the Trusteeship Council to assume the functions under Article 87, then the Trusteeship Council is acting under the 'authority' of the General Assembly in carrying out the functions. The Trusteeship Council does not act under the 'authority' of the Security Council; it *assists* the Security Council. Likewise, in the case of Article 88, the Security Council is supposed to draw up the Questionnaire,[4] and to avail itself of the Trusteeship Council's assistance in so doing; it is not merely supposed to receive the Questionnaire from the Trusteeship Council after it has been formulated. The same applies to the rest of the substance of the draft resolution. Instead of merely receiving reports from the Trusteeship Council on the functions mentioned, the Security Council should actually undertake the functions with the help of the Trusteeship Council.

The Trusteeship Council itself was generally in favour of the draft resolution, and accordingly it adopted a resolution to implement the Security Council's request.[5] However, a minority view considered that it was the right and duty of the Security Council to carry out in respect of strategic areas, the functions exercised by the General Assembly and Trusteeship Council for

[4] This follows from Article 83 (1) by which 'all functions . . . of the United Nations relating to strategic areas . . . shall be exercised by the Security Council.'

[5] *Official Records of the Trusteeship Council,* Fourth Session, Resolution 46 (IV).

non-strategic areas. The Security Council could not delegate the functions stated in Articles 87 and 88 to the Trusteeship Council, but could merely avail itself of the assistance of the Trusteeship Council. This minority view held further that the Security Council itself should formulate the Questionnaire for strategic territories.

The Economic and Social Council

The Rules of Procedure of the Economic and Social Council contain provisions for the rendering of assistance to the Trusteeship Council,[6] and the Charter provides that the Trusteeship Council shall avail itself of such assistance.[7] These provisions provide the basis for the co-operation of these two organs in the matter of trusteeship.

At its First Session, the Trusteeship Council decided to appoint a committee of three to meet with a similar committee of the Economic and Social Council for the purpose of discussing matters of concern to them both.[8] These two committees submitted a joint report to both the Trusteeship Council and the Economic and Social Council suggesting methods of co-operation between the two organs.[9] Among the suggestions made were that the Economic and Social Council, whilst being permitted to make general recommendations and studies on economic and social problems, should not single out trust territories for special recommendations without the prior approval of the Trusteeship Council; all petitions to the United Nations originating from, or relating to, trust territories should be dealt with first by the Trusteeship Council, which might subsequently seek the assistance of a specialised commission of the Economic and Social Council; the date and place of the first meeting of a session of either Council, together with the agenda for the session, should be communicated to the President of the other body; the President of either Council or his representative was to be per-

[6] Rules 10, 12, and 13 (Doc. E/2424, May 12, 1953, pp. 4–5).

[7] Article 91 states that 'the Trusteeship Council shall, when appropriate, avail itself of the assistance of the Economic and Social Council and of the specialised agencies in regard to matters with which they are respectively concerned.'

[8] See *Resolutions Adopted by the Trusteeship Council During its First Session,* p. 1 (Resolution 1 (I)).

[9] Doc. E & T/C.1/2/Rev. 1 (*Official Records of the Trusteeship Council,* Second Session, First Part, Supplement, pp. 225–234).

mitted to participate in the deliberations of the other Council, when matters within the concern of his own Council were under discussion. Thus the Economic and Social Council was to be enabled to act as an advisory body to the Trusteeship Council, and also to include trust territories in its general recommendations.

The Economic and Social Council's activities with regard to trusteeship are not confined to advising the Trusteeship Council and including trust territories within the sphere of its general recommendations. It has a part to play with respect to the General Assembly and the Security Council. In view of the fact that primary responsibility for the supervision of trust territories is vested in the General Assembly and the Security Council, and since the economic and social advancement of the inhabitants of trust territories figures among the basic objectives of the Trusteeship System,[10] the assistance of the Economic and Social Council is very important to these two organs. Article 62 of the Charter authorises the Economic and Social Council to make recommendations to both the General Assembly and to Members of the United Nations, with respect to international economic, social, cultural, educational, health and other related matters. The basis for the co-operation of the Security Council and the Economic and Social Council is provided by Article 65: 'The Economic and Social Council may furnish information to the Security Council and shall assist the Security Council upon its request.' This authorises both the Security Council to seek the Economic and Social Council's assistance, and the Economic and Social Council to provide such assistance.

10 See Article 76 (b).

Chapter 9

THE TRUSTEESHIP COUNCIL

The Charter provides for a special trusteeship body which is to be one of the principal organs of the United Nations.[1] In furtherance of this provision, and in pursuance of Resolution 64 of the First Session of the General Assembly,[2] the Trusteeship Council was established. In spite of its being named in the Charter as a principal organ, the Trusteeship Council is subordinate to the General Assembly[3] or Security Council[4] in the exercise of its functions, except in the formulation of the Questionnaire.[5] In carrying out the functions of the United Nations for trust territories elaborated in Article 87, the Trusteeship Council acts as the agent of the General Assembly, the latter having primary responsibility for all non-strategic trust territories.[6]

Under the League of Nations Mandate System, responsibility for mandates rested with the League Council who established the Permanent Mandates Commission in accordance with Article 22 of the Covenant. This was a specialist body which operated entirely under the jurisdiction of the League Council and made no pretence at being a principal League organ. Since the Permanent Mandates Commission acted as the agent of the League Council, its activities were subject to the unanimous vote of a body of limited membership[7]; in the case of the Trusteeship System, the Trusteeship Council operates under the authority of an organ of universal membership which votes by a two-thirds majority on all trusteeship matters.[8] Thus the Trusteeship Council is controlled by a much more representative forum than was the Permanent Mandates Commission.

The Trusteeship Council is an unique organ of the United

1 Article 7 (1).
2 See *Resolutions Adopted by the General Assembly During the Second Part of its First Session,* Doc. A/64/Add. 1, pp. 122–123.
3 Articles 85 (2) and 87.
4 Article 83 (3).
5 See above, Chap. 8, pp. 151–153.
6 See *ibid.*
7 *i.e.,* the League Council.
8 Article 18 (2) of the Charter.

Nations inasmuch as it has powers over only certain Members—the administering authorities—and is concerned with only certain territories—trust territories. Thus the non-administering members of the Trusteeship Council may discuss and criticise the actions and policies of the administering members, whilst invoking the 'domestic jurisdiction' clause [9] to protect themselves from attack. The Trusteeship Council is the only organ in which its members may participate in the proceedings whilst remaining outside its jurisdiction. As a result of this, the Trusteeship Council has witnessed a line-up of its members on offensive and defensive sides.

Composition

The Trusteeship Council bears a similarity to the Economic and Social Council and the Security Council in that it consists of only certain Members of the United Nations, of which some are elected by the General Assembly. The original Working Paper at the San Francisco Conference [10] envisaged a Trusteeship Council consisting of all the administering Powers and an equal number of non-administering Powers elected by the General Assembly. As in the case of the Economic and Social Council, it was not proposed that the five Great Powers would necessarily be represented on the Trusteeship Council. However, this was subsequently altered to ensure permanent seats on the Trusteeship Council to the five permanent members of the Security Council, regardless of whether or not they administered trust territories.[11]

Article 86, paragraph 1 (c), provides for equality of representation on the Trusteeship Council as between administering and non-administering Members. This is in contrast to the Permanent Mandates Commission where a majority of nationals of non-mandatory States sat, although the League Covenant did not require this nor did it have anything to say as regards the composition of the Commission. It was in the Constitution of the Permanent Mandates Commission [12] that it was laid down that nationals of non-mandatory States should be in a majority

9 Article 2 (7).

10 U.N.C.I.O. Doc. 323, II/4/12, May 15, 1945, p. 3 (*U.N.C.I.O. Docs.*, Vol. 10, p. 677).

11 See *Summary Report of Thirteenth Meeting of Committee II/4* at San Francisco, pp. 4–5 (*U.N.C.I.O. Docs.*, Vol. 10, pp. 516–517). See further above, Chap. 2, pp. 28, 33–34.

12 League of Nations, *Official Journal* I (1920), p. 87, paragraph (a).

on this body and where the total membership was fixed at nine.[13] These provisions of the Commission's Constitution allowed for nationals of only four of the seven mandatory States to sit on the Commission,[14] and three mandatory States were never represented.[15] Under the Trusteeship System the non-representation of an administering State can only happen in the case of a non-Member administering State, since Article 86 assures membership on the Trusteeship Council to all Members administering trust territories who, in this article, are mentioned even before the permanent members of the Security Council.

Since paragraph 1 (c) of Article 86 requires that there shall be equality of representation on the Trusteeship Council as between administering and non-administering Powers, the Trusteeship Council could not be established until at least some trust agreements had been concluded by Members in order to provide the administering members of the Council. Furthermore, since the five permanent members of the Security Council were automatically accorded seats on the Trusteeship Council, it was necessary either for five other United Nations Members to become administering authorities or for some of the five permanent members and a sufficient number of others to do so. In this connection, it is interesting to note that, had all the trust agreements designated the Organisation as administering authority, the Trusteeship Council could not have been established, since there would have been no administering Members to sit on the Council.[16] Any change in status from a non-administering to an administering Power by a permanent member of the Trusteeship Council necessitates an adjustment in the membership. Thus when the United States became an administering authority

13 The membership of the Permanent Mandates Commission was increased to ten in 1927 in order to give a seat to a German national.

14 Great Britain, France, Belgium and Japan.

15 New Zealand, Australia and the Union of South Africa. If all the mandatory States had been included it would have been necessary for the Commission to consist of at least fifteen members, which it was felt were too many to enable the Commission to function satisfactorily. Therefore all the British Empire was lumped together for the purpose of Commission representation, as was also done in the case of membership of the League Council. See further, Van Maanen-Helmer, *The Mandates System* (1929), p. 79 *et seq.*

16 This was pointed out by the United States delegate, Mr. Dulles, in 1946 (*Official Records of the General Assembly,* Second Part of the First Session, Fourth Committee, Part 2: Summary Records of Meetings of Sub-Committee 1, p. 35).

in 1947 it was necessary for two extra members to be elected to restore the balance of the Council.

Since the establishment of the Trusteeship Council rested on the prior conclusion of some trust agreements, it was conceivable in 1945 that the Trusteeship Council would never be set up. This was a very real fear felt by the non-colonial Members of the United Nations with the result that, after much discussion in the General Assembly, a resolution was adopted in 1946 calling on Members responsible for non-self-governing territories to submit trusteeship agreements for some of them in order that the Trusteeship Council might be established.[17]

The provisions of Article 86 of the Charter raise an interesting problem should some of the trust agreements be terminated, for instance, through the granting of independence to the territories. An administering State loses its seat on the Trusteeship Council when it ceases to administer a trust territory, unless it is one of the permanent members of the Security Council in which case it becomes a non-administering member of the Trusteeship Council. Thus if a sufficient number of trust agreements are terminated, the number of administering members on the Trusteeship Council will fall below the number of non-administering members, since the five permanent members referred to in Article 86, paragraph 1 (b), must remain. This would upset the balanced membership required by Article 86, paragraph 1 (c). Considering that Chapter XIII forms the constitution of the Trusteeship Council, it follows that it is unconstitutional for this body to continue to function in violation of a provision of this Chapter of the Charter. However, the Trusteeship Council is not authorised to cease operating whilst there are any trust territories left in existence, since its assistance is still required by the General Assembly in the exercise of the supervision over the remaining trust territories. The problem does not appear to have occurred to the drafters of the Charter at San Francisco, and therefore the records of the proceedings of this Conference throw no light on the matter.

A precedent for the functioning of the Trusteeship Council without the equality of representation required by Article 86 was set by the Trusteeship Council itself when it first came into existence. For the first year, the Trusteeship Council functioned

[17] See *Resolutions adopted by the General Assembly*, First Session, First Part, Doc. A/64, p. 13, Resolution 9 (I).

with a membership in which the administering Powers exceeded the non-administering Powers, due to the absence of the Soviet Union.[18] In this case, however, the Soviet Union was technically a member of the Trusteeship Council, having been named as such in the General Assembly's resolution establishing the Trusteeship Council[19]; she merely failed to take her seat. There is nothing in the Charter requiring a member of the Trusteeship Council to have a representative present at every meeting of the Council; in fact Article 89 (2) indicates that it is expected that all members will not always be represented. This article speaks of decisions being taken by a majority of the members present and voting; if all members were expected to be always present it is difficult to understand why the word 'present' was included here. The possible illegality in the Council's functioning without the presence of the Soviet Union stems from Article 86 (2). This requires that each member of the Trusteeship Council shall designate a representative to the Council.[20] It might be argued that a State is not really a true member of the Trusteeship Council until it has completed its part of the contract—the designation of a representative. The mere absence of a representative from the Council table upon occasion is not the same as the failure of a member to designate a representative.

A possible interpretation of the requirement of equality of representation on the Trusteeship Council is that it is applicable only to members of the Trusteeship Council who fall under paragraph 1 (c) of Article 86. In this way it would apply only to the question of elected members of the Trusteeship Council and not to the members holding seats by virtue of paragraphs

[18] The Soviet Union boycotted the Trusteeship Council for the first year of its existence, maintaining that it was illegally constituted since the trust agreements were not in conformity with the Charter and therefore could not legally be approved by the General Assembly. See above, Chap. 2, p. 35.

[19] Resolution 64 (I) (*Resolutions adopted by the General Assembly during the Second Part of its First Session,* Doc. A/64/Add. 1, pp. 122–123).

[20] Adapting the Opinion of the International Court of Justice on the *Interpretation of Peace Treaties* (1950), to this case, it can be held that the Soviet Union was violating her obligations in failing to designate a representative to the Trusteeship Council. 'In view of the fact that the Treaties provide that any dispute shall be referred to a Commission "at the request of either party," it follows that either party is obligated, at the request of the other party, to co-operate in constituting the Commission, in particular by appointing its representative. Otherwise the method of settlement by Commission provided for in the Treaties would completely fail in its purpose' (*I.C.J. Reports 1950,* p. 65).

1 (a) and 1 (b). Paragraph 1 (c) requires that the General Assembly shall elect 'as many other Members . . . as may be necessary to ensure that the total number of members of the Trusteeship Council is equally divided between those Members of the United Nations which administer trust territories and those which do not.' However, if the non-administering Powers holding seats on the Trusteeship Council under paragraph 1 (b) already exceed the number of administering Powers, then the election of additional members by the General Assembly can only aggravate the situation. Thus paragraph 1 (c) must be held to be inoperative in this instance. The requirement of equality of representation is relevant only when the question of electing *additional* members of the Trusteeship Council is under consideration; if the Trusteeship Council consists of only members holding seats under paragraphs 1 (a) and 1 (b), it is not contrary to Article 86 for the membership to be unequally divided between the two. Paragraph 1 (c) comes into operation only when the administering Powers are in the majority, for the purpose of restoring the balance. This interpretation of Article 86 would appear to be the only one consistent with the Charter provisions on trusteeship as a whole. If the equality of representation requirement were intended to restrict the representation on the Trusteeship Council of members referred to in paragraph 1 (b), then it should have been mentioned in this paragraph or in the preamble to Article 86 (1), as well as in paragraph 1 (c).

One fact that Article 86 makes very clear is that only Members of the United Nations may become members of the Trusteeship Council. Since the permanent members of the Security Council mentioned in paragraph 1 (b) are by definition Members of the United Nations, and since it is hardly conceivable that the General Assembly would wish to elect a non-Member to a place on the Trusteeship Council, only in the case of an administering authority does the Membership question assume importance. Article 86 uses very definite language, mentioning the word 'Members' twice with regard to the administering authorities: not only does it specify that the Trusteeship Council is to be composed of 'Members of the United Nations,' but it further states that these are to include 'those Members administering trust territories.' Thus, although the language used in the Charter legally permitted the designation of non-Member

Italy as the administering authority for a United Nations trust territory,[1] for so long as she remained outside the Organisation, Italy was excluded from membership of the Trusteeship Council by the wording of Article 86.

There is no provision in the Charter for a non-member of the Trusteeship Council to participate in the discussions of this organ, with or without a vote, and provision for non-Member Italy to do so had to be inserted into the Trusteeship Council's Rules of Procedure. This gap in the trusteeship provisions of the Charter is strange considering that other organs of the United Nations provide for the participation in their proceedings of States other than their members. The Economic and Social Council is authorised to invite Members of the United Nations who are not members of the Council to participate without vote in its discussions.[2] The Security Council is permitted, under certain circumstances, to invite even non-Members of the United Nations to take part in its deliberations.[3] In the case of the International Court of Justice, a non-Member may become a party to the Statute of the Court.[4] The only authorisation in the Charter for the General Assembly to include a non-Member in its work is found in Article 35 (2), where the non-Member is limited to bringing a dispute to which it is a party to the attention of the General Assembly.[5]

Since the Charter did not provide for the participation of a non-member of the Trusteeship Council in its discussions, the Trusteeship Council was left to formulate provisions for this participation which could then be included in its Rules of Procedure. These provisions were based on the pattern set for the other organs of the United Nations and on a joint statement annexed to the Report of the Rapporteur of Committee II/4 at San Francisco. For although the possibility of a non-Member of the United Nations *becoming* an administering authority was not envisaged at San Francisco, consideration was given to the possibility of a State withdrawing from the United Nations but *continuing* to administer a trust territory—an event which had

[1] See below, Chap. 11, pp. 206–207.
[2] Article 69.
[3] Article 32.
[4] Article 93 (2) of the Charter.
[5] See further Goodrich and Hambro, *Charter of the United Nations, Commentary and Documents* (1949), pp. 252–254.

occurred in the case of Japan under the League of Nations. In a Joint Statement on the subject at San Francisco, the Delegates of the United Kingdom and the United States[6] expressed the view that if a State withdrew for reasons which reflected no discredit upon it, it could continue to administer a trust territory provided that it was willing to abide by the terms of the Trusteeship System. Although ceasing to be a member of the Trusteeship Council, it might attend meetings of the Council when matters affecting its trust territories were under consideration. It is not clear why it was considered even then that the State would necessarily cease to be a member of the Trusteeship Council since according to the Report of the Rapporteur of Committee II/4, the Trusteeship Council was to be composed of '*States* administering trust territories'—it was only later that this was changed to '*Members* administering trust territories,' the form in which it appears in the Charter. The Trusteeship Council followed the pattern set out in this report in drafting additional Rules of Procedure: non-Member Italy was to participate in the proceedings of the Council, without vote, when matters concerning her trust territory were under consideration.[7] In actual fact, Italy's position with regard to participation in the Trusteeship Council was similar to that afforded a Member of the United Nations which is not represented on the Trusteeship Council.[8] Whilst Italy participated in the Council's proceedings when her trust territory was under discussion, United Nations Members who are not members of the Trusteeship Council are entitled to be represented therein when items they have proposed are considered by the Council.[9] In neither case does this participation include the right to vote.

[6] *Report of the Rapporteur of Committee II/4,* Annex C (U.N.C.I.O. Doc. 1115, p. 14, see *U.N.C.I.O. Docs.,* Vol. 10, p. 620).

[7] The rights accorded Italy were greater than those possessed by the Mandatory Powers in the Permanent Mandates Commission. The Mandatory Powers had the right to be present at meetings of the Commission for the discussion of their own reports only (see League of Nations, Permanent Mandates Commission, *Minutes of Second Session* (1922), p. 97). Italy had the right to be present at meetings of the Trusteeship Council not only when her reports were being discussed, but whenever matters concerning Somaliland were under consideration.

[8] See Rule 12 of the Trusteeship Council's Rules of Procedure (Doc. T/1/Rev. 3, 1952, p. 3).

[9] In practice, there has to date (*i.e.,* up to 1956) been no instance of a Member of the United Nations not represented on the Trusteeship Council being invited to participate in the Council's proceedings as the

The exclusion of an administering authority from active participation in the Trusteeship Council has its precedent in the Permanent Mandates Commission, where nationals of three Mandatory Powers—Australia, New Zealand and the Union of South Africa—never took part. In this case there was no provision for them even to attend meetings without a vote. In fact, these three Mandatories were at times not even represented on the League Council, although they were entitled to send delegates to participate in debates when their mandates were under discussion.[10] It was the practice of the League to afford these delegates at such times full Council rights including voting, although they were not Council members.[11] This practice of affording voting rights on the League Council to non-members of that body without granting them membership, provides a pattern which might be adapted in favour of a non-Member administering authority by the Trusteeship Council.

Another interesting point with regard to membership of the Trusteeship Council is whether, in the case of a trust territory being administered by a joint administering authority of more than one United Nations Member, each Member State comprising the joint administering authority is entitled to a seat on the Trusteeship Council. Since the Trusteeship Council is stated, in

result of the inclusion in the Council's agenda of an item proposed by that Member. However, there have been instances where such Members have been invited to participate in Council discussions for other reasons—generally that the item under consideration concerned the Member. This occurred notably in connection with the questions of the Italian colonies and the International Statute for Jerusalem: in the former case, representatives of Colombia, Egypt, Ethiopia and India were invited to participate in the preparation of a trust agreement for Somaliland (*Official Records of the Trusteeship Council,* Second Special Session, Second Meeting, p. 16); in the latter case, Egypt, Syria, Lebanon and Argentina were invited to participate in the Council's preparation of an international statute for Jerusalem (*Official Records of the Trusteeship Council,* Second Special Session, Fourth Meeting, p. 41).

Italy was not the only non-Member of the United Nations to participate in the Trusteeship Council's deliberations: at its Sixth Session, the Trusteeship Council invited Jordan to send a representative to the Council to present Jordan's views on the revision of the Draft Statute for Jerusalem (*Official Records of the Trusteeship Council,* Sixth Session, Resolution 118 (VI)).

10 Resolution adopted by the League Council on August 31, 1923 (see League of Nations, *Official Journal* IV (1923), p. 1328), under the terms of Article 4 (5) of the Covenant.

11 See League of Nations, *The Council of the League of Nations: Composition, Competence, Procedure* (Geneva: Information Section, 1938), p. 57.

Article 86, as consisting of 'those Members administering trust territories,' the answer would appear to be in the affirmative. The case of Nauru is no test for two reasons: firstly, actual administration is exercised by one State on behalf of the other two[12]; and secondly, all three States mentioned in the trust agreement as forming the joint administering authority, administer other trust territories, and therefore are automatically members of the Trusteeship Council.

The members of the Trusteeship Council are each required by Article 86 (2) to designate a representative to the Council. Thus the individuals sitting on the Trusteeship Council are national delegates who are there to represent the views of their respective States. They are politicians in a position of dependence on their governments. This is especially borne out in practice, where heads of delegations and even ambassadors[13] are sometimes designated as representatives. It is the States who are the members of the Trusteeship Council; the individual delegates are the agents through which the States act. The Trusteeship Council's Rules of Procedure bear out this fact, by providing that an alternate delegate or advisor may represent his State when the representative so decides.[14] In this way the State may continue to be represented even when its chief representative is unable to attend meetings of the Council; thus recognition is given to the importance of the *State* being represented regardless of whether a particular individual is present.

In the case of the Permanent Mandates Commission the situation was different and more complex. According to the Constitution of the Commission,[15] the members of the Commission were to be *nationals* of States. They were not to hold any office which put them in a position of direct dependence on their governments, and they were to be selected by the Permanent Mandates Commission on the basis of their personal merits and competence.[16] Thus they were to be experts and not State

12 See further above, Chap. 6, pp. 107–108.

13 *e.g.*, Sir Carl Berendsen of New Zealand who, besides being a colonial expert, was Ambassador to the United States at the same time as being a representative on the Trusteeship Council; likewise with Prince Wanaiken of Thailand.

14 Rule 18 (Doc. T/1/Rev. 3, p. 3).

15 Paragraph (a) of the Constitution of the Permanent Mandates Commission (League of Nations, *Official Journal* I (1920), pp. 87–88).

16 *ibid.*

delegates. But at the same time the nationality question did play its part as is evidenced by the fact that the majority of the Commission were required to be nationals of non-Mandatory States.[17] According to the Constitution of the Permanent Mandates Commission, the entire membership of the Commission could have come from two States, the majority from a single State, which was not a Mandatory and the rest from a single Mandatory State; but in practice a further consideration of nationality was taken into account. Only one expert was ever chosen from a single State, and of the experts from Mandatory States there was always a national from each of the same four of the seven Mandatory Powers—there was always a British, French, Belgian and Japanese[18] expert on the Commission and never an Australian, New Zealand or South African expert. The nationality consideration was in further evidence in 1927 when the membership of the Commission was increased from nine to ten to enable a German national to take his seat thereon. On the other hand, the practice of appointing alternates to take the place of members of the Commission who were unable to attend meetings was never adopted; thus a State that normally had a national sitting on the Commission might not have a national there at any given time.

Thus, although the Members of the Permanent Mandates Commission were primarily individual experts, it cannot be said that politics were ignored. The nationality aspect certainly played its part, although the fact that the appointments were made by the League Council rather than by individual States, and the insistence on appointees holding no office of dependence on their governments, went a long way towards giving the Commission a membership of independent experts.

The Charter makes no provision for the inclusion of representatives of specialised commissions or bodies on the Trusteeship Council, although Article 91 provides a possible basis for this. This article states that 'the Trusteeship Council shall, when appropriate, avail itself of the assistance of the Economic and Social Council and of the specialised agencies in regard to matters with which they are respectively concerned.' Whether this assist-

17 *ibid.*

18 The Japanese member remained on the Commission until 1938 although Japan withdrew from the League in 1935.

ance is to be forthcoming at the Council table, or whether it is merely to extend to the provision of specialised data by the Economic and Social Council and the 'specialised agencies, is not mentioned. Whilst there is no authority in the Charter for these bodies to assume membership in the Trusteeship Council,[19] and therefore the voting rights resulting from such membership cannot be accorded them,[20] the possibility of a representative of the Economic and Social Council or one of the specialised agencies participating in the deliberations of the Trusteeship Council in an advisory capacity is not ruled out.

The Rules of Procedure of the Trusteeship Council as originally adopted provided that the representatives of the specialised agencies, but not of the Economic and Social Council, might be invited to attend meetings and to participate without vote in the Trusteeship Council's deliberations.[1] In August 1947, a joint committee of representatives of the Trusteeship Council and the Economic and Social Council, set up to discuss methods of co-operation between the two organs, recommended that the President of the Economic and Social Council, or his representative, be permitted to participate in discussions of the Trusteeship Council on matters of concern to the Economic and Social Council, in return for reciprocal privileges to the Trusteeship Council.[2] This recommendation was approved by the Trusteeship Council on November 25, 1947. Thus the Trusteeship Council has followed the practice of the Permanent Mandates Commission, where non-voting rights of participation in the Commission's deliberations were accorded to an International Labour Office representative.[3]

Functions and Powers

The only function which the Charter allocates entirely and specifically to the Trusteeship Council is the formulation of the questionnaire, which is to provide the basis for the annual reports of the administering powers on the trust territories under

[19] Membership is open only to Members of the United Nations (see Article 86 (1) of the Charter).
[20] Article 89 (1).
[1] Rule 13 (Doc. T/1/Rev. 1 of April 23, 1947).
[2] See report of this joint committee (Doc. E & T/C.1/2/Rev. 1).
[3] See Quincy Wright, *Mandates Under the League of Nations* (1930), p. 140.

their administration.[4] Presumably this function includes the revision of the questionnaire when this is considered necessary, since a revision amounts to the formulation of a new questionnaire.[5]

Apart from the formulation of the questionnaire, the function of the Trusteeship Council is to assist the General Assembly and Security Council in the manner indicated in Articles 85, 87 and 83. Articles 83 and 87 are concerned with the Trusteeship Council's assisting in the exercise of the United Nations' supervisory functions over trust territories.[6]

Interesting problems are raised by Article 85. The first paragraph of this article states that the functions of the United Nations for all non-strategic trust agreements, including the approval of the terms of the trust agreements and of their alteration or amendment, are to be exercised by the General Assembly. The second paragraph then goes on to provide that the Trusteeship Council 'shall assist the General Assembly in carrying out these functions'—'these functions' referring to those outlined in paragraph 1. Taking Article 85 by itself, it appears that the Trusteeship Council is to assist the General Assembly in the conclusion of the trust agreements and in their alteration or amendment. However, this is obviously not the intention of Article 85, since the Trusteeship Council could not be constituted until a sufficient number of trust agreements had been concluded[7]; therefore, the Trusteeship Council did not exist at the time at which the first trust agreements came up for United Nations' approval. It must be assumed that the phrase 'including the approval of the terms of the trusteeship agreements and of their alteration or amendment' applies only to the General Assembly. The only interpretation of the Trusteeship Council's functions with regard to a trust territory that can be reconciled with Chapters XII and XIII of the Charter, is that these functions begin after the trust agreement has been approved and that they do not extend to the alteration or termination of the agreement.

The San Francisco proceedings support the above interpreta-

4 Article 88.

5 For a discussion of the Questionnaire see below, Chap. 10, pp. 183–185.

6 For an elaboration of these functions, see above, Chap. 8, pp. 152–158.

7 This was necessary in order to satisfy the requirements of Article 86 with regard to the composition of the Trusteeship Council. See above, p. 161 *et seq.*

tion. In the Report of the Rapporteur of Committee II/4,[8] the Trusteeship Council was not mentioned in the article which accorded powers regarding the trust agreements to the General Assembly. In this draft of the International Trusteeship System, paragraph 10 allocated the United Nations' functions with regard to non-strategic trust agreements, including the approval and alteration of the terms of the agreements, to the General Assembly alone.[9] The Trusteeship Council was not introduced until paragraph 11, which provided that 'in order to assist the General Assembly to carry out those functions under the trusteeship system not reserved to the Security Council, there shall be established a Trusteeship Council, which shall operate under the authority of the Assembly.'[10] Quite clearly this authorises the exercise of functions by the Trusteeship Council only under the Trusteeship System, and not until a trust agreement has been concluded do functions with regard to it fall under the Trusteeship System. A function which in itself *brings* a territory under the Trusteeship System, or *removes* it from the System,[11] is not the same thing as a function *under* the Trusteeship System. With this consideration in mind, it does not appear that the Trusteeship Council is authorised to take part in the actual drawing up of a trust agreement, as occurred in the case of the agreement for Somaliland. In allocating the task of negotiating a trust agreement with the proposed administering authority to the Trusteeship Council,[12] the General Assembly was overstepping its authority. Only with regard to functions under the Trusteeship System is the General Assembly authorised by the Charter to make use of the assistance of the Trusteeship Council.[13]

In two notable instances, the Trusteeship Council appears to have acted illegally in exercising functions quite outside the Trusteeship System, which it is not authorised to do by the Charter. The first of these cases took place when the Trusteeship Council examined the report from the Union of South Africa on South-West Africa, which was not a trust territory.[14] As in the

[8] U.N.C.I.O. Doc. 1115 (*U.N.C.I.O. Docs.*, Vol. 10, p. 607 *et seq.*).
[9] *ibid.*, p. 618.
[10] *ibid.*, p. 618.
[11] *i.e.*, through termination of the agreement.
[12] See *Official Records of the General Assembly*, Fourth Session, Resolution 289 (IV).
[13] Articles 85 (2) and 87.
[14] See below, Chap. 12, p. 240.

case of the drawing up of the trust agreement for Somaliland, the General Assembly authorised the Trusteeship Council to take this action,[15] and was thus overstepping its authority. The second instance of the Trusteeship Council's acting outside the Trusteeship System occurred when it proceeded to draw up a statute for the City of Jerusalem at its Second Session. Once more the Trusteeship Council was acting in accordance with instructions from the General Assembly, which called on the Trusteeship Council to 'elaborate and approve a detailed Statute of the City.'[16]

In carrying out its trusteeship functions, the Trusteeship Council, like the General Assembly, is limited to making recommendations to Members. It does not make binding decisions. Thus, although recommendations are passed by a majority vote of the Trusteeship Council, and often against the wishes of one or more of the administering authorities, no state becomes bound by any action of the Council against its will. It is true that Article 89 mentions 'decisions' of the Trusteeship Council, but there is no article requiring Members to carry out these decisions, as there is in the case of the Security Council.[17] The good faith of the administering authorities is necessary for the implementation of the Trusteeship Council's resolutions. The same is true of the resolutions of the General Assembly. Only with regard to a strategic trust territory is it possible for an organ of the United Nations to make a decision binding on an unwilling administering authority[18]; and this is only possible when the administering authority is not a permanent member of the Security Council and, thus, unable to exercise the veto. Thus, to date there has been no possibility of the United Nations

15 *Official Records of the General Assembly,* Second Session, Resolution 141 (II).

16 *Official Records of the General Assembly,* Second Session, Resolution 181 (II), Part III.

17 Article 25. There are other instances in the Charter of the use of the word 'decision' in its non-technical sense: Article 18 (2) provides that 'decisions of the General Assembly on important questions . . . shall include: *recommendations* with respect to the maintenance of international peace and security . . .' (italics added); decisions by the Security Council under Article 27 include the Security Council's non-binding recommendation to the General Assembly on the expulsion of a Member under Article 6: by Article 67 (2) the Economic and Social Council makes decisions which include 'recommendations' under Article 62.

18 By means of Article 27 (3).

making a binding decision with regard to a trust territory against the will of the administering authority.[19]

In the case of the Mandates System, a similar position prevailed with regard to specific mandates, since all Mandatories were represented on the League Council when their territories were under consideration, and decisions were taken by unanimous vote. However, in the case of a *general* resolution on mandates, this might be passed against the wishes of certain Mandatory powers since they were not all members of the League Council,[20] and such resolution would nevertheless be binding on the unwilling and unrepresented Mandatories. This situation cannot occur under the Trusteeship System.

Article 87 of the Charter allocates the supervision of trust territories to the General Assembly, and under its authority to the Trusteeship Council. Thus, according to the Charter, the Trusteeship Council is to exercise as much authority in this respect as the General Assembly grants to it. The implication is that the General Assembly should expressly authorise the Trusteeship Council to undertake functions under Article 87. Without such authorisation, strictly speaking, the Trusteeship Council has no right to assume trusteeship functions. Whilst the Trusteeship Council was authorised by Article 90 to adopt its own Rules of Procedure, it was not legally permitted to assume to itself in these Rules the functions outlined in Article 87. In adopting its Rules of Procedure, the Trusteeship Council not only assumed to itself the United Nations' trusteeship functions with regard to annual reports, visiting missions and petitions without the prior authorisation of the General Assembly, but it also assumed these functions to itself absolutely. In the entire twenty-eight Rules devoted to annual reports, visiting missions and petitions, no mention is made of the General Assembly or of the fact that the Trusteeship Council functions under the authority of the General Assembly.[1]

It is true that the Trusteeship Council's Rules of Procedure were based upon the Provisional Rules of Procedure of the Trusteeship Council drafted by the United Nations Preparatory

[19] See further below, p. 222 *et seq.*

[20] Australia, New Zealand, the Union of South Africa, and Belgium were not permanently represented on the League Council.

[1] See Rules 72–99 inclusive of the Rules of Procedure of the Trusteeship Council (Doc. T/1/Rev. 3 of 1952, pp. 11–17).

Commission, and that these latter were transmitted to the Trusteeship Council by the Secretary-General on the request of the General Assembly.[2] It might be argued that in requesting that these Provisional Rules of Procedure be transmitted to the Trusteeship Council, the General Assembly was approving their contents. However, this is not the same thing as specifically authorising the Trusteeship Council to assume certain trusteeship functions. Furthermore, as far as concerns the absolute assumption by the Trusteeship Council of the trusteeship functions under Article 87, the General Assembly is not permitted to grant these functions to the Trusteeship Council except where the Trusteeship Council is to exercise the functions under the authority of the General Assembly. Article 87 requires the continual supervision of the General Assembly over the Trusteeship Council in the exercise of the Council's functions. Nor is the General Assembly permitted to surrender the role granted to it by Article 87.

Subsidiary Organs

The assumption by the Trusteeship Council of the functions specified in Article 87 of the Charter has necessitated the establishment of subsidiary organs. These have taken the form of a number of *ad hoc* committees and of two standing committees—the Committee on Administrative Unions,[3] and the special Petitions Committee.[4] There is no authority in the Charter for the Trusteeship Council to establish any subsidiary organs, with the exception of visiting missions under Article 87 (c),[5] and it is doubtful whether such a right exists. The Trusteeship Council bases this right on Rule 66 of its Rules of Procedure, although there seems to be no authority for this Rule ever having been adopted. In the cases of the General Assembly, the Security Council, and the Economic and Social Council, specific provisions

[2] See *Resolutions Adopted by the General Assembly During the First Part of its First Session,* Doc. A/64, p. 13.

[3] For details of this Committee, see above, p. 65.

[4] This Committee was established by the Trusteeship Council in 1952 (*Official Records of the Trusteeship Council,* Resolution 425 (X)) to undertake a preliminary examination of petitions received under Article 87 (b) (see below, p. 189 *et seq.*) and to prepare proposals on action to be taken by the Trusteeship Council.

[5] Since this article authorises the Trusteeship Council, under the authority of the General Assembly, to 'provide for periodic visits' to the trust territories, it must be assumed that the Council is authorised to establish missions for this purpose—these are in the nature of subsidiary organs.

are found in the Charter for them to establish such subsidiary organs as may be necessary for the exercise of their functions,[6] and it can be assumed that a similar provision would have been included in Chapter XIII of the Charter if it were intended that the Trusteeship Council should do likewise. The absence of such provision in the light of the provisions concerning the other three organs, suggests that the Trusteeship Council does not have similar rights. Even if it is contended that, since the Trusteeship Council is not forbidden to establish subsidiary organs, it may do so, Article 85 (2) definitely establishes that such subsidiary organs may only be set up with the prior approval of the General Assembly. In the light of this it should be noted that even the establishment of visiting missions under Article 87 (c) is to be undertaken only with the prior approval of the General Assembly, since the preamble of Article 87 states that it is under the authority of the General Assembly that the Trusteeship Council may exercise the functions mentioned in paragraphs (a), (b), (c) and (d).[7]

In practice the Trusteeship Council has acted as though it possesses full authority to establish subsidiary organs at will. Whether the organs established have been temporary—as the Committee on Rural Economic Development of the Trust Territories[8]—or standing committees—as the Committee on Petitions, the pattern of the Trusteeship Council itself has been generally followed as regards composition. Thus, the principle of equality of representation between administering and non-administering States has been observed with three exceptions: the Special Visiting Mission to Western Samoa in 1947, the Committee established in 1947 to discuss matters of common interest with the Economic and Social Council, and the Committee set up to confer with the Security Council on strategic areas under trusteeship.[9] In each of these cases, the established organ was composed of two representatives from non-administering States and one representative from an administering State.

In 1951, an attempt was made to have the subsidiary organs employ the Trusteeship Council's practice of associating non-

6 Articles 22, 29, and 68.
7 See above, pp. 175–176.
8 Established on March 16, 1951, in furtherance of General Assembly Resolution 438 (V).
9 For details of the activities of these Committees, see below, p. 181, and above, pp. 158–159, 156–157.

Council members in its deliberations[10]: a draft resolution recommending that the Trusteeship Council 'associate countries which are not members of the Council with the activities of its subsidiary organs' was introduced into the General Assembly's Fourth Committee.[11] It failed to obtain the necessary two-thirds majority in the General Assembly, however, and was therefore rejected—the administering States and the Soviet bloc opposing it.[12] The defeat of this proposal was unfortunate for two reasons: firstly, it prevented administering Power Italy, who was until the end of 1955 not a member of the Trusteeship Council, from participating in the work of the subsidiary organs even when matters concerning her trust territory were under consideration.[13] Secondly, non-permanent members of the Trusteeship Council are required to vacate their seats on the subsidiary organs simultaneously with the expiration of their term of office in the Council: this deprives the subsidiary organs of the benefit of the experience of States so effected, and it creates an atmosphere of instability within the organs which is especially pronounced in the case of the standing committees. Whilst the first disadvantage has been removed through the admission of Italy to the United Nations, and subsequently to the Trusteeship Council, the second drawback remains. The fear on the part of the administering authorities is that adoption of the practice of associating non-members of the Trusteeship Council in the subsidiary organs would result in the permanent outnumbering of administering States by non-administering States in these organs. This fear is not, however, necessarily valid, since the Trusteeship Council has adopted the practice with no such results. The difficulties anticipated might well be overcome by allowing non-Members of the Trusteeship Council to participate in the subsidiary organs without voting rights, or in maintaining the equality of representation as between administering and non-administering Powers by not insisting that the latter be members of the Trusteeship Council.

[10] See above, pp. 167–168, n. 9.

[11] Doc. A/2061, January 16, 1952 (see *Official Records of the General Assembly*, Annexes).

[12] *Official Records of the General Assembly*, Sixth Session, 361st Plenary Meeting, pp. 348–349.

[13] Italy was excluded from membership of the Trusteeship Council because she was not a United Nations Member (see further above, p. 171, n. 19). This situation was rectified when, on December 14, 1955, Italy was admitted to Membership in the United Nations and thus became entitled to a permanent seat on the Trusteeship Council. At the opening of the Trusteeship Council's Seventeenth Session on February 7, 1956, Italy was seated as a full member.

Chapter 10

THE MEANS OF TRUSTEESHIP SUPERVISION

The basis of the Trusteeship System, as in the Mandates System, lies in the concept that the administration of backward peoples should be subject to international supervision. This does not mean that the actual administration should be undertaken by an international body; it has been generally recognised that administration by a single State is more efficient and of greater benefit to the peoples concerned. The few cases of international administration to date have been undertaken internationally rather than nationally because of the strategic or political importance of the area concerned. It is significant that no use has been made of the provision in the Charter for trusteeship administration to be undertaken by the United Nations directly. Somaliland would seem to have been an obvious territory to be administered directly by the United Nations under the Trusteeship System, but this opportunity was passed over in favour of a single State administration.

The United Nations Charter provides for the supervision of trusteeship administration to be exercised by the Organisation through its principal organs.[1] The means to be employed by the United Nations in the exercise of this supervision are stated in Article 87: they include the consideration of reports submitted by the administering authorities, the acceptance and examination of petitions, and the provision of periodic visits to the trust territories. Since, to exercise its supervisory role over trusteeship administration, the United Nations must be kept supplied with detailed and balanced information, the means of supervision permitted by Article 87, paragraphs (a), (b) and (c), assume great importance. They provide information on a particular trust territory from the three most interested sources: the administering authority through its reports; the inhabitants by means of petitions; and the United Nations directly from the observations of visiting missions to the trust territories. This represents an

[1] See above, Chap. 8, for a discussion of the part played by the various United Nations organs in the exercise of trusteeship supervision.

advance over the Mandates System where the League was forced to rely on annual reports and petitions only.[2] The practice of sending visiting missions to make a routine examination of conditions in a trust territory was never adopted by the League, on the grounds that it would tend to undermine the authority of the Mandatory.[3] The only instances of the League's sending any visiting missions to a mandated territory occurred in connection with particular disputes or problems which were before the League Council; then, occasionally special commissions of inquiry were dispatched by the Council.[4]

The Nature of United Nations Supervision

The question arises whether, in its supervision of trusteeship administration, the United Nations is limited to criticism of the accomplished acts of the administering authority, or whether this supervision may also include a constructive policy-forming element. The means of supervision specifically accorded the United Nations by Article 87 suggest that the United Nations' functions are to weigh and pass judgment upon the way in which the administering authorities have been exercising their administrative role. The United Nations is 'to consider reports submitted by the administering authority,' these reports being the annual reports referred to in Article 88 which presumably are to provide a record of the administering authorities' actions in the trust territories during the previous year. In utilising its power 'to accept petitions and examine them in consultation with the administering authority,' the United Nations is examining a situation which already exists in a trust territory, and in some cases is passing judgment on the actions of the administering authority. The 'periodic visits to the respective trust territories'

2 Only annual reports were mentioned in the Covenant (Article 22 (7) and (9)). Petitions were introduced into the Mandates System as a result of the adoption of additional rules of procedure by the League Council (see League of Nations, *Official Journal* IV (1923), p. 300).

3 See opinion of the British member of the Permanent Mandates Commission, Lord Lugard, who strongly opposed the Commission's adopting the policy of 'challenging the whole administration of any Mandatory Power by visiting the territory in order to listen to all who criticised it' (P.M.C., *Minutes* VII (1925), p. 128).

4 In 1930, in pursuance of a British proposal, the League Council gave its consent to the despatch of an *ad hoc* Commission of enquiry to Palestine to investigate claims regarding the Wailing Wall of Jerusalem (see Quincy Wright, *Mandates Under the League of Nations* (1930), pp. 182–184).

which the United Nations is authorised to make are for the purpose of discovering facts at first hand about the administration of the trust territories, and these facts will eventually be subject to the approval or censure of the United Nations. All this suggests that the most the United Nations can do is to provide constructive criticism of the administration of the trust territories. However, consideration of additional factors does not bear out this conclusion.

To interpret the United Nations' functions with regard to petitions as merely to examine and pass judgment on the administering authority's acts, is to assume that all petitions are concerned with complaints against the administering authority in question. Practice does not support this assumption, and an example to the contrary was given as early as the First Session of the Trusteeship Council. In 1947, the Trusteeship Council received a petition from the leaders and representatives of Western Samoa, requesting self-government for the trust territory with New Zealand acting as protector and advisor to the territory. This petition was in no way a complaint against the administering authority; rather it was a sign of approval of the administering authority for the inhabitants of the trust territory to ask for the same State to act as its advisor and protector. However, the petition called for some constructive suggestions on the part of the United Nations. On the basis of the report from a special visiting mission which the Trusteeship Council dispatched to Western Samoa,[5] the Trusteeship Council did make some constructive proposals on the future of Western Samoa. These proposals were incorporated in a resolution.[6]

Apart from utilising the system of annual reports, petitions and visiting missions, the United Nations is permitted to take 'other actions in conformity with the terms of the trusteeship agreements.'[7] What these 'other actions' include is not

5 By a resolution (*Official Records of the Trusteeship Council,* First Session, Resolution 4 (I)), the Council authorised the dispatch of a special mission to Western Samoa to investigate the petition. The mission was instructed to report its finding to the Trusteeship Council.

6 The Trusteeship Council resolved that the people of Western Samoa should be accorded such measures of self-government as were indicated in the visiting mission's report. The people should be encouraged and assisted to assume increasing responsibilities for self-government, and ultimately be accorded full self-government as soon as they were capable of assuming the responsibilities involved (*Official Records of the Trusteeship Council,* Second Session, Resolution 13 (II)).

7 Article 87 (d).

indicated, but the importance of this provision lies in the fact that the means of supervision stated in paragraphs (a), (b) and (c) of Article 87 are not exhaustive. The General Assembly is authorised by Article 10 to make recommendations to the administering authorities, and there is no reason to assume that these must be confined to the subject matter of accomplished acts of the administering authorities; nor has the General Assembly interpreted it this way in practice. At the Third Session of the General Assembly, it was recommended that a university be set up in each of the trust territories.[8] This was not a criticism of the administering authorities, but a suggestion as to the way in which the educational advancement of the inhabitants of the trust territories could be best achieved. At its Sixth Session, the General Assembly invited the administering authorities to include in their annual reports estimates of the time which they considered necessary for the attainment of self-government or independence by the trust territories.[9]

Further evidence of the United Nations' extra-supervisory powers stems from Articles 79, 83 and 85 of the Charter. Under these articles the United Nations has authority to give or withhold its consent to the termination of a trust agreement, which introduces an administrative element into the United Nations' supervisory role. Since the termination of a trust agreement involves a change in status of the trust territory concerned, in exercising its decisive powers in this respect the United Nations is engaging in policy-making.

Annual Reports

Mention of reports from the administering authorities is made in two articles of the Charter. Article 87 (a) empowers the General Assembly and, under its authority, the Trusteeship Council to 'consider reports submitted by the administering authority'; and Article 88 provides that 'the administering authority for each trust territory within the competence of the General Assembly shall make an annual report to the General Assembly upon the basis of such questionnaire' formulated by the Trusteeship Council. Article 88 *requires* the administering

[8] *Official Records of the General Assembly,* Third Session, Resolution 225 (III).

[9] *Official Records of the General Assembly,* Sixth Session, Resolution 558 (VI).

authority to submit the report; Article 87 *permits* the United Nations to consider it.

Since the administering authority is required to compile its annual report on the basis of the Trusteeship Council's Questionnaire, it is important to consider the true nature of this Questionnaire. The Charter says only that it shall cover the 'political, economic, social, and educational advancement of the inhabitants of each trust territory'[10]; details within these categories are left to the actual drafting. The Charter does not expressly authorise questions on additional subjects, nor does it limit the questions to the topics mentioned. However, the Questionnaire must be in conformity with the Charter and the trust agreements. Furthermore, the scope of the Questionnaire is restricted to matters concerning the Trusteeship System, and therefore questions referring to an adjacent non-self-governing territory with which the trust territory forms an administrative union must not be included.[11] This restriction on the subject matter of the Questionnaire follows from the fact that the Trusteeship Council is only competent to act within the Trusteeship System.[12] Therefore, it is competent to formulate a Questionnaire only on matters which fall within the Trusteeship System.

Even when formulating questions within the scope of the Trusteeship System, the problem arises as to whether the Trusteeship Council is entitled to ask for information which the Charter does not state as required. A resolution adopted by the General Assembly at its Sixth Session requested that the annual reports of the administering authorities include information on the time in which the objective of self-government or independence by the territory is to be achieved.[13] It must be considered whether the Trusteeship Council is entitled to include a question on the lines of the General Assembly's resolution in the Questionnaire. Nowhere in the Charter or the trust agreements, with the exception of the trust agreement for Somaliland, is an administering authority required to fix a time limit for the achievement of self-

10 Article 88.

11 This has provided serious difficulties in practice, especially in the case of statistical data which the Trusteeship Council requires, but which is often not available separately for the trust territory due to its being administered as an integral part of an adjacent territory.

12 See further above, Chap. 9, pp. 172–174.

13 *Official Records of the General Assembly,* Sixth Session, Resolution 558 (VI).

government or independence by a trust territory. In fact neither of these alternate goals need ever be reached, since development is only required to be *towards* self-government or independence. However, the Trusteeship Council is required to formulate a Questionnaire on the political advancement of the inhabitants,[14] and Article 76 (b) requires the development of the territory towards self-government or independence; therefore a question concerning the time-limit for the achievement of these alternative goals is presumably within the sphere of the Trusteeship System and the competence of the Trusteeship Council. The administering authority could answer that, whilst development towards self-government or independence was taking place in the trust territory, it was expected that the territory would never *reach* that goal.

Since it is compulsory for the annual report on a trust territory to be compiled on the basis of the Questionnaire, presumably all the questions must be answered. This obligation arises from Article 88 of the Charter. Thus the Questionnaire for trust territories differs from the questionnaires for the Mandates and the Standard Form[15] for non-self-governing territories, these latter having come into existence through the practices of the League and United Nations respectively rather than through the Covenant and the Charter. The obligation to reply to all questions on the Mandates' questionnaires and the Standard Form is at least questionable.

The language of Article 88 does not indicate whether a separate Questionnaire is to be formulated for each trust territory, or whether one standard Questionnaire is to be used for all the trust territories. Whilst it would clearly prove impractical to draw up a separate Questionnaire for each trust territory—although Article 88 permits this, it would appear that it is quite permissible for the Trusteeship Council to attach additional questions to the Questionnaire in the case of any particular trust territory. Likewise, Article 88 does not state whether or not a new Questionnaire is to be formulated each year, which leaves open to the Trusteeship Council the power to revise the Questionnaire at will.[16]

14 Article 88.
15 See below, Chap. 12, p. 243 *et seq.*
16 A Revised Questionnaire was approved at the Trusteeship Council's Eleventh Session. See *Official Records of the Trusteeship Council,*

Whilst the Trusteeship Council is required to formulate a Questionnaire for all non-strategic trust territories, it is not clear from Article 88 whether it is authorised to do likewise for a strategic trust territory. This Article states that the Trusteeship Council shall formulate a Questionnaire on the advancement of the inhabitants of *each* trust territory, although it only requires the administering authorities to submit annual reports on trust territories within the competence of the General Assembly. However, taking into account Article 83, it would seem that it is the Security Council which should formulate a Questionnaire for a strategic territory, unless the Security Council delegates this power to the Trusteeship Council, as it may do under Article 83 (3). In practice the Security Council has delegated this duty to the Trusteeship Council.[17]

The problem now arises as to whether there is any obligation on an administering authority to submit an annual report—and, if so, to whom the report must be submitted, and whether it must be compiled on the basis of the Trusteeship Council's Questionnaire. Since all trust territories must be subject to United Nations supervision in order to qualify as United Nations' trusteeships, and since the methods of supervision authorised for the United Nations are found in Article 87, it seems that all trust territories are subject to the forms of supervision outlined in this article. For this supervision to be exercised with respect to any particular trust territory, the United Nations must be in possession of reports from the administering authority concerned. In the case of a strategic territory, if Article 83 is read in conjunction with Article 87, the Security Council is substituted for the General Assembly as the organ to exercise the United Nations' supervision. Thus the administering authority reports to the Security Council in place of the General Assembly.[18] However,

Eleventh Session, Resolution 463 (XI). For the text of this Revised Questionnaire, see Doc. T/1010 (*Official Records of the Trusteeship Council,* Special Supplement, New York 1952).

17 By a resolution adopted during its Fourth Year (see *Official Records of the Security Council,* Fourth Year, No. 18, pp. 6, 7), the Security Council requested the Trusteeship Council to transmit a Questionnaire for the strategic trust territory to the Security Council (see further above, Chap. 8, p. 155 *et seq.*). The Trusteeship Council transmits this Questionnaire one month before forwarding it to the administering authority of the trust territory (see *Official Records of the Trusteeship Council,* Fourth Session, Resolution 46 (IV)).

18 See further below, Chap. 10, pp. 217–218.

it does not appear from the Charter that the administering authority for a strategic trust territory is required to make a report annually, since it is Article 88 not 87 which refers to *annual* reports; nor need the reports be based on the Trusteeship Council's Questionnaire. So long as some reports are submitted by the administering authority, the United Nations supervisory function under Article 87 (a) is able to be exercised.

Article 88 states that the General Assembly is to be the recipient of the annual reports from the administering authorities, a role which it exercises exclusively according to this article. Under Article 87 (a), the General Assembly is empowered to 'consider' reports submitted by the administering authorities, a function it may delegate to the Trusteeship Council if it wishes.[19] The question arises as to what this power to 'consider' includes, and whether it includes the making of recommendations with respect to the reports. Elsewhere in the Charter, when the word 'consider' has been used, an additional word has been included if it was intended that further action should follow upon the consideration of a problem. Thus in Article 11, the General Assembly is authorised to 'consider the general principles of co-operation in the maintenance of international peace and security' and to 'make recommendations' to Members of the Security Council, or both. Similarly, in Article 17 (1) the General Assembly is authorised to 'consider and approve the budget of the Organisation.' If a narrow interpretation of 'consider' in Article 87 (a) is adopted, then the role of the General Assembly and Trusteeship Council with regard to annual reports appears to be limited to empty examinations of the reports without the power to suggest administrative improvements or to recommend future courses of action. This can scarcely be called supervision.

However, Article 10 can be called in to supplement the provisions of Article 87 (a) in favour of the General Assembly. When these two articles are read together, they permit the General Assembly to make recommendations to an administering authority as a result of the examination of the annual report. The same is not true of the Trusteeship Council, since this general

[19] In practice, the Trusteeship Council undertakes the consideration of the annual report. See Rule 72 of the Trusteeship Council's Rules of Procedure (Doc. T/1/Rev. 3 of 1952, p. 11).

power of making recommendations to Members granted to the General Assembly by Article 10 is not accorded to the Trusteeship Council by the Charter. Since the Trusteeship Council operates under the authority of the General Assembly and is supposed to assist the General Assembly in its exercise of trusteeship functions,[20] the General Assembly can empower the Trusteeship Council to make suggestions and recommendations to the General Assembly on the basis of the annual reports. However, the General Assembly may not empower the Trusteeship Council to make such recommendations to the administering authorities. If the General Assembly accepts the suggestions and recommendations of the Trusteeship Council, they can be passed on to the administering authorities by means of General Assembly resolutions.

In actual practice, this pattern is not followed, although the Trusteeship Council has not attempted to make recommendations in furtherance of the annual reports directly to the administering authorities, without the specific authorisation of the General Assembly in each case. In the case of each annual report, the Trusteeship Council draws up a report on its examination of the annual report for submission to the General Assembly. Included in the Council's report is a section on the Council's conclusions and recommendations. This report is then examined by the General Assembly,[1] and such of the recommendations as are approved become the subject of General Assembly resolutions. So far the practice is in conformity with the Charter. However, the General Assembly's resolutions have tended to recommend that the Trusteeship Council make recommendations to the administering authorities on specific matters arising out of the annual reports, whereas the General Assembly's resolutions should address the administering powers directly.[2]

20 Article 85 of the Charter. See further above, Chap. 9, pp. 171–173, and Chap. 8, pp. 152–155.

1 These reports are all included in the annual *Report of the Trusteeship Council* to the General Assembly.

2 In the *Report of the Trusteeship Council* to the General Assembly's Third Session (*Official Records of the General Assembly,* Third Session, Suppl. No. 4), the Council's comments on the annual reports of the administering authorities expressed concern at the inadequacy of educational facilities in the territories (*ibid.,* pp. 10, 18, and 32). As a result of the Council's comments, the General Assembly adopted a resolution recommending that the Council should request the administering authorities to increase educational facilities, and should propose to them

Since Article 88 states that annual reports are to be transmitted to the General Assembly by the administering authorities, the President of the General Assembly would seem to be the correct person to receive these reports, or alternatively a copy might be distributed to each member of the General Assembly. Rule 72 of the Trusteeship Council's Rules of Procedure does not conform with Article 88, inasmuch as it states that the annual reports are to be submitted to the Secretary-General by the administering authorities. Furthermore, this Rule requires the Secretary-General to transmit the annual reports directly to the Members of the Trusteeship Council, completely ignoring the role of the General Assembly as the recipient of the annual reports. The Secretary-General cannot even be considered to be acting as the agent of the General Assembly, since in that case he would be required to pass the reports on to the General Assembly promptly. It can be argued from Rule 72 that the Secretary-General is acting as the agent of the Trusteeship Council, but this is not what is required by Article 88 of the Charter.[3]

Rule 74 of the Trusteeship Council's Rules of Procedure permits the relevant administering authority to appoint a special representative to participate in the examination of the annual report by the Trusteeship Council. Since this is not authorised by the Charter, it is a matter which requires the agreement of both parties concerned—the Trusteeship Council and the administering authority. The language is correct in that it permits, but does not require, the administering authority to make use of the provision. In practice, however, the administering authorities have been glad to utilise this provision and a special representative, well-informed on the territory concerned, has invariably been present during consideration of an annual report. Only two exceptions to this have occurred: the first was during preliminary consideration of the first annual report on New

that primary education be free and higher education not dependent on means (*Official Records of the General Assembly,* Resolution 225 (III)). Subsequently the Trusteeship Council, acting on the General Assembly's resolution, adopted a resolution on the lines indicated by the General Assembly (*Official Records of the Trusteeship Council,* Fourth Session, Resolution 83 (IV)).

[3] Cf. the case of petitions where the Secretary-General legally acts as the agent of the Trusteeship Council in receiving the petitions. See below, p. 189 *et seq.*

Guinea,[4] and the second was during the examination of the annual report on Nauru in 1953.[5] It should be noted that, since each member of the Trusteeship Council may have only one vote,[6] a special representative must be considered a voteless participant.

Article 87 (a) mentions reports submitted by the administering authorities but it does not specify that these are 'annual' reports. Thus, the General Assembly and Trusteeship Council are not limited to the consideration of the annual reports mentioned in Article 88, although these are included in Article 87 (a). Any reports which the administering authorities may submit to the United Nations may be considered and used to supplement the annual reports.

Petitions

The General Assembly and Trusteeship Council are authorised to 'accept petitions and examine them in consultation with the administering authority.' No mention is made of the source of these petitions, whether it is to be restricted to the inhabitants of the trust territory or to include outsiders too. Since the Charter leaves the question open, it rests with the General Assembly and Trusteeship Council, who alone are authorised by the Charter to receive petitions, to decide on the admissibility of a petition from any particular source.

The question of petitions from anonymous sources being examined was raised at the Fifth Session of the General Assembly, when India proposed that anonymous petitions should not be regarded as inadmissible merely on account of their source.[7]

4 At the Second Session of the Council, final action on the report on New Guinea was postponed until the Third Session when a special representative was to be present (*Official Records of the Trusteeship Council,* Second Part of the Second Session, 60th Meeting, pp. 7–8).

5 At its Twelfth Session, the Trusteeship Council considered the annual report on Nauru after the Australian Delegate had announced that a special representative would not be present. Due to the fact that the Council had become familiar with the affairs of the small trust territory and that a Visiting Mission had just returned from there, the Australian Government considered it unnecessary to send a special representative to the Council on this occasion (*Official Records of the Trusteeship Council,* Twelfth Session, 470th Meeting, par. 28). During the examination of the report, the Australian Delegate answered questions raised by Council members (*ibid.,* 470th and 471st Meetings).

6 Article 89 (1).

7 Doc. A/C.4/L. 101 (*Official Records of the General Assembly,* Fifth Session, Fourth Committee, pp. 169–170).

The United Nations, however, may refuse to accept petitions on any ground that it pleases, since it is not compelled to accept petitions at all. The grounds mentioned in Rule 81 of the Trusteeship Council's Rules of Procedure as rendering petitions inadmissible, are not exhaustive.[8] No 'right of petition' is granted to any one by Article 87; the 'right' arising out of this article belongs to the General Assembly and Trusteeship Council, who have the right to accept petitions and examine them if they wish. The Trusteeship Council's Rules of Procedure grant the 'right of petition' to 'inhabitants of the Trust Territories or other parties,'[9] but they do not require that the Trusteeship Council accept such petitions; they merely permit the Trusteeship Council to do so.[10] The right of petition does not imply that the petitioners have a right to have the Trusteeship Council accept their petitions.

At the Second Session of the Trusteeship Council the President of the Council correctly stated that he interpreted it as a matter of grace, not of right, that under Rule 80 of the Trusteeship Council's Rules of Procedure, this body could grant the hearing of oral petitions.[11] What is true of oral petitions is also true for all petitions.

Only the General Assembly and the Trusteeship Council are authorised by the Charter to accept petitions.[12] Thus Rules 82 and 84 of the Trusteeship Council's Rules of Procedure, authorising the Secretary-General and members of visiting missions to the trust territories to accept petitions, are in conformity with the Charter only in so far as the Secretary-General and members of the visiting missions can be said to be acting as intermediaries and not actually *accepting* the petitions. The Rules of Procedure support this interpretation. With regard to petitions accepted by members of visiting missions to the trust territories, Rule 84 says that these 'shall be transmitted promptly to the Secretary-General for circulation to the members of the Council.' Similarly,

[8] Rule 81 states that 'normally petitions shall be rendered inadmissible if they are directed against judgments of competent courts of the Administering Authority or if they lay before the Council a dispute with which the courts have competence to deal' (Doc. T/1/Rev. 3, 1952, p. 13).

[9] Rule 77 (Doc. T/1/Rev. 3, 1952, p. 12).

[10] Rule 76 states that 'petitions *may* be accepted and examined by the Trusteeship Council' (*ibid.*, italics added).

[11] *Official Records of the Trusteeship Council*, Second Session, First Part, p. 27.

[12] Article 87 (b).

Rule 85 states that 'the Secretary-General shall circulate promptly to the members of the Trusteeship Council all written petitions received by him.' In both cases, the final destination of the petitions is the Trusteeship Council, and the Secretary-General or member of the visiting mission is merely the intermediary. In fact the compulsive wording of Rules 84 and 85 establish that it is the positive duty of the Secretary-General or the member of the visiting mission to pass the petitions promptly to the members of the Trusteeship Council. Neither the Secretary-General nor a member of a visiting mission is authorised to refuse to take a petition, since to reject a petition is to imply the power of acceptance, a power which only the General Assembly and Trusteeship Council possess. Nor is it legal for the Secretary-General to screen petitions before they are examined by the Trusteeship Council, since he is not authorised to accept or examine petitions; in any case, petitions may only be examined 'in consultation with the administering authority.'[13]

In practice, the Trusteeship Council has often ruled petitions outside its competence, and therefore rejected them.[14] The main criterion for deciding if a petition is within the competence of the General Assembly or Trusteeship Council is whether such petition comes within the scope of the Trusteeship System. A limitation not found in the Charter is provided by Rule 81 of the Trusteeship Council's Rules of Procedure, to the effect that 'petitions shall be considered inadmissible if they are directed against judgments of competent courts of the Administering Authority or if they lay before the Council a dispute with which the courts have competence to deal.' This is modified by the provision that this rule shall not be interpreted so as to prevent

13 Article 87 (b).

14 *e.g.*, At the Second Session, the Trusteeship Council ruled out of its competence a petition requesting the international control of strategic raw materials in non-self-governing territories, three petitions containing proposals for the internationalisation of the Polar regions of the globe, and a petition requesting the international control of strategic areas and their protection by the United Nations (see *Official Records of the Trusteeship Council,* Second Session, Resolutions 24 (II), 22 (II), and 23 (II)). At its Fourth Session, the Trusteeship Council rejected a petition from a former Tanganyika chief, who had been dismissed, requesting a pension (*Official Records of the Trusteeship Council,* Fourth Session, Resolution 78 (IV)). At its Sixth Session, the Trusteeship Council ruled outside its competence two petitions concerning the unification of parts of the two Cameroons with a part of Nigeria (*Official Records of the Trusteeship Council,* Resolution 165 (VI)).

consideration by the Trusteeship Council of petitions against legislation on the grounds of its incompatibility with the provisions of the Charter or of the trusteeship agreements, irrespective of whether decisions on cases arising under such legislation have previously been given by the courts of the administering authority. The part of Rule 81 which excludes from the Trusteeship Council's competence petitions concerning disputes with which the local courts have competence to deal, amounts to a requirement that local remedies be exhausted. But it should be considered whether the inadmittance of petitions on account of their being 'directed against judgments of competent courts of the Administering Authority' amounts to 'denial of justice.' It would appear that the second part of Rule 81 prevents denial of justice, inasmuch as petitions concerning legislation which is held incompatible with the Charter or the trust agreements are held to be admissible. Presumably, the 'judgments of competent courts of the Administering Authority' to which Rule 81 refers concern legislation, and only with legislation which is within the scope of the Trusteeship System—in other words, within the scope of the Charter or trust agreements—is the Trusteeship Council competent to deal. Therefore, apart from the limitation requiring that local remedies be exhausted, Rule 81 does not restrict the Trusteeship Council in any way.

Whilst Rule 81 may limit the action of the Trusteeship Council, it cannot limit the right of the General Assembly to accept and examine a petition which the Rules seek to render inadmissible. This gives rise to the point as to whether, if a petition has been ruled outside the competence of the Trusteeship Council yet remains within the competence of the General Assembly, it should be passed on to the General Assembly. This is so only if the petition falls within the scope of the Trusteeship System, since the General Assembly is not authorised to accept petitions except under the Trusteeship System. However, it is possible for a petition to be within the scope of the Trusteeship System yet outside the competence of the Trusteeship Council. Such a case might arise with a petition concerning the termination of a trust agreement; in this case it would seem that the Trusteeship Council should pass the petition on to the General Assembly, who may accept or reject it.[15]

[15] On relationship between the Trusteeship Council and General Assembly, see further above, Chap. 8, pp. 152–155.

The Charter does not state whether petitions are to be written or oral; therefore both are permissible. The Trusteeship Council's Rules of Procedure specifically allow for the hearing of oral petitions,[16] and nowhere is the General Assembly forbidden to do so. However, to satisfy Article 87 (b), oral petitions must be examined in consultation with the administering authority. An attempt was made at the Third Session of the Trusteeship Council in 1948 to limit the source of oral petitions. The Delegate of the United Kingdom proposed that only a resident of a trust territory and a spokesman of its inhabitants should be entitled to appear in person before the Trusteeship Council. The Trusteeship Council correctly held that this matter could only be decided in each individual case in the light of the particular circumstances, and it refused to make a hard and fast ruling on the subject.[17] At the Seventh Session of the General Assembly, objections were raised to the hearing of oral petitions directly by the General Assembly on the grounds that the petitioners should first apply to the Trusteeship Council; only afterwards might they be heard by the General Assembly, when this body examined the Trusteeship Council's report.[18] It is true that the Trusteeship Council's Rules of Procedure[19] indicate that it is the proper body to hear oral petitions, but these Rules cannot be allowed to limit the right which the General Assembly enjoys under the Charter: the right to accept and examine petitions without any requirement that they be examined first by another body.[20] Since the Charter accords this right to the General Assembly, there can be no question of the General Assembly's by-passing the Trusteeship Council and its organs, as the Australian Delegate to the General Assembly held was occurring.[1] The fact that the Trusteeship Council's Rules of Procedure provide that the Council shall hear oral petitions does not preclude or limit the right of the General Assembly to do so too, nor does it mean that the General Assembly must exercise this right only after the Trusteeship Council has done so.

16 Rule 80 (Doc. T/1/Rev. 3, 1952, p. 12).

17 For the view of the United Kingdom Delegate, see *Official Records of the Trusteeship Council,* Third Session, Third Meeting, pp. 21, and 26–27.

18 See *Official Records of the General Assembly,* Fourth Committee, Seventh Session, pp. 13–16.

19 Rule 80.

20 See Article 87 (b).

1 *Official Records of the General Assembly,* Seventh Session, Fourth Committee, p. 14.

The practice of hearing oral petitions was never adopted under the League of Nations Mandates System; this, however, provided no precedent for the Trusteeship System since no mention of petitions of any sort was made in the Covenant, the Constitution of the Permanent Mandates Commission, or in the terms of the Mandate treaties themselves. Although Great Britain proposed that provision be made in the Covenant for petitions to be received from mandated territories,[2] this was never done. Nevertheless, petitions had begun to arrive by the time the Permanent Mandates Commission came into being, and Great Britain submitted proposals to the League Council for dealing with them. As a result of this, additional rules of procedure for the Permanent Mandates Commission were adopted by the League Council to cover the receipt and examination of petitions.[3] In practice, such petitions were limited to written petitions.[4]

The possibility exists in the Charter for the General Assembly or Trusteeship Council to investigate the subject matter of a petition through sending a fact-finding mission to the trust territory concerned. The principle of United Nations visits to trust territories is introduced in Article 87 (c), where it is provided that these visits shall take place at times agreed upon with the administering authorities. The purpose of these visits is not stated in the Charter; therefore, presumably the United Nations may instruct a visiting mission to investigate a petition, although the timing of

[2] See *U.S. Foreign Relations: Paris Peace Conference, 1919,* Vol. 3, p. 719.

[3] League of Nations Doc. *C.P.M.* 38 (I).

[4] In 1926, the League Council asked the Mandatory Powers for their views on the subject of oral petitions; all the Mandatories were against it. Recognising the justice of their objections, the League Council decided that 'there is no occasion to modify the procedure which has hitherto been followed by the Commission in regard to this question'. The Rapporteur, however, observed in his report that if, in a particular case, the circumstances showed that it was impossible for all the necessary information to be secured by the usual means, the Council might 'decide on such exceptional procedure as might seem appropriate and necessary in the particular circumstances' (see League of Nations, *Mandates System–Origins–Principles–Application,* p. 42). In a recent Advisory Opinion, the International Court expressed the view that 'the Council having established the right of petition, and regulated the manner of its exercise, was, in the opinion of the Court, competent to authorise the Permanent Mandates Commission to grant oral hearings to petitioners, had it seen fit to do so.' (*Admissibility of Hearings of Petitioners by the Committee on South-West Africa,* Advisory Opinion: *I.C.J. Reports 1956,* p. 29).

this investigation must be consented to by the administering authority. An example of a fact-finding mission being sent to a trust territory to investigate a petition occurred in 1947, when the Trusteeship Council authorised the sending of a special mission to Western Samoa for the purpose of investigating a request for self-government from leaders and representatives of the territory.[5] This was done on the proposal of the administering authority. At other times regular United Nations Visiting Missions have been instructed to investigate the subject matter of petitions.[6]

The practice of the Trusteeship Council in the case of a petition is, after examination, to adopt a resolution by majority vote. Whether the resolution is permitted to include recommendations to the administering authority concerned is doubtful. The General Assembly and Trusteeship Council are only authorised to 'examine' a petition, not to take any further action thereon. The General Assembly can call in Article 10 to authorise the making of recommendations to the administering authority, but the Trusteeship Council has no such authority. Therefore, the Trusteeship Council is restricted to advising the General Assembly to make recommendations to the administering authority, and then only if the General Assembly asks for the Trusteeship Council's advice.[7]

VISITS

The General Assembly and Trusteeship Council may 'provide for periodic visits to the respective trust territories at times agreed upon with the administering authority.'[8] For the first time the principle of periodic international inspection of dependent territories is introduced. This was proposed in the case of the Mandates System, but was rejected by the Mandatories on the grounds that it would tend to undermine the authority of the

[5] *Official Records of the Trusteeship Council,* First Session, Resolution 4 (I). See further above, pp. 181–182.

[6] The terms of reference laid down by the Trusteeship Council in 1949 for the United Nations Visiting Mission to West Africa included the instruction 'to investigate on the spot, after consultation with the local representative of the Administering Authority concerned, such petitions dealing with the conditions of the indigenous inhabitants as are, in its opinion, sufficiently important to warrant special investigation' (Doc. T/348).

[7] See above, pp. 186–187.

[8] Article 87 (c).

Mandatories. Occasionally the League Council sent special investigating missions to a mandated area in connection with disputes before the Council; but it never sent missions to investigate general conditions in the mandates.[9]

Since periodic visits may be made to a trust territory only at times agreed upon with the administering authority, such visits can be prevented from ever taking place through the refusal of the administering authority to agree on a time. The administering authority, however, is required to submit to the supervision by the United Nations of its administration of a trust territory, and it would seem that this must include the submission to the means of supervision specifically stated in the Charter. Furthermore, a Member administering authority is required to 'give the United Nations every assistance in any action it takes in accordance with the present Charter.'[10] Therefore, there is at least a strong moral requirement for the administering authority to agree on a time for a visit to be made by a United Nations mission. There is perhaps more than a moral requirement, for presumably it was the intention of the drafters of the Charter that Article 87 (c) should be made operative; otherwise it would not have been included in the Charter. As was stated in the *Timor Case* (1914): 'In case of doubt, treaties ought to be interpreted conformably with the real mutual intention.'[11] Since the intention at San Francisco was to constitute a system of visiting missions to the trust territories, the administering authorities have an obligation to carry out in good faith their part in putting the system into effect. The purpose of the wording of Article 87 (c) is to ensure that United Nations' visits do not take place without prior notice being given to the administering authority concerned, or at times which are inconvenient to the administering authority for technical or administrative reasons.

United Nations visits are not required to be at any fixed intervals of time; they are merely to be periodic. Nor is the United Nations *required* to make visits; it is merely permitted to do so. It is entirely up to the General Assembly or Trusteeship

[9] See Quincy Wright, *Mandates Under the League of Nations* (1930), p. 183.

[10] Article 2 (5).

[11] P.C.A., *Netherlands* v. *Portugal* (1 Scott, *Hague Court Reports*, p. 355 at p. 365), and see further Bin Cheng, *General Principles of Law as Applied by International Courts and Tribunals* (1953), p. 107.

Council to decide whether to take advantage of this means of supervision, and they are at liberty to send missions to some trust territories and not to others. No uniformity of treatment as between the trust territories is required.

The duties of a visiting mission are determined by its terms of reference. These may include instructions to investigate general conditions in a trust territory, or they may be devoted to a directive to investigate a particular problem.[12] Special investigations are quite in accord with Article 87 which neither forbids nor expressly authorises them. Rules 84 and 89 of the Trusteeship Council's Rules of Procedure permit representatives of a visiting mission to receive written or oral petitions. These Rules are only in accordance with the Charter so long as the petitions are passed straight on to the General Assembly or Trusteeship Council, since the receipt of petitions by a representative of a visiting mission must not amount to the acceptance of them.[13]

A visiting mission may make recommendations to the Trusteeship Council or General Assembly only if such recommendations come within its terms of reference. If these terms include only instructions to investigate a particular problem, the mission's recommendations must be confined to the subject matter of this problem. The United Nations Visiting Mission to East Africa in 1948 suggested in its report on Tanganyika that the Trusteeship Council should avail itself of the assistance of the International Labour Organisation and UNESCO, when considering reports on problems arising in connection with the new communities established for Africans working on the Ground Nuts Scheme.[14] This was within the scope of the Mission's terms of reference,[15] which included the instruction to give attention to issues raised in connection with the administering authority's annual report.

As with the case of annual reports and petitions, only the General Assembly is permitted to make recommendations to the

12 See Rule 97 of the Trusteeship Council's Rules of Procedure (Doc. T/1/Rev. 3, p. 17).

13 See above, pp. 190–191.

14 See *United Nations Visiting Mission to East Africa: Report on Tanganyika and Related Documents*, p. 109 (*Official Records of the Trusteeship Council*, Fourth Session, Suppl. No. 3, Doc. T/218).

15 *Official Records of the Trusteeship Council*, Third Session, Resolution 37 (III).

administering authorities as a result of visits to the trust territories.[16]

Article 87 (c) does not say by whom the periodic visits are to be made; according to this provision they could be made by one or more persons. It appears to be entirely up to the General Assembly and Trusteeship Council to determine the composition of a visiting mission. They are at liberty to include representatives to the Trusteeship Council, individuals who are not representatives to the Trusteeship Council, or even outside experts. A further problem is to decide whether the appointment to a visiting mission is a State or personal appointment. The Charter provides no answer to this, so it is left to the Trusteeship Council and General Assembly to fix any criteria for the selection of members of a visiting mission.

In practice, member States of the Trusteeship Council have been selected to compose the visiting missions, the governments of these States being asked to nominate nationals who are then subject to the approval of the Trusteeship Council itself.[17] Thus in the last analysis, the appointment is a personal one but based on nationality. Since, however, it is the Trusteeship Council and General Assembly alone who are authorised to provide for visits to trust territories, the members of a visiting mission are responsible only to the Trusteeship Council or General Assembly as the case may be. This is reflected in Rule 96[18] of the Trusteeship Council's Rules of Procedure. Although in practice the balance between administering and non-administering States found on the Trusteeship Council has been maintained in the visiting missions, if the members of a mission exercise their roles correctly this is a needless precaution. It reflects a mistrust of the ability of an individual to act independently of his government.

16 See above, pp. 186–187, 195.

17 The only exception to this practice occurred in the case of the Special Visiting Mission to Western Samoa in 1947. In this instance, the Trusteeship Council made its own appointments from among representatives of the Member States represented on the Council (*Official Records of the Trusteeship Council,* First Session, 27th Meeting, p. 735), without requesting selected Member States to nominate individuals. A further departure from usual practice was the appointment of an individual to the Mission who was not himself a representative on the Trusteeship Council (*i.e.,* Dr. E. Cruz-Coke of Chile)—the only occasion that this has happened.

18 'A mission and the individual members thereof shall, while engaged in a visit, act only on the basis of the instructions of the Council and shall be responsible exclusively to it'.

A further question to be considered in the composition of a visiting mission is whether interest groups should be represented. In 1951, the Economic and Social Council adopted a resolution, on the proposal of the Commission on the Status of Women, inviting Member States to nominate, and the Trusteeship Council to consider, the appointment of women as members of visiting missions.[19] There is no legal reason why this should be either prohibited or authorised, but the practical difficulties involved in accepting the principle would be immense. If women were to be represented, there would inevitably arise the question of racial, and perhaps even religious, representation. The matter presents too many administrative problems for the Trusteeship Council to adopt this practice.

[19] Resolution 385 (XIII), Part E (*Official Records of the Economic and Social Council,* Sixth Year, Thirteenth Session, Suppl. No. 1, p. 38).

PART FIVE

THE ADMINISTRATION OF TRUST TERRITORIES

CHAPTER 11

THE ADMINISTERING AUTHORITY AND ITS OBLIGATIONS

IN the application of the Trusteeship System to any territory, two entities are involved: the supervisory body (the United Nations acting through its organs)[1] and the administering authority. In this chapter, it is proposed to examine the types of administering authority provided for in the Charter and the obligations which the administering authority undertakes.

THE ADMINISTERING AUTHORITY

Under Article 81 of the Charter, the administering authority of a trust territory 'may be one or more states or the Organisation itself' and must be designated in the trust agreement. No further mention of the nature of the administering authority is made, nor are any rules laid down for the selection of such an authority. In one respect the Covenant of the League of Nations was more specific in the matter of the choice of the Mandatory than is the Charter in its choice of an administering authority, for under the Covenant the Mandatory was to be an 'advanced nation.'[2] Under the Charter, the stage of development of the administering authority itself is not considered relevant. At San Francisco, there was a proposal put forward by the Egyptian Delegate to the effect that 'due regard being given to the wishes of the population in the selection of the trustee authority . . .' be added to Article 81 of the Charter.[3] This proposal was similar in substance to Article 22 (4) of the Covenant, which provided that in the case of A Mandates the wishes of the communities formerly belonging to the Turkish Empire 'must be a principal consideration in the selection of the Mandatory.' The Egyptian proposal at San Francisco was rejected, however, and the inhabitants of the trust territories had no hand in choosing the authority that was to administer them. A provision along the lines of that

[1] See above, Chaps. 8 and 9.
[2] Article 22 (2) of the Covenant.
[3] *Summary Report of the Fourteenth Meeting of Committee II/4* (*U.N.C.I.O. Docs.*, Vol. 10, p. 541).

suggested by Egypt did find its way into the terms of the Italian Peace Treaty, where the Governments of the United States, the United Kingdom, France, and the Soviet Union undertook to make the final disposition of the former Italian colonies accord with the wishes and welfare of the inhabitants of the territories concerned.[4] This was of practical interest from the point of view of the Trusteeship System inasmuch as all the former Italian colonies were at one time or another considered as possible future trust territories. However, an examination of the proceedings, inside and outside of the United Nations, which led to the disposal of these former colonies, does not reveal that much attention was paid to this provision of the Italian Peace Treaty.[5]

The definition of the administering authority given in Article 81 allows for four different kinds of administration: administration by a single State, joint administration by more than one State, administration by a non-Member, and administration by the Organisation itself.

Administration by a single State

The simplest type of administering authority is that of a single State. This was the form which the Mandatory invariably took under the League Mandates System, although a joint administration of States was not ruled out by the provisions of the Covenant. Article 22 merely provided that the administration should be exercised by 'advanced nations,' which allowed for one or more States to become a Mandatory. In practice, however, the territories in question were allocated by the Allied Supreme Council to single States to be administered as mandates by them, with the exception of Nauru which was assigned to 'His Britannic Majesty' without any instructions as to which State should exercise the administration on his behalf. This

4 Peace Treaty with Italy, Annex XI, paragraph 2 (Cmd. 7481 (1948)).

5 For discussions on the question of the disposal of the former Italian colonies, see *Official Records of the General Assembly,* Second Part of the Third Session, First Committee, 238th Meeting onwards (p. 1 *et seq.*). See also G. Schwarzenberger, *Power Politics* (1951), pp. 407–411, and 671–674. In the case of Libya and Eritrea, it is true that opposition by the local population to the return to any kind of Italian rule was successful. However, the opposition of the population to Italy was not heeded in the case of Somaliland. The representative of the Somali Youth League expressed, before the General Assembly, opposition 'to the restoration of Italian administration in any form or guise whatsoever' (*Official Records of the General Assembly,* Second Part of the Third Session, First Committee, 248th Meeting, pp. 96–97).

matter was solved through a tripartite agreement between Australia, Great Britain and New Zealand, of July 2, 1919, which vested the administration in Australia for a five-year period; administration continued to be undertaken by Australia right up to the time of the territory's being placed under the Trusteeship System.[6] Thus, by the time the Mandate for Nauru entered into force, Australia had become the administering authority and was thus the actual Mandatory.

The practice of a single State administration has been followed under the Trusteeship System. There have been many cases where a joint administration has been proposed, and it has been held by some that the trust territory of Nauru provides an example of a joint administering authority in practice.[7] But to assert this is to use the term 'administering authority' differently from the way in which it is used in the Charter.[8] This confusion owes its origin to the terms of the trust agreement for Nauru itself. Article 1 of this agreement says that the Governments of Australia, New Zealand and the United Kingdom are designated as the joint administering authority 'which will exercise the administration of the Territory.' Article 4 states that Australia will 'exercise full powers of legislation, administration and jurisdiction' over the territory on behalf of the administering authority, which this article says is Australia, New Zealand and the United Kingdom. But, according to Article 81 of the Charter, the term 'administering authority' refers to the authority 'which will exercise the administration of the trust territory.' Thus, a strict interpretation of this article places Australia as the administering authority, and consequently Nauru is not subject to an administering authority of more than a single State. No other view is tenable taking into account the definition of 'administering authority' in Article 81. Furthermore, Article 87 requires annual reports to be submitted by the *administering authority;* in the case of Nauru, these reports are submitted by the Government of Australia.

6 See Duncan Hall, *Mandates, Dependencies and Trusteeship* (1948), p. 147.

7 See Oppenheim (ed. Lauterpacht), *International Law* (seventh ed.), Vol. 1, p. 208.

8 See above, Chap. 6, pp. 107–108.

Joint administration

Consideration has been given at various times to the possibility of placing a territory under trusteeship with a joint administering authority of several States, but this has never materialised.[9] The most notable example of this was Korea. At the Second Moscow Conference in December 1945, the Foreign Ministers present decided to set up a joint commission consisting of representatives of the United States' and Soviet Commands in Korea. This commission was to draw up proposals to be submitted to the Soviet Union, the United States, the United Kingdom and China for joint consideration 'for the working out of an agreement concerning a four-Power trusteeship of Korea for a period of up to five years.'[10] This plan never materialised and we have no example of a trust territory under joint administration.

Non-member as administering authority

The wording of Article 81 of the Charter has made it possible for a non-Member to become an administering authority,[11] a situation which was not considered at San Francisco. However, consideration was given to the possibility of a State withdrawing from the United Nations but continuing to administer a trust territory, an event which had occurred under the League Mandates System in the case of Japan.

The Egyptian Delegation at San Francisco attempted to have a provision inserted into the Charter, which would have provided that withdrawal from United Nations Membership by an administering authority was grounds for the transfer of the trust territories it administered to another administering authority.[12] Syria pursued this line later in the Security Council when she suggested that the Security Council adopt the principle that 'when a trustee or a Mandatory Power withdraws from the United Nations, or

9 At the Bandung Conference in April 1955, Sir John Kotelawala (Prime Minister of Ceylon) proposed that Formosa be placed under the joint trusteeship of the Colombo Powers (8 *Chronique de Politique Étrangère*, No. 4, July 1955, p. 393).

10 Communique of the Moscow Conference, issued December 24 and 25, 1945 (see Royal Institute of International Affairs, *United Nations Documents 1941–1945*).

11 Article 81 states that the administering authority 'may be one or more states or the Organisation itself.' It does not specify that the administering authority must be a United Nations Member.

12 *Summary Report of the Fourteenth Meeting of Committee II/4*, p. 5 (*U.N.C.I.O. Docs.*, Vol. 10, p. 543).

is expelled from it, its right to that trust or to that mandate would not persist, and the General Assembly of the United Nations should be free to deprive it of that right for as long as it is not a Member.'[13] Had any such principle been adopted, the possibility of designating a non-Member as an administering authority would not have existed.

The Egyptian proposal at San Francisco led to a Joint Statement on the subject by the Delegates of the United Kingdom and the United States, which was annexed to the Report of the Rapporteur of Committee II/4.[14] It was proposed herein that if a State withdrew from the Organisation for reasons which reflected no discredit upon it, the State could continue to administer a trust territory provided that it declared its willingness to abide by the terms of the Trusteeship System. Although ceasing to be a Member of the Trusteeship Council, it could be given the opportunity to attend meetings of the Trusteeship Council when matters affecting its trust territories were under consideration. It is not clear why it was considered that the State would necessarily cease to be a Member of the Trusteeship Council since, according to the Report of the Rapporteur of Committee II/4, the Trusteeship Council was to be composed of '*states* administering trust territories.'[15] It was only later that this phrase was changed to 'Members administering trust territories,' the form in which it appears in the Charter; the records of the San Francisco Conference, however, do not indicate the reason for this change.

There has as yet been no case of an administering Power withdrawing from the United Nations, but in 1950 a non-Member, Italy, was designated as the administering authority for Somaliland. To a large extent the pattern of the Joint Statement of the United Kingdom and United States was followed: for so long as Italy remained a non-Member she was excluded from Membership of the Trusteeship Council by the wording of Article 86, but participated in the work of the Trusteeship Council without vote whenever matters concerning Somaliland were under discussion.

[13] *Official Records of the Security Council,* Second Year, No. 23, p. 470.

[14] U.N.C.I.O. Doc. 1115, Annex C, pp. 14–15 (*U.N.C.I.O. Docs.,* Vol. 10, p. 620).

[15] *Report of the Rapporteur of Committee II/4,* Doc. 1115, p. 6 (*U.N.C.I.O. Docs.,* Vol. 10, p. 612).

The Organisation as administering authority

According to Article 81 of the Charter, the Organisation itself is permitted to become the administering authority of a trust territory. Administration of this type was not provided for under the Mandates System, and it has been of no practical significance under the Trusteeship System. There is no example of the Organisation becoming the administering authority of a trust territory, although it has been proposed at many times. In 1946, the United States Delegate to the General Assembly, Mr. Dulles, suggested that the former Italian colonies might be placed under direct United Nations trusteeship and thus provide a chance for the Organisation to become an administering authority.[16] This idea was taken up when the question of the disposal of the former Italian colonies came before the United Nations General Assembly in 1949. Both the Indian[17] and Soviet[18] Delegates dwelt at some length on this proposal but eventually the idea was discarded. In 1947, the Trusteeship Council went so far as to draft a trust agreement for the City of Jerusalem in which the United Nations was designated as the administering authority, with the Trusteeship Council discharging the responsibilities of administration on behalf of the Organisation.[19] This draft trust agreement never came into operation, however, and a solution to the problem of Jerusalem was found outside the Trusteeship System.[20]

The possibility of the Organisation becoming an administering authority raises numerous practical difficulties which would have the effect of changing the whole conception of United Nations trusteeship, if indeed it is feasible at all for the Organisation to assume this administrative role. Certain delegates at San Francisco expressed the opinion that direct international administration was likely to be unsatisfactory, but they did not press the matter and provision for it remained in the draft charter.[21]

16 *Official Records of the General Assembly,* Second Part of the First Session, Fourth Committee, Part 2, p. 36.

17 *Official Records of the General Assembly,* Second Part of the Third Session, First Committee, p. 65. 18 *ibid.,* p. 23.

19 See *Official Records of the Trusteeship Council,* Second Session, Third Part, Annex, p. 4ff.

20 As with other aspects of the Palestine problem, the United Nations was faced with a series of *faits accomplis* and it is these that determined the fate of Jerusalem.

21 See *Summary Report of Eleventh Meeting of Committee II/4,* p. 4 (*U.N.C.I.O. Docs.,* Vol. 10, p. 499).

The difficulties pertaining to direct international administration fall under four headings: the drawing up of the trust agreement, the exercise of administration, supervision, and the duties of the administering authority.

The drawing up of the trust agreement

The pattern of the two stages in the negotiation of a trust agreement breaks down when the designated administering authority is the United Nations itself. The second stage in the conclusion of a trust agreement comprises the acceptance of the terms by the administering authority,[1] and approval of them by the Organisation. In the case where the United Nations is the administering authority, this would amount to an agreement between the Organisation and itself. The practical way round this difficulty would be for the agreement between the 'States directly concerned' to be followed by a resolution of the General Assembly approving it. The Organisation as administering authority would not be permitted to take part in the actual drawing up of the terms of trusteeship, since this is reserved to 'States.'[2] However, since the Organisation is made up of Member States, these Member States might all take part in the drawing up of the terms of trusteeship, claiming that since the Organisation was to become the administering authority all Member States were *ipso facto* 'States directly concerned.'

The exercise of administration

There is no indication as to whom the actual administration is to be delegated when the Organisation assumes the status of an administering authority. As has been mentioned above,[3] in the case of the City of Jerusalem it was proposed to entrust administration to the Trusteeship Council. With respect to the Italian colonies, the Soviet Union proposed that for each colony the Trusteeship Council should appoint an administrator who would be assisted by an advisory council of seven Members of the

1 This is true whether there is specific acceptance of the terms of the agreement, as in the case of the Pacific Islands where the approval by the United States Government in accordance with its constitutional requirements took place, or implied acceptance. See above, p. 77 *et seq.*

2 Article 79 of the Charter: 'The terms of trusteeship for each territory to be placed under the trusteeship system . . . shall be agreed upon by the states directly concerned.'

3 See above, p. 208.

United Nations.[4] There seems to be little basis for attributing authority to the Trusteeship Council to appoint such an administrator or even to set up a subsidiary body to exercise administration,[5] although this latter power can be attributed to the General Assembly under Article 22 of the Charter.[6]

Supervision

The machinery of supervision, which is such an essential element of the Trusteeship System, completely breaks down when the administering authority is the Organisation itself. In the case of the annual report to the General Assembly (or to the Security Council for strategic areas) by the administering authority, the Organisation would be reporting to itself, which would render this supervisory operation meaningless. If the General Assembly should delegate the duty of administration to the Trusteeship Council, or to a specially established organ, then there could be an annual report from this body to the General Assembly. However, this would merely be an internal administrative matter, analogous to the submitting of annual reports to the General Assembly by all the organs of the United Nations under Article 15 of the Charter. It would be similar to a report to the Government of an administering Power by that Power's representative in the trust territory.

If a report to the General Assembly by the body carrying out the administration—whether it be the Trusteeship Council, a special organ or an administrator—is considered as an annual report under Articles 87 and 88, then the body submitting the report is the actual administering authority, not the Organisation.[7] This follows from the fact that Article 88 requires that the report be submitted by the actual administering authority. Furthermore, the Charter does not permit the Trusteeship

[4] See *Official Records of the General Assembly,* Second Part of the Third Session, First Committee, p. 23. For text of the Soviet proposal, see Doc. A/C.1/433.

[5] See further above, Chap. 9, pp. 176–178.

[6] Under Article 22, 'the General Assembly may establish such subsidiary organs as it deems necessary for the performance of its functions.'

[7] In the case of Tanganyika, the Cameroons and Togoland under United Kingdom administration, the administration of these territories is delegated to the Governors of Tanganyika, Nigeria and the Gold Coast respectively; but the annual reports on the territories to the United Nations are made by the United Kingdom Government—the actual administering authority.

Council, a special organ or an individual to become an administering authority; this is reserved to 'one or more states or the Organisation itself.'[8] The sending of United Nations Visiting Missions to a trust territory administered by the Organisation itself, is rendered meaningless, since a United Nations Mission could visit the territory in its capacity as administering authority. If a supervisory mission were dispatched to the territory, the Organisation would be acting as judge in its own cause. Any petitions sent to the United Nations from the inhabitants of a trust territory so administered, would be mere petitions to the administering authority of the trust territory, and they could scarcely be examined by the Organisation 'in consultation with the administering authority'[9] since the latter is the Organisation itself. In this way, the Organisation as administering authority would be operating without any supervision whatsoever, and this is hardly the system of trusteeship as envisaged in Chapters XII and XIII of the Charter.

What should have been provided in the Charter is for the Organisation to administer a trust territory by delegating power to one of its organs or to a body specially created for the purpose, and this is probably the intention behind Article 81. This becomes more likely when it is considered that the Organisation can act only through individuals. Thus, it is necessary, from a practical point of view, for the Organisation to delegate its administrative role to individuals in order to assume the role of the administering authority for a trust territory. Viewed in this way, United Nations supervision over a trust territory which it administers itself is neither so meaningless or ridiculous as it appears at first. It is not mere supervision by the United Nations of its own activities, but rather supervision by the United Nations (presumably the General Assembly) of the activities of its agents to whom it has delegated administration. As the Permanent Court of International Justice held in its judgment on the *Chorzow Factory* (1927), in the interpretation of a provision of a treaty 'account must be taken . . . of the functions which, in the intention of the contracting Parties, is to be attributed to this provision.'[10] In the case of Article 81 of the

[8] Article 81 of the Charter.
[9] Article 87 (b).
[10] P.C.I.J. Series A, No. 9, p. 24 (1 Hudson, *World Court Reports*, p. 589 *et seq.*).

Charter, the function of the provision 'such authority, hereinafter called the administering authority, may be . . . the Organisation itself' is to provide for the exercise of trusteeship administration to be undertaken by the Organisation. Since, as has already been mentioned, the Organisation can act only through individuals, therefore Article 81 must be interpreted liberally enough to permit the United Nations to exercise administration through its appointed agents.

Duties of the administering authority

Since the United Nations is authorised to administer a territory directly only under the Trusteeship System, there is no way in which a trust agreement for a territory under the United Nations administration can be terminated, except through the granting of independence to the territory. The achievement of the alternative goal of self-government, which is envisaged in Article 76 (b), is not grounds for the termination of the trusteeship status in this case, since the United Nations is not authorised to exercise such external control over a territory as would be needed for this, except under the Trusteeship System. Thus, the Organisation as administering authority has the duty to guide the trust territory under its control towards full independence, not merely towards self-government.

The provisions of Article 84 [11] do not apply in their entirety to the case where the Organisation is the administering authority. Whilst there is nothing irreconcilable in the United Nations having the duty to see that a territory plays 'its part in the maintenance of international peace and security,' the way in which this duty is elaborated presents difficulties. The administering authority is authorised to make use of 'volunteer forces, facilities, and assistance from the trust territory in carrying out the obligations towards the Security Council undertaken in this regard by the administering authority, as well as for local defence and the maintenance of law and order within the trust territory.'

[11] Article 84 reads as follows: 'It shall be the duty of the administering authority to ensure that the trust territory shall play its part in the maintenance of international peace and security. To this end the administering authority may make use of volunteer forces, facilities, and assistance from the trust territory in carrying out the obligations towards the Security Council undertaken in this regard by the administering authority, as well as for local defence and the maintenance of law and order within the trust territory.'

Since it is under Article 43 (1) that obligations are undertaken towards the Security Council involving forces, facilities and assistance for the maintenance of international peace and security, it is presumably to obligations under this article that Article 84 refers. By Article 43 (1), 'all Members of the United Nations, in order to contribute to the maintenance of international peace and security, undertake to make available to the Security Council, on its call and in accordance with a special agreement or agreements, armed forces, assistance, and facilities, including rights of passage, necessary for the purpose of maintaining international peace and security.' However, it is only Members of the United Nations who have undertaken obligations towards the Security Council under this article. The Organisation itself has undertaken no obligations towards the Security Council, and therefore the part of Article 84 referring to 'obligations towards the Security Council undertaken . . . by the administering authority' does not apply where the United Nations is the administering authority. In this case, Article 84 only specifically authorises the trust territory to play its part in the 'maintenance of international peace and security' through 'local defence and the maintenance of law and order within the trust territory.'

The use of volunteer forces, facilities and assistance for other than 'local defence and the maintenance of law and order within the trust territory' may, however, be arranged by special agreement. The Organisation may enter into a special agreement with the Security Council on behalf of the trust territory, by means of which agreement the administering authority undertakes to make available to the Security Council the forces, facilities and assistance of the territory, similarly to the way in which Member administering authorities do under Article 43 (1) and 84.

In view of the difficulties mentioned, it is not surprising that no trust agreements have been approved designating the Organisation as administering authority. It would appear that the doubts expressed at San Francisco concerning the practicability of direct international administration were not without foundation.[12]

Obligations of the Administering Authority

The obligations of the administering authority of a trust territory

12 See above, p. 208, and *U.N.C.I.O. Docs.*, Vol. 10, p. 499.

are derived from four sources: Chapter XI of the Charter, Chapters XII and XIII, the terms of the trust agreements, and other international instruments. A more controversial problem which has arisen in the practice of the United Nations is whether there is not a fifth source of obligations—United Nations resolutions.

Obligations under Chapter XI

All trust territories are necessarily non-self-governing, since trusteeship involves administration by other than the inhabitants of the territory, and since the goal of a trust territory is 'self-government or independence.' Therefore, Chapter XI of the Charter applies to trust territories. It was obviously intended that this should be the case, inasmuch as the drafters of the Charter saw it necessary specifically to exempt trust territories from the requirements of Article 73 (e), leaving the implication that the rest of Chapter XI did apply to them. Likewise, the *Report of the Rapporteur of Committee II/4* at the San Francisco Conference endorsed this view. It stated that the Declaration regarding Non-Self-Governing Territories applied to all dependent territories under the administration of a Member of the United Nations and not *merely* to those placed under trusteeship,[13] thus indicating that there was no doubt that it applied to trust territories. Members of the United Nations themselves are bound to apply Chapter XI in any trust territories they administer, by virtue of Article 2 (2) of the Charter.

The essence of Chapter XI is that *Members* of the United Nations undertake certain obligations with respect to any non-self-governing territories they administer. It is only Members who have obligations by reason of this Chapter; non-Member administering authorities, or the Organisation as administering authority, have none of these obligations unless they specifically agree to undertake them. The only example to date of an administering authority not being a Member of the United Nations has been Italy during the period from 1950 to 1955. In this case, no acceptance of the obligations under Chapter XI was undertaken by Italy with respect to the trust territory of Somaliland. In the text of the trust agreement, Italy undertakes to administer the territory in accordance with

[13] U.N.C.I.O. Doc. 1115, p. 3 (*U.N.C.I.O. Docs.*, Vol. 10, p. 599).

Chapters XII and XIII of the Charter,[14] but there is no mention of Chapter XI. However, the very detailed obligations which Italy undertakes in the Trust Agreement itself with regard to the welfare of the inhabitants of the territory go far beyond the obligations of Members of the United Nations under the provisions of Chapter XI.

Under Article 73, Members specifically recognise that the interests of the inhabitants of the dependent territories they administer are paramount. This is in direct contrast to Article 76 of Chapter XII where the interests of the inhabitants appear to have been made subordinate to those of the rest of the world.[15] The difference is actually one of emphasis since Chapter XII does not ignore the interests of the inhabitants,[16] and the obligation to maintain international peace and security arises out of Articles 1 and 2 and, therefore, applies to the administration by Members of territories under both Chapters XI and XII. The importance of Chapter XI is that it lays primary stress on the welfare of the dependent peoples themselves; it thus places a clear obligation on the Members of the United Nations administering trust territories to take cognisance of this welfare aspect.

Obligations under Chapters XII and XIII

The obligations of the administering authority under Chapters XII and XIII apply whatever the type of the administering authority. The provisions of Chapters XII and XIII must apply even to a non-Member or to the Organisation as administering authority; otherwise such administration cannot be said to be administration under the United Nations Trusteeship System. In the only example of a non-Member administration, a provision was included in the trust agreement in question specifically recognising the applicability of Chapters XII and XIII.[17] The special problems which would arise should the Organisation become an administering authority, and which lends serious doubts to the practicability of direct United Nations administration, have already been dealt with earlier in this chapter.[18]

14 Article 3 of the trust agreement for Somaliland (see *Official Records of the General Assembly,* Fifth Session, Suppl. No. 10, p. 5).

15 See further Chap. 4, pp. 54–55.

16 See Article 76 (b) and (c).

17 See Article 3 of the trust agreement for Somaliland.

18 See above, pp. 208–213.

The obligations of the administering authority arising out of Chapter XII are found in Articles 76 and 84. The obligation in Article 76 (a) to further international peace and security is substantially reinforced by Article 84, where it is made the positive *duty* of the administering authority to see that a trust territory plays its part in maintaining international peace and security. The trust territory is assigned a very active role, and the administering authority is instructed in the way in which the trust territory is to exercise this role. The duty of the administering authority is considerably lessened in the case where such an authority is a non-Member,[19] since a non-Member has undertaken no obligations towards the Security Council and therefore has no need of the assistance of the trust territory in carrying out such obligations.

By Article 76 (b) and (c), an administering authority is obligated to guide a trust territory towards 'self-government or independence,' and 'to encourage respect for human rights and fundamental freedoms for all.' These obligations are fairly straightforward and provide no complications except in the case of the Organisation as administering authority, when the goal of self-government becomes inapplicable.[20] The obligation of the administering authority to practice the open-door in a trust territory would lead to the ridiculous if strictly applied, for it would rule out any form of monopoly in a trust territory. This would prohibit the establishment by the administering authority of even such essential administrative monopolies as a Postal System, and presumably the clause 'without prejudice to the attainment of the foregoing objectives' was intended to prevent such absurdity. Many of the trust agreements specifically allow for the creation of essential administrative monopolies,[1] and this can be reconciled with the open-door principle by means of the above clause. The wording of Article 76 (d) is interesting in so

[19] Also in the case where the Organisation is the administering authority. See further above, pp. 208–213.

[20] See above, p. 212.

[1] Article 10 of the agreements for Tanganyika (*United Nations Treaty Series,* Vol. 8, p. 91), Ruanda-Urundi (*ibid.*, p. 105), British administered Cameroons (*ibid.*, p. 119), and British administered Togoland (*ibid.*, p. 151); Article 9 of the agreements for French administered Togoland (*ibid.*, p. 165), and French administered Cameroons (*ibid.*, p. 135); Article 16 of the agreement for Somaliland (*Official Records of the General Assembly,* Fifth Session, Suppl. No. 10, p. 8). See further, above, Chap. 6, pp. 109–110.

far as it affects a non-Member administering authority. The obligation is 'to ensure equal treatment in social, economic, and commercial matters for all *Members* of the United Nations and their nationals'[2]; it does not prevent the non-Member administering authority adopting preferential treatment for itself and its nationals. In the case of the trust agreement for Somaliland, this possibility was ruled out in so far as it affected Italian nationals,[3] but a preferential status for the Italian Government was possible so long as Italy remained a non-Member.

The obligations of an administering authority under Chapter XIII are much more specific than under Chapter XII. They arise out of Articles 86, 87 and 88. Under Article 86, Members of the United Nations who administer trust territories are obliged to 'designate one specially qualified person to represent it' in the Trusteeship Council. The wording of this article is clearly more than permissive inasmuch as it states that a Member 'shall' designate a representative. Under Articles 87 and 88, an administering authority is obliged to co-operate with the United Nations in the prescribed manner to enable the machinery of supervision to function satisfactorily. Thus, an administering authority has the duty of playing its part in the matters of annual reports, petitions and visiting missions.

'The administering authority for each trust territory within the competence of the General Assembly shall make an annual report to the General Assembly' upon the basis of a questionnaire prepared for this purpose by the Trusteeship Council.[4] Whether the administering authority for a strategic trust territory is obliged to make a similar report to the Security Council is not apparent at first. Article 88 clearly does not impose any obligations on the administering authority of a strategic trust territory; the question is whether Article 87 does so. Article 87 is concerned with outlining the functions of the General Assembly and Trusteeship Council, and it appears that they are permitted, but not compelled, to take action with respect to annual reports, petitions, and visiting missions. However, these are the only methods of supervision which the Charter specifically authorises, and if these are not used, no supervision is being exercised by the

2 Italics added.

3 See Article 15 of the trust agreement for Somaliland (*Official Records of the General Assembly,* Fifth Session, Suppl. No. 10, p. 8).

4 Article 88 of the Charter. See above, Chap. 10, pp. 182–189.

Organisation. This cannot be reconciled with Article 75 which says that the International Trusteeship System is established for the purpose of the administration and supervision of such territories as are placed under it. If either the administrative or supervisory aspect is missing, it would seem that this is not trusteeship as defined by the Charter. If it is United Nations trusteeship that is under consideration, then the United Nations must exercise its supervisory role over the trust territories, and this must be done in the manner prescribed in Article 87.

A possible interpretation of the permissive language used in the preamble to Article 87 is that it was adopted to coincide with paragraph (b)—the acceptance and examination of petitions by the Organisation. The discretion of the Organisation is needed in the case of the examination of the petitions, since many petitions may be outside the competence of the United Nations and therefore ought not to be examined by it. If the position is accepted that the Organisation is obliged to exercise supervision over the trust territories in the manner prescribed in Article 87, then it becomes apparent that the administering authorities have an obligation to act in such a manner as permits this supervision. Thus, even without Article 88, they must submit reports to the United Nations, since otherwise there would be no reports for the United Nations to examine. In the case of a strategic trust territory, Article 83 provides for the substitution of the Security Council in place of the General Assembly and Trusteeship Council. Thus, the obligation arising out of Article 87 for the administering authority to submit reports is for such reports to be submitted to the Security Council in the case of strategic trust territories.

Once the United Nations has decided that a petition is within its competence and that it requires examination, the administering authority has a duty to co-operate in this examination. This follows from the fact that the United Nations is empowered to examine petitions only in consultation with the administering authority. Any discretionary powers which arise from Article 87 in the matter of petitions do not belong to the administering authority but to the United Nations.[5] Once the Organisation has decided that a petition is within its competence and that it requires examination, the administering authority has a duty to

[5] See above, p. 189 *et seq.*

co-operate in this examination, since the United Nations is empowered to examine petitions only in consultation with the administering authority. The administering authority also has the duty of passing on to the United Nations any petitions from the trust territory which may be submitted through the administering authority. Likewise, the administering authority must do nothing to prevent the inhabitants of the trust territory from sending petitions to the United Nations.

The times at which the United Nations' periodic visits are to be made to trust territories are to be agreed upon with the administering authority.[6] This involves an obligation on the part of the administering authority to facilitate such visits once a time has been agreed upon. If the administering authority is a Member of the United Nations, this obligation is perhaps reinforced by Article 2 (5), where it is stated that 'all Members shall give the United Nations every assistance in any action it takes in accordance with the present Charter . . .' Whether this paragraph is of any relevance depends on the interpretation of the word 'action' as used here. An extensive interpretation would include in 'action' any resolution or recommendation adopted by a United Nations organ. Thus, by being required to 'give the United Nations every assistance in any action it takes . . .' all Members would be required to carry out every United Nations resolution or recommendation. It is questionable whether such is true. The most prevalent view is that 'action' referred to in Article 2 (5) refers only to enforcement action under Articles 39, 53 and 106.[7] In this case, Article 2 (5) is not relevant to the facilitating of United Nations' visits by the administering authorities.

Obligations under the terms of the trust agreements

As is stated in Article 81 of the Charter, the trust agreements must in each case include the terms under which the trust territory is to be administered. Thus, in addition to the obligations incumbent upon the administering authority by reason of the provisions of the Charter, supplementary obligations may arise out of the terms of the trust agreement itself. These are likely

[6] Article 87 (c).
[7] See Hans Kelsen, *The Law of the United Nations* (1951), p. 91; L. Goodrich and E. Hambro, *Charter of the United Nations, Commentary and Documents* (1949), pp. 107–108.

to be particular to the territory concerned. Obligations incurred by an administering authority under the terms of a trust agreement are binding only so long as they do not contravene the terms of the Charter. So far as Member administering authorities are concerned, this is clearly stated in Article 103 of the Charter, where it is provided that, in the case of conflict, their obligations under the Charter override those under any other international instrument. In the case of a non-Member administering authority the matter is not so clear, although the Organisation is certainly not entitled to approve a trust agreement which violates the provisions of the Charter. From the point of view of the non-Member administering authority, a good case can be made out for holding that its obligations under the trust agreement—to which it is a party, take precedence over the Charter provisions—to which the non-Member is not a party. However, if the obligations of the non-Member administering authority under the Charter conflict with those under the trust agreement, the latter are not permitted to override the former when this would be detrimental to the maintenance of international peace and security. The Organisation is required by Article 2 (6) to 'ensure that states which are not Members of the United Nations act in accordance with these Principles [the Principles in Article 2 of the Charter] so far as may be necessary for the maintenance of international peace and security.' Among these principles is the obligation to 'fulfil in good faith the obligations assumed . . . in accordance with the present Charter.'[8]

Article 2 (6), however, does not place any obligation on non-Members, it is upon the Organisation that the obligation rests—an obligation to ensure that non-Members act in a certain manner. As has been stated by Professor Goodrich and Dr. Hambro, 'the Charter does not of course create any legal obligations for non-Member States.'[9] It is therefore the Organ-

[8] Article 2 (2).

[9] L. Goodrich and E. Hambro, *Charter of the United Nations, Commentary and Documents* (1946), p. 70. See also the Second Edition published in 1949: 'It is doubtful whether an international instrument like the Charter can impose legal obligations on States which are not parties to it' (pp. 108–109). This general principle of *pacta tertiis nec nocent nec prosunt* was upheld by the Permanent Court of International Justice in its Order of 1929 concerning the *Free Zones of Upper Savoy and District of Gex:* 'in any event, Article 435 of the Treaty of Versailles is not binding on Switzerland, which is not a Party to this Treaty, except to the extent to which that country has itself accepted it' (*P.C.I.J.* Series A, No. 22, p. 17).

isation, not the non-Member administering authority, that is obligated to ensure that the Charter overrides the trust agreement when such is necessary for the maintenance of international peace and security. Professor Kelsen, on the other hand, holds that Article 2 (6) claims to be legally binding on non-Members.[10] However, included in the Principles of the Charter mentioned in Article 2 (6) is Article 2 (2). This latter obligates Members to 'fulfil in good faith the obligations assumed by them in accordance with the present Charter' in order to 'ensure to all of them the rights and benefits resulting from membership.' If Professor Kelsen's interpretation of Article 2 (6) is accepted, then under Article 2 (2) non-Members are required to fulfil obligations arising out of Article 2 (6) for a purpose that does not exist—since, by definition, non-Members have no 'rights and benefits resulting from membership.' This seems to be an indication that Article 2 (6) was not intended to place any legal obligations upon non-Members,[11] but rather obligations upon the Organisation.

Obligations under other international instruments

There are certain multilateral conventions which apply to the territories of a particular region. The most notable of these are the Berlin and Brussels Acts. These Acts imposed obligations on States administering territories in the 'Conventional Basin of the Congo.' Certain of the trust territories fall within the area covered by these treaties, and although they are not under the same administration as they were at the time of the conclusion of the treaties, the present administering authorities[12] were all parties to these treaties. Whilst any inconsistencies between these treaties and the United Nations Charter would clearly result in the provisions under the latter prevailing,[13] a different situation arises in the case of a clash between the provisions of such treaties as the Berlin and Brussels Acts and those of the trust agreements. Since the trust agreements are concluded between the United

10 H. Kelsen, *Sanctions in International Law under the Charter of the United Nations* (31 *Iowa Law Review*, 1946, pp. 499–543 at p. 502).

11 See further, J. L. Kunz, *Revolutionary Creation of Norms in International Law* (41 *American Journal of International Law*, 1947, pp. 119–126).

12 Belgium, France and the United Kingdom. The territories concerned were formerly under German rule.

13 Article 103 of the Charter.

Nations and the administering authority in each case, these trust agreements can only override a previous treaty between the same parties. Any obligations towards other parties previously incurred by an administering authority must prevail over its obligations under a trust agreement.

Obligations arising out of United Nations Resolutions

The question has arisen in the operation of the Trusteeship System whether the administering authorities are under any obligation to implement the resolutions of the General Assembly and Trusteeship Council. Inasmuch as it is through resolutions, in furtherance of the exercise of the means of supervision stated in Article 87, that the United Nations exercises its supervisory functions under the Trusteeship System,[14] this question assumes great importance. The Security Council is clearly authorised to make decisions binding on Members, and the obligation of an administering authority of a strategic area to implement such decisions is not in dispute.[15] It is only the resolutions of the General Assembly and Trusteeship Council which are considered here from the point of view of establishing obligations upon the administering authorities.

It is generally accepted that what powers the General Assembly possesses to make binding decisions do not extend to resolutions addressed to Members,[16] but are confined to resolutions such as those 'adopted under articles of the Charter by which the General Assembly is authorised to take specific action.'[17] Similarly, whilst certain articles of the Charter authorise the Trusteeship Council to take specific action of binding legal effect, such as the adoption of Rules of Procedure under Article 90 (1), such binding decisions do not cover resolutions addressed to Members. Moreover, nowhere in the Charter

14 See above, Chap. 10.

15 This is of no practical importance at the moment inasmuch as the only administering authority so affected can prevent the Security Council from making distasteful decisions through use of the veto.

16 See L. Goodrich and E. Hambro, *Charter of the United Nations: Commentary and Documents* (1949), pp. 151–152; H. Kelsen, *The Law of the United Nations* (1951), pp. 195–196.

17 F. B. Sloan, *The Binding Force of a Recommendation of the General Assembly of the United Nations* (23 *British Yearbook of International Law*, 1948, pp. 1–33 at p. 15). Examples of such resolutions are those admitting new Members to the Organisation, or electing members to the various Councils under Article 18 (2).

do Members in their capacity as administering authorities undertake to implement trusteeship resolutions. Therefore, if the administering authorities do have any obligation to implement General Assembly and Trusteeship Council resolutions, such obligation must arise from their particular relationship to the United Nations.

The question has been discussed frequently by both the General Assembly and the Trusteeship Council, notably in connection with the Use of the Flag of the United Nations in Trust Territories.[18] The fullest debate, however, occurred in 1950 when the General Assembly requested the Secretary-General to compile a report on the measures taken by Members to implement the resolutions of the General Assembly and Trusteeship Council. It was proposed that the following clause be inserted into the General Assembly's request: 'Considering that the administering authorities have a clear obligation to implement the resolutions of the General Assembly and the Trusteeship Council in matters relating to Chapters XII and XIII of the Charter.'[19] The argument in favour of this proposal was based on Article 75 of the Charter providing that 'the United Nations shall establish under its authority an international trusteeship system'; this provision was held to establish that ultimate authority over a trust territory rested with the United Nations, which implies that an administering authority acts as the agent of the United Nations in the administration of a trust territory.[20] If the clause quoted above is a correct statement of the administering authorities' obligations, then the General Assembly and Trusteeship Council possess legislative powers over trust territories, the role of the administering authorities being to administer this legislation (*i.e.*, the resolutions and recommendations). According to Article 75, however, the Trusteeship System was established 'for the administration and supervision' of trust territories. If it were intended that the United Nations should have a legislative position in regard to the administration of trust territories, then the

18 *Official Records of the General Assembly,* Fourth Session, Plenary Meetings, pp. 174–190; *ibid.,* Fourth Session, Fourth Committee, pp. 33–37; *Official Records of the Trusteeship Council,* Sixth Session, pp. 603–613.

19 *Official Records of the General Assembly,* Fifth Session, Fourth Committee, p. 84.

20 This view was expressed by the Philippine Delegate (*Official Records of the General Assembly,* Fourth Session, Fourth Committee, p. 33).

purpose of the Trusteeship System in Article 75 should have been stated as the 'administration of United Nations' legislation' in trust territories or the 'administration of trust territories under United Nations direction.' Supervision is not the same thing as legislation or direction and it does not imply the same binding powers. Furthermore, Article 75 only states that the *establishment* of the Trusteeship System shall be under United Nations' authority, it does not state that the actual *functioning* of the two elements of the System—administration and supervision—shall be under the authority of the United Nations. Article 75 may well be interpreted to mean that whilst the establishment of the Trusteeship System is solely within the powers of the United Nations, once the System is in operation the power and responsibility over trust territories is divided between the supervisory and administering authorities. Only where both these rôles are exercised by the United Nations (*i.e.*, when the Organisation acts as administering authority) does the United Nations exercise supreme authority over the trust territories and do United Nations resolutions acquire legislative force. The administering authority is not even subordinated to the United Nations to the extent of being assigned the duty to 'assist' the organs of the United Nations in the operation of the Trusteeship System, as the Trusteeship Council is obligated to 'assist' the General Assembly.[1] None of the other articles in the Trusteeship Chapters of the Charter define the relationship of the administering authority to the United Nations more precisely than Article 75, nor do they give any more reason to attribute legislative authority to the United Nations organs.

Article 81 states that 'the terms under which the trust territories will be administered' will be included in the trust agreements. In some of the trust agreements, the administering authorities undertake to apply to the territories such General Assembly resolutions as are appropriate to them.[2] Thus, an obligation to implement certain resolutions exists as a result of these trust agreements. It should be noted, however, 'that while a recommendation of the General Assembly may possess binding force by virtue of a special agreement between States, this legal effect is not derived from the recommendation itself but from

[1] See above, pp. 152–155.

[2] *e.g.*, Article 7 of the agreement for Tanganyika, see above, pp. 103–104.

the instrument in which the special agreement is found'[3]—in this case the trust agreement.

It thus seems reasonable to conclude that, in general, an administering authority is not bound to implement General Assembly or Trusteeship Council resolutions, except as a result of special agreement. This is not to say, however, that an administering authority is entitled to ignore such resolutions completely. Inasmuch as the administering authorities are supposed to administer trust territories under United Nations supervision, the view expressed by Judge Lauterpacht before the International Court of Justice provides a reasonable interpretation of the obligations of the administering authorities arising out of resolutions. In his Separate Opinion on *South-West Africa—Voting Procedure* (1955),[4] Judge Lauterpacht, whilst agreeing that General Assembly resolutions addressed to Members 'are not legally binding upon them in the sense that full effect must be given to them,'[5] strongly denies that these resolutions have no legal effect whatsoever. 'A Resolution recommending to an administering State a specific course of action creates *some* legal obligation which, however rudimentary, elastic and imperfect, is nevertheless a legal obligation and constitutes a measure of supervision. The State in question, while not bound to accept the recommendation, is bound to give it due consideration in good faith. If, having regard to its own ultimate responsibility for the good government of the territory, it decides to disregard it, it is bound to explain the reasons for its decision.'[6] Adopting this interpretation, the resolutions of the General Assembly fall short of legislation in that there is no compulsion to *implement* them, but at the same time the obligation to *consider* them exists. United Nations practice has shown that the administering authorities, whilst frequently refusing to implement resolutions, have generally explained the grounds for their non-compliance. This may result from their desire to justify their attitudes in the light of the political influence of United Nations resolutions, rather than from any recognition of their legal obligations in this

[3] F. B. Sloan, *op. cit.*, p. 18.
[4] Advisory Opinion of June 7, 1955, see *I.C.J. Reports 1955*, p. 67 *et seq.*
[5] *ibid.*, p. 118.
[6] *ibid.*, pp. 118–119.

respect.[7] In this case, it should be borne in mind, however, that through consistent practice a custom can develop whereby administering authorities become legally obliged to consider United Nations resolutions and explain any non-compliance.[8]

[7] Judge Lauterpacht considers that the latter is true, see *ibid.*, p. 119.

[8] For elaboration on the possibility of General Assembly resolutions becoming binding through custom, see F. B. Sloan, *op. cit.*, p. 21.

PART SIX

TRUSTEESHIP AND NON-SELF-GOVERNING TERRITORIES

CHAPTER 12

THE TRUSTEESHIP SYSTEM AND CHAPTER XI OF THE CHARTER

WHILST there is no doubt that the 'Declaration Regarding Non-Self-Governing Territories' embodied in Chapter XI of the Charter covers all dependent territories, both those inside and outside the Trusteeship System, the Trusteeship System itself is restricted to such dependent territories as have been specifically placed under it. The separateness of the two systems cannot be emphasised too strongly, in view of the disagreement which has arisen in the United Nations with regard to the nature of Chapter XI, and the relationship between it and Chapters XII and XIII. Were it not for such disagreement, a discussion of Chapter XI within a study of 'The Trusteeship System of the United Nations' would be merely incidental. The importance of Chapter XI from this point of view stems from the continual and persistent attempts in the United Nations to assimilate it into the Trusteeship System, and from concurrent opposing attempts to minimise the effect of Chapter XI.

THE NATURE OF CHAPTER XI

Chapter XI applies to all non-self-governing territories, whether or not they are placed under the International Trusteeship System. The obligations accepted by Members of the United Nations under Chapter XI came into force with the rest of the Charter, and were in no way contingent upon the conclusion of trust agreements or the establishment of the Trusteeship Council. This fact was never disputed, and the General Assembly's resolution at the First Part of its First Session noting that the provisions of Chapter XI of the Charter were already in force,[1] was merely expressing in words the general opinion of United Nations Members.

The main source of controversy in the United Nations with regard to non-self-governing territories, has been the extent of the

[1] *Resolutions adopted by the General Assembly during the First Part of its First Session*, p. 13, Resolution 9 (I).

obligations arising out of Chapter XI. The colonial powers asserted that, as its title suggests, Chapter XI was merely a unilateral declaration of principles by certain States for their guidance in governing dependent territories. This may have been the original intention at San Francisco inasmuch as this Chapter stems largely from the proposals of two colonial powers, Australia [2] and the United Kingdom,[3] but its embodiment in the Charter makes it more than a mere declaration: it is an integral part of a multilateral treaty capable of imposing obligations upon Members in the same way as any other part of the Charter. The terms of the provisions of Chapter XI leave no doubt that obligations are imposed upon Members responsible for the administration of non-self-governing territories. These Members 'accept as a sacred trust the obligation to promote to the utmost, within the system of international peace and security established by the present Charter, the well-being of the inhabitants of these territories.'[4] The way in which the 'well-being of the inhabitants' is to be promoted is elaborated in Article 73.[5] By Article 74, Members agree to apply the 'principle of good-neighbourliness' in their policy towards non-self-governing territories.[6]

Article 73 (e) imposes a very specific obligation upon Members of the United Nations, requiring them to submit regular information to the Secretary-General on non-self-governing territories not under the Trusteeship System.[7] It would seem that the Secretary-General himself is authorised to insist that he be supplied with this information, since Article 73 (e) requires that he receive it: if no information is forthcoming on a particular territory, then the Secretary-General cannot play the part assigned to him. The General Assembly is authorised to 'recommend' to Members that they transmit the information required under Article 73 (e), this power of recommendation stemming from Article 10. In this case, where there is an obligation on the

[2] U.N.C.I.O. Doc. 2, G/14 (1) (*U.N.C.I.O. Docs.*, Vol. 3, p. 543).
[3] U.N.C.I.O Doc. 2, G/26 (d) (*U.N.C.I.O. Docs.*, Vol. 3, p. 609).
[4] Preamble to Article 73.
[5] See below, Appendix.
[6] *ibid.*
[7] The supplying of information on dependent territories by the administering power has a precedent in the practice of the United Kingdom under the League of Nations. The United Kingdom Government was in the habit of sending copies of all colonial annual reports to Geneva for deposit in the League of Nations Library. (See Duncan Hall, *Mandates, Dependencies and Trusteeship* (1948), p. 63, n. 25.)

part of the Members concerned to act,[8] the 'recommendation' of the General Assembly assumes the character of a decision and is not mere advice to Members.[9] It is Article 10 which transforms Chapter XI into more than the unilateral declaration which the colonial Powers insist it is. Under this article, the General Assembly is authorised to discuss any matter within the scope of the Charter and to make recommendations to Members of the United Nations on any such matters. With this in mind, it is hard to see how any article in the Charter can be considered a mere unilateral declaration by Members, except where Article 2 (7) removes an article from the authority of the United Nations.[10] The right of the General Assembly under Article 10 extends to the discussion of any matter arising out of Chapter XI and to the making of recommendations with respect to it, subject only to the limitation of Article 2 (7).

The real problem is to decide to what extent Article 2 (7) limits the rights enjoyed by the General Assembly under Article 10. The administering Powers have continually held that non-self-governing territories are 'essentially within the domestic jurisdiction' of the administering State. This view was expressed by the United States Delegate who said that 'unless Non-Self-Governing Territories, through particular agreements, are brought under the trusteeship system, the United Nations has no authority to intervene in such territories. That authority remains with their own national government.'[11] A point to note is that Article 2 (7) refers to 'matters' within the domestic jurisdiction of a State, not to 'territories' within the domestic jurisdiction; therefore this article may prohibit the United Nations intervening in certain 'matters' concerning non-self-governing territories, but it does not remove the territories themselves from the field of the concern of the United Nations. One matter relating to non-self-governing territories with which the United Nations

[8] *i.e.*, to transmit information.

[9] It should be noted, however, that the legal basis of the obligation upon Members would be Article 73 (e) of the Charter, not the General Assembly's recommendation. See further above, p. 222 *et seq.*

[10] Article 2 (7) reads: 'Nothing contained in the present Charter shall authorise the United Nations to intervene in matters which are essentially within the domestic jurisdiction of any state or shall require the Members to submit such matters to settlement under the present Charter.'

[11] *Official Records of the General Assembly*, Second Part of the First Session, 64th Plenary Meeting, p. 1332.

has obviously a right to be concerned is the transmission of information under Article 73 (e). Since this information is required to be sent to the Secretary-General by Members, any failure on their part to do so is of concern to the United Nations and as such may be discussed by the General Assembly, who may adopt recommendations on this matter. Furthermore, under Article 73, Members of the United Nations responsible for non-self-governing territories undertake certain obligations with regard to the administration of these territories,[12] and in Article 2 (2) Members undertake to fulfil the obligations assumed by them in the Charter. This is especially important inasmuch as Article 2 enumerates the principles of the United Nations, and for violation of these principles a Member may be expelled from the Organisation by the 'General Assembly upon the recommendation of the Security Council.'[13] In order to be able to determine whether the principle of the Charter expounded in Article 2 (2) is being violated, the General Assembly must be able to discuss whether the obligations assumed by Members under Article 73 are being fulfilled. Only by discussing non-self-governing territories can this be done. Therefore in discussing matters under Chapter XI, the United Nations is not intervening in matters which are essentially within the domestic jurisdiction of States; these matters are equally within the jurisdiction of the United Nations. However, this does not sanction the intervention of the United Nations in matters regarding non-self-governing territories which are not essential for discovering whether Members are fulfilling their obligations under Article 73. Such matters may well be subject to Article 2 (7).[14]

Although there was no doubt that the provisions of Chapter XI came into force with the Charter as a whole, there was considerable difficulty in deciding to whom these provisions applied. Whilst the title of Chapter XI refers to non-self-governing terri-

[12] See above, p. 229 *et seq.*

[13] Article 6.

[14] *e.g.*, the attempts to get the United Nations to deal directly with the non-self-governing peoples without going through the administering authorities (see proposal that the General Assembly should request the Economic and Social Council to convoke a conference of non-self-governing peoples to which Chap. XI applies: *Official Records of the General Assembly*, Second Part of the First Session, Sixth Committee, Annex 18, p. 285), and the attempts to assimilate non-self-governing territories into the Trusteeship System without trust agreements having been concluded (see below, p. 239 *et seq.*).

tories, nowhere is there any definition of what comprises a non-self-governing territory. One certainty, however, is that Chapter XI applies only to 'non-self-governing territories' under the control of a Member of the United Nations. This becomes obvious in reading Article 73 in which 'Members of the United Nations which have or assume responsibilities for the administration of territories whose peoples have not yet attained a full measure of self-government . . .' recognise and accept certain principles, and Article 74 in which 'Members of the United Nations also agree . . .' to base their policies on the principle of good-neighbourliness. The essence of Chapter XI is that *Members* of the United Nations undertake certain obligations; the non-self-governing territories are merely the recipients of the benefits of these obligations. Even were Chapter XI not worded in this manner it could not be held to apply to territories under the control of non-Members, since the latter are not signatories to the Charter and therefore cannot be bound by it.

Chapter XI does not include in its definition of a non-self-governing territory, non-self-governing minority groups within a metropolitan State. This has been a constant source of grievance to the colonial States, who feel that they are being singled out from among a much larger group of States who morally, if not legally according to Chapter XI, are responsible for the administration of territories 'whose peoples have not yet attained a full measure of self-government.' It is evident from the records of the United Nations that this opinion was held by the colonial Powers as far back as 1946,[15] but it did not assume much prominence until it appeared in the form of the 'Belgian Thesis' in 1952. The essence of this 'Thesis' is that Chapter XI applies to backward indigenous, minority and other unassimilated non-self-governing groups within a metropolitan territory as much as to colonial areas.[16] Whilst this view has much to commend it

[15] See view expressed by the United Kingdom Delegate to the Fourth Committee in 1946: 'the adoption of this resolution (recognising Chapter XI as already in force), however, would not completely dispose of the problem of Non-Self-Governing Peoples. There were subject peoples within sovereign States, for whom the United Nations must care as it had for peoples under the control of imperial Powers' (*Official Records of the General Assembly,* First Part of First Session, Fourth Committee, p. 34).

[16] See *Official Records of the General Assembly,* Seventh Session, Fourth Committee, p. 23; *ibid.,* Ninth Session, Fourth Committee, p. 150. See also the document submitted by the Belgian Government to the Secretary-General in reply to General Assembly Resolution 567 (VI)

de lege ferenda, it can scarcely be considered *lex lata*: the wording of Article 74 distinguishes non-self-governing territories from metropolitan territories, and Article 2 (1) ('The Organisation is based on the principle of the sovereign equality of all its Members') read with Article 2 (7) (the domestic jurisdiction clause) does not sanction interference in the internal affairs of a State, except where there is a threat to the peace, or where a State specifically agrees to permit interference. The San Francisco records give no indication that the participating States intended to include metropolitan areas within Chapter XI, and therefore no agreement to permit United Nations interference therein can be assumed.

In 1946, Members were asked to give their opinions on the factors which should be taken into consideration in determining which were the non-self-governing territories,[17] and to enumerate those under their control. At first, disputes arose, not over the failure of Members to list *all* their non-self-governing territories as one might have expected, but from Members enumerating territories which it was claimed by other Members they had no right to include.[18] Later this situation was reversed when Members ceased to transmit information on territories which it was felt fell within Chapter XI. Certain colonial Powers claimed that territories under their control had advanced beyond the stage where they could be considered non-self-governing. This raised the fundamental questions of who is competent to decide what constitutes a non-self-governing territory—the United Nations or the administering Power, and what conditions must be fulfilled to remove a territory from this category. The French

requesting the opinion of Members on factors to be taken into account in deciding whether a territory is or is not one in which the inhabitants are still non-self-governing (6 *Chronique de Politique Étrangère,* No. 4, July 1953, pp. 530–538).

17 Letter from the Secretary-General, dated June 29, 1946 (see *Yearbook of the United Nations,* 1946–1947, p. 208).

18 Argentina claimed that the United Kingdom had no right to include the Falkland Islands amongst her dependencies since Argentina did not recognise British sovereignty here (*Official Records of the General Assembly,* First Part of the Third Session, Fourth Committee, p. 7). Guatemala claimed the same as regards British Honduras (*ibid.,* p. 23). The Soviet Union called attention to the inclusion of information on Indonesia by the Netherlands Government, and proposed that since the Republic of Indonesia had been established as an independent State the information should not be considered (*ibid.,* p. 22).

Government felt that 'the determination of territories whose peoples have not yet attained a full measure of self-government lies exclusively within the competence of the states which have responsibilities for the administration of such territories.'[19] The United States expressed a similar view when explaining its action in ceasing to transmit information on the Panama Canal Zone.[20] The United Kingdom went further, stating that since economic, social and educational conditions in Malta were now the exclusive concern of the Government of Malta, the United Kingdom found it 'inappropriate, and indeed impossible' to continue to transmit information under Article 73 (e).[1]

The view of the United Kingdom is one which raises an interesting point. If the United Nations is to decide when a territory is no longer non-self-governing, then the administering Power must retain enough control over the territory to be able to provide information for the United Nations. It might well be argued that such a course, in delaying self-government, would be running contrary to the Charter. The view, however, of the non-colonial States was that once the General Assembly had accepted the list of non-self-governing territories, then only the General Assembly itself had the right to determine when these territories no longer fell within this category. The General Assembly itself endorsed this view at its Fourth Session in 1949.[2] The discussion was continued in 1950 when the Netherlands announced that it was no longer transmitting information on Indonesia to the

19 Letter from the French Government to the Secretary-General, dated April 29, 1949 (Doc. A/915) (see *Yearbook of the United Nations, 1948–1949*, pp. 730–731).

20 Note from the Government of the United States to the Secretary-General, dated August 18, 1949 (see *Yearbook of the United Nations, 1948–1949*, p. 731).

1 Letter from the United Kingdom Government to the Secretary-General, dated March 16, 1949 (see *ibid.*, p. 730). See also a statement by the Netherlands Delegate to the General Assembly in 1954, concerning the cessation of information on Surinam and the Netherlands Antilles: 'Legally the Netherlands Government had no right to interfere with the complete self-government of the Netherlands Antilles and Surinam on the matters mentioned in Article 73 (e) . . . To transmit such information the Netherlands Government would first have to obtain it from the Governments of Surinam and the Netherlands Antilles, and, as the representatives of those countries had informed the Fourth Committee . . . their Governments and Parliaments were not prepared to furnish such information since, in their opinion, that would constitute an infringement of their autonomy' (*Official Records of the General Assembly*, Ninth Session, Fourth Committee, p. 226).

2 *Official Records of the General Assembly*, Fourth Session, Resolution 334 (IV).

Secretary-General, since sovereignty had been transferred to the Republic of Indonesia. In this case, however, the United Nations had tangible proof of this: Indonesia had been admitted to the United Nations and was therefore by definition a self-governing State.

Although both the Fourth Committee and the Committee on Information from Non-Self-Governing Territories[3] have set up committees to consider the problem of what is a non-self-governing territory and at what stage it might be said to have become 'self-governing,' the question has not been settled. The General Assembly, in 1953, adopted a list of factors for guidance in this matter,[4] at the same time instructing the Committee on Information to continue studying the question. The colonial Powers objected to this list of factors which the General Assembly had adopted, reiterating the view that final responsibility for determining when a territory had reached full self-government lay not with the United Nations but with the administering Power concerned.[5] However, the General Assembly's list of factors was realistic in that it was flexible. It recognised that 'self-government' is not a specific term but that it may take several forms. Three forms specifically mentioned were independence,[6] some other separate system of self-government, or a free association of the territory 'on an equal basis with the metropolitan or other country as an integral part of that country or in any other form.'[7] Thus the way was paved for some self-

[3] This Committee was established by General Assembly Resolution 332 (IV) for a three-year period, renewed for further three-year periods in 1952 and 1955. In 1952, its name was changed from the 'Special Committee on Information Under Article 73 (e)' to the 'Committee on Information from Non-Self-Governing Territories.'

[4] See *Official Records of the General Assembly,* Eighth Session, Suppl. No. 17, p. 21, Resolution 742 (VIII).

[5] See *Official Records of the General Assembly,* Eighth Session, Fourth Committee, pp. 40, 65, 67. A practical use of this argument came from the United States Government who, on January 19, 1953, informed the Secretary-General that since the Puerto Rican constitution had come into force, establishing a commonwealth status for the Caribbean Island, it was no longer 'necessary or appropriate' for the United States to continue to submit information (U.N. Doc. A/AC.35/L. 121 of 1953). The cessation of information was approved at the next session of the General Assembly, but not the right of the United States to decide unilaterally.

[6] One is reminded of the attempts at San Francisco to insert the goal of independence into Article 73 (b) (see *Summary Report of the Sixth Meeting of Committee II/4, U.N.C.I.O. Docs.,* Vol. 10, p. 452).

[7] By the end of 1955, three instances of the achievement of self-government without independence had been approved by the General

governing status such as within the British Commonwealth or within a federal system, all this provided that the dependent peoples enter freely into the new arrangement and that they are self-governing.

According to the list adopted by the General Assembly, the factors to be considered in determining whether a territory has reached independence consist of its international status and the degree of internal self-government. The first factor relates to the attainment of external sovereignty by the territory—its recognition as a sovereign State by the international community; the second factor relates to the nature of the government of the territory. Thus it is self-government in the Western sense, democratic self-government involving political self-determination. Since, by Article 73 (b), Members of the United Nations are obligated to develop self-government in all their non-self-governing territories, the granting of a form of independence to a territory which does not include internal self-government is not permitted; hence the inclusion of the second factor in determining independence.[8] In determining the attainment of some 'other separate system of self-government' by a territory, the two factors mentioned above are supplemented by a collection of 'general' factors, these latter including the opinion of the population, their political advancement and other similar matters. It is not clear why these additional factors are included here separately, since they would appear to be an integral part of the consideration of the attainment of 'internal self-government.' With regard to the achievement of self-government within the metropolitan or other country, the same 'general' factors as for the achievement of self-government are to be considered. In place of the international status of the territory, the status of the territory within the federal or other structure is to be considered. In place of internal self-government, 'internal constitutional conditions' are substituted. However, since the territory must be developed towards self-government, these 'internal constitutional conditions' must constitute self-government.

Assembly: Puerto Rico—now a self-governing entity in political association with the United States as regards foreign affairs (General Assembly Resolution 748 (VIII)); Greenland—now integrated with Denmark (General Assembly Resolution 849 (IX)); the Netherlands Antilles and Surinam—now two self-governing integral parts of the Kingdom of the Netherlands (General Assembly, Resolution 945 (X)).

8 See further above, Chap. 4, pp. 57–58.

Relationship with the Trusteeship System

Whilst Chapter XI applies to all non-self-governing territories under the control of Members of the United Nations, the International Trusteeship System is limited in its operation to territories which have been specifically placed thereunder. In spite of attempts by certain Members to establish that the Trusteeship System should apply to *all* non-self-governing territories,[9] this was obviously not the intention of the drafters of the Charter. If it was intended that all non-self-governing territories should be brought under trusteeship, then it is difficult to explain the inclusion of Article 73 (e) in the Charter. For Article 73 (e) specifically exempts Members from sending information to the Secretary-General on trust territories under their administration; if all non-self-governing territories were intended to become trust territories, then Article 73 (e) is superfluous.

There is no doubt that Chapter XI does apply to all trust territories under the administration of a Member of the United Nations. When the Charter came into operation there were no trust territories, since specific agreements were required for their creation. Therefore those territories which subsequently became trust territories were non-self-governing immediately prior to being placed under trusteeship. As the General Assembly recognised in a resolution adopted during the First Part of its First Session,[10] Chapter XI came into force with the rest of the Charter and Members of the United Nations immediately assumed obligations with regard to their non-self-governing territories. Among these territories were the majority of those that were subsequently placed under the Trusteeship System. The obligations assumed under Chapter XI with regard to these territories did not cease once they were placed under trusteeship; Members placing territories under trusteeship were assuming additional obligations. The obligations previously assumed under Chapter XI were in no way diminished except in so far as concerns Article 73 (e).

Ever since 1945, there has been dissatisfaction concerning Chapter XI among certain Members of the United Nations.

9 *e.g.*, India asked for the extension of the Trusteeship System to all or some of the non-self-governing territories in 1947 (see *Official Records of the General Assembly*, Second Session, Fourth Committee, Annex 5a, pp. 217–218).

10 *Resolutions Adopted by the General Assembly during the First Part of its First Session*, p. 13, Resolution 9 (I).

This has been due to the fact that no special machinery for the supervision of non-self-governing territories, other than those placed under the Trusteeship System, was provided by the Charter. The provisions of Chapter XI rested to a large extent on the good faith of the colonial Powers for their realisation. This was a most unsatisfactory situation from the point of view of some of the non-colonial Powers, who turned their attention towards the more exacting provisions of Chapters XII and XIII.

Attempts to Alter this Relationship

The dissatisfaction felt by many Members of the United Nations with the lack of supervisory machinery in Chapter XI, resulted in attempts by them to alter the relationship established by the Charter between this Chapter and the International Trusteeship System. These attempts have been to assimilate Chapter XI into the Trusteeship System, at first by direct methods, and when these failed by indirect methods. At the same time there has been a notable tendency on the part of the colonial Powers to underestimate the legal effect of Chapter XI. The frequency with which Article 2 (7) has been invoked to remove dependent territories from the scrutiny of the United Nations has alarmed certain of the non-colonial Powers, and this has resulted in an intensification of their efforts to get all non-self-governing territories placed under the Trusteeship System.

At the Second Session of the General Assembly, India introduced a draft resolution into the Fourth Committee stating that 'whereas at the time of the creation of the United Nations it was intended that non-self-governing territories be voluntarily placed under the International Trusteeship System by States responsible for their administration and such intention was embodied in Article 77 (c) of the Charter of the United Nations . . . the General Assembly Resolves that Members of the United Nations responsible for the administration of such territories be requested to submit Trusteeship Agreements for all or some of such territories as are not ready for immediate self-government.'[11] Although this proposal was defeated in the General Assembly, the closeness of the vote startled the colonial powers. Another less direct, but hardly less obvious attempt to assimilate Chapter XI into the Trusteeship System occurred when Poland proposed

[11] *Official Records of the General Assembly,* Second Session, Fourth Committee, pp. 217–218, Annex 5a.

to the Third Session of the General Assembly that in cases where an administrative union between a trust and a non-self-governing territory was in the interests of the peoples concerned, the non-self-governing territory included in it should be brought under the Trusteeship System.[12] Whilst these attempts to place non-self-governing territories under trusteeship failed, other indirect means were being employed to accomplish the same end.

At the Sixty-Fourth Meeting of the General Assembly, the United Kingdom Delegate stated that 'the Charter itself provides no organ for the supervision of the application of Chapter XI.' Whilst it is true that the Charter provides no *special* organ for this purpose, it is not correct to say that it provides no organ. Under Article 10, the General Assembly is authorised to concern itself with Chapter XI. Similarly, Article 22 permits the General Assembly to establish a special organ to assist it in this.

The trend to narrow down the differences between the two systems began when the General Assembly assigned matters concerning non-self-governing territories to its Fourth Committee, the same committee that deals with the Trusteeship System. Following upon this, consideration was given to the possibility of having the information submitted to the Secretary-General under Article 73 (e) examined by some organ of the United Nations. Cuba proposed that this should be undertaken by the Trusteeship Council,[13] but the proposal was objected to and overruled. However, in the case of South-West Africa, a report from a non-trust territory was examined by the Trusteeship Council, although it is difficult to justify this action legally. As the Soviet Delegate pointed out, the examination of the report on South-West Africa by the Trusteeship Council could not be justified by any article of the Charter, because the only article which authorises the Trusteeship Council to examine a report is Article 87 (a) which concerns only reports from trust territories.[14]

12 *Official Records of the General Assembly,* First Part of the Third Session, Fourth Committee, Annexes to the Summary Records of Meetings, pp. 9–10.

13 *Official Records of the General Assembly,* Second Part of the First Session, Fourth Committee, Part III, Sub-Committee 2, p. 89.

14 See *Report of the Trusteeship Council to the General Assembly Covering its Second and Third Sessions,* p. 42 (*Official Records of the General Assembly,* Third Session, Suppl. No. 4).

Establishment of a Special Organ for Chapter XI

Although it was obvious that the illegality of having the Trusteeship Council examine reports from non-self-governing territories would prevent the General Assembly agreeing to make a practice of this, the matter was not dropped by Members. Proposals were made for the General Assembly to establish a special organ for this purpose, a course permitted by Article 22 of the Charter. There is no doubt of the legality of the General Assembly's establishing a special committee; the doubt lies in whether the information transmitted by Members under Article 73 (e) may be examined at all. According to the Charter, the information is to be transmitted to the Secretary-General for *information* purposes; nothing is said about its being examined, or about the Secretary-General passing it on to some organ of the United Nations.[15] However, it can be argued that only by having this information examined can it be ascertained whether the principles in Chapter XI are being put into practice, since no other machinery of supervision exists.

After a previous unsuccessful attempt, a Cuban proposal to establish a special committee to receive and examine the information transmitted under Article 73 (e) was accepted by the General Assembly in 1946. An *ad hoc* Committee was established composed of an equal number of Members transmitting information and representatives elected by the General Assembly,[16] the similarity to the Trusteeship Council being evident. In 1947, a Special Committee on Information Transmitted under Article 73 (e) was established,[17] identical to the *ad hoc* Committee of the previous year.

Special Committees continued to be established for fixed

15 At the First Session of the General Assembly, the administering Powers had consented to the information transmitted under Article 73 (e) being summarised and analysed and thus brought to the attention of the Assembly (see *Resolutions Adopted by the General Assembly During the First Part of its First Session*, p. 13). However, they opposed any form of United Nations supervision over colonial territories, holding that 'there is no warrant for such supervision in the Charter' (see Gt. Britain, Colonial Office: *Information on Non-Self-Governing Territories: Memorandum by the Colonial Office on Proceedings in the General Assembly of the United Nations*, 1947, p. 3 (Colonial No. 228)).

16 *Official Records of the General Assembly*, Second Part of the First Session, Resolution 66 (I).

17 *Official Records of the General Assembly*, Second Session, Resolution 146 (II).

periods of time, at first for one-year periods [18] and then in 1949 for a three-year period.[19] In 1952 the title was changed to the Committee on Information from Non-Self-Governing Territories [20]; the omission of the word 'special' in the title may well have been a subtle move towards permanency. In 1952, the General Assembly was faced again with the problem of this Committee. A proposal that it continue on a permanent basis so long as there existed any territories which were non-self-governing was not unexpectedly opposed by France,[1] Belgium,[2] and the United Kingdom,[3] who announced that they could not undertake to participate in the work of the Committee if it were placed on a permanent or quasi-permanent basis. The United Kingdom added that the establishment of a permanent Committee would constitute an attempt to transform non-self-governing territories into trust territories, despite the clear distinction between them established by the Charter.[4] The final decision was merely to continue the Committee for a further three-year period, during which time Belgium ceased to participate in its work and France announced her intention of doing the same.[5] In 1955, the Committee was again renewed for a three-year period on exactly the same basis as before,[5a] after the United Kingdom had announced that she would continue participation in the Committee only on these terms. Proposals for the creation of a permanent committee were again defeated.

18 *Official Records of the General Assembly,* Second Session, Resolution 146 (II), and Third Session, Resolution 219 (III).

19 *Official Records of the General Assembly,* Fourth Session, Resolution 332 (IV).

20 *Official Records of the General Assembly,* Sixth Session, Resolution 569 (VI).

1 *Official Records of the General Assembly,* Seventh Session, Fourth Committee, p. 108.

2 *ibid.*, p. 111.

3 *ibid.*, p. 109.

4 *Official Records of the General Assembly,* Seventh Session, 402nd Plenary Meeting, p. 344.

5 In a communication to the Chairman of the Committee on Information, dated August 14, 1953, the Belgian Delegation announced its decision not to participate in the Committee's work further (Doc. A/AC.35/L. 142). At a meeting of the French Cabinet on October 2, 1955, following the vote in the General Assembly to include Algeria on the agenda of the Tenth Session, the Minister for Overseas France announced that France would no longer furnish to the Secretary-General information under Article 73 (e) nor participate in the Committee's discussions (see *Le Monde,* October 4, 1955, p. 3, col. 5).

5a *Official Records of the General Assembly, Tenth Session,* Resolution 933 (X).

Scope of the Information Transmitted under Article 73 (e)

Controversy arose over the scope of the information to be transmitted and the use to which it might be put. The colonial Powers, adopting a strict interpretation of Article 73 (e), held that only the classes of information enumerated therein—educational, economic and social—were required[6] and that these were to be used for information purposes only.[7] They held that any other course was contrary to the 'domestic jurisdiction' clause in Article 2 (7). It was argued by the non-colonial Powers that the United Nations required additional information to ascertain the extent to which the obligations undertaken in Articles 73 and 74 were being carried out. For the first year it was left to the individual States to determine what information to provide, but this did not last long. The *ad hoc* Committee, once established, decided that the information so far transmitted did not give a clear enough picture of life in the territories; it thereupon proceeded to draw up a Standard Form[8] for the guidance of Members transmitting information—an obvious similarity to the Questionnaire of the Trusteeship System.

With the adoption of the Standard Form by the General Assembly began the attempts to go beyond the requirements of Article 73 (e) and extract political information from the colonial Powers. An optional category of questions was included in the Standard Form, designed to discover the extent of indigenous participation in the administration of the territories and the extent to which racial discrimination affected this participation. A few States furnished information in this optional category stressing, however, the purely voluntary nature of their actions. Other States ignored this section, fearful of creating an unhealthy precedent which could later be used to their disadvantage. The next move was to get the questions in the optional category transferred to the compulsory category, against the arguments of the colonial Powers who said that such a course would go beyond the Charter.[9] In spite of these objections, the General

6 *Official Records of the General Assembly,* Second Part of the First Session, Fourth Committee, Part III; Sub-Committee II, pp. 12–13.

7 *ibid.*, pp. 25–26.

8 Doc. A/385 of September 18, 1947.

9 See discussion in the Fourth Committee at the Fourth Session of the General Assembly (*Official Records of the General Assembly,* Fourth Session, Fourth Committee, pp. 138–142).

Assembly adopted a resolution which recommended that when the revision of the Standard Form was undertaken, general information on geography, history, people and human rights would cease to be classified under the optional category. At the same time it expressed the hope that Members who had not already done so would include details of the government of their non-self-governing territories in their reports.[10] When the Revised Standard Form was adopted in 1951,[11] only political information was left in the optional category, everything else being transferred to the compulsory category. A resolution of the Third Session of the General Assembly considered that it was essential that the United Nations be informed of any changes in the constitutional position and status of any non-self-governing territory, as a result of which the responsible Government concerned thought it unnecessary to continue to transmit information under Article 73 (e).[12] The Members concerned were requested to furnish the Secretary-General, within six months, with such information as may be appropriate including the constitution, legislative act or executive order providing for the government of the territory, and the relationship of the territory to the Government of the metropolitan country. This was another attempt to establish the authority of the United Nations over political developments of the non-self-governing territories.

When the Revised Standard Form was adopted on December 7, 1951,[13] the similarity to the Questionnaire of the Trusteeship System, which had been noticeable when the original Standard Form was adopted, was even more pronounced. The questions in the Revised Standard Form were more detailed and many ideas gathered from the Trusteeship Council's Questionnaire had crept in. The questions were divided into categories under headings similar to those used in the Questionnaire, and the main distinction between the Questionnaire and the Revised Standard Form lay in the fact that political questions were grouped in an optional category under the latter.

10 *Official Records of the General Assembly,* Fourth Session, Resolution 327 (IV).

11 *Official Records of the General Assembly,* Sixth Session, Resolution 551 (VI).

12 *Official Records of the General Assembly,* Third Session, Resolution 222 (III).

13 *Official Records of the General Assembly,* Sixth Session, Suppl. No. 20, pp. 40–54, Resolution 551 (VI).

Use of the Information Transmitted

Although Article 73 (e) states that the information to be transmitted is for the purpose of information, it does not restrict its use to information purposes *only*. However, it is arguable that Article 73 (e) should be interpreted strictly to impose the least obligation on the administering Powers; this interpretation would mean that the administering Powers are obligated to transmit information *only* for information purposes. In practice, the United Nations has not recognised any restriction on the use of the information. A procedure similar to that of the Trusteeship System is followed, in which the information is analysed and summarised by the Secretariat and then examined by the Special Committee. The Specialised Agencies are authorised to co-operate with the Committee in an advisory capacity, as is the Economic and Social Council. This again is similar to the procedure permitted in the Trusteeship Council. The Secretary-General is empowered by an Assembly resolution to make use of all relevant and comparable official information communicated to the United Nations and the Specialised Agencies on economic, social, and educational conditions in dependent territories, in order to provide a better means of assessing the information transmitted.[14]

Attempts to Introduce Petitions into Chapter XI

Another tendency which started harmlessly enough but which has developed into an issue, has been the attempt to give the inhabitants of non-self-governing territories a voice in the work of the international organisation. This began in November 1946 in the General Assembly, when the Delegate of the Philippines suggested that a conference system be set up for the representatives of non-self-governing peoples to which Chapter XI applies. The proposal as originally submitted[15] met so many legal objections in both the General Committee and the Legal Committee that it was withdrawn and a revised resolution submitted. The resolution finally adopted by the General Assembly merely recom-

14 *Official Records of the General Assembly,* Third Session, Resolution 218 (III).

15 A proposal to include on the General Assembly's agenda a request that the Economic and Social Council call such a conference and subsequently submit a report thereon to the General Assembly (*Official Records of the General Assembly,* Second Part of the First Session, Sixth Committee, Annex 18, p. 285).

mended to Members having responsibility for non-self-governing territories that they set up regional commissions to give means of expression to the traditions, wishes and aspirations of non-self-governing peoples.[16]

There was nothing new in this resolution as it was proposed that the commissions should be along the lines of the already existent Caribbean Commission. Matters were not allowed to rest there, however. Next came an attempt to allow indigenous participation in the work of the United Nations itself, although there is no authorisation for this in the Charter. An attack was launched in the General Assembly in 1951 to get indigenous participation in the work of the Special Committee, simultaneously with a parallel move to associate the indigenous inhabitants of trust territories in the work of the Trusteeship Council.[17] The Special Committee was invited to examine the possibility of associating the non-self-governing territories more closely in its work,[18] and to report to the next session of the General Assembly, when a resolution was adopted inviting Members to make possible the participation of qualified indigenous representatives in the work of the Committee.[19] Many arguments against this resolution were advanced by the administering Powers. They argued that the proposal implied dual representation of States on the General Assembly's committees[20] which should remain associations of sovereign governments. They further argued that the committees of the General Assembly should not be converted into tribunals in which Member States would be confronted by the indigenous inhabitants of the territories they administered.[1] But the main reason was not stated, which was that the administering Powers feared that this would prove to be a back-door way in which to introduce the practice of petitions—an integral part of the Trusteeship System—into the realm of non-self-

16 *Official Records of the General Assembly,* Second Part of the First Session, Resolution 67 (I), p. 126.

17 *Official Records of the General Assembly,* Sixth Session, Resolution 554 (VI).

18 *ibid.,* Resolution 556 (VI).

19 *Official Records of the General Assembly,* Seventh Session, Resolution 647 (VII).

20 See view of the Australian Delegate (*Official Records of the General Assembly,* Seventh Session, Fourth Committee, p. 140), the United Kingdom Delegate (*ibid.,* p. 133), and the French Delegate (*ibid.,* p. 134). See also *Official Records of the General Assembly,* Seventh Session, Plenary Meetings, pp. 342–356.

1 *ibid.,* p. 344.

governing territories. The view was expressed that the only way in which the inhabitants could be associated in the work of the Committee was through the inclusion of one of their representatives on the delegation of the administering Member. In answer to this, it was argued that such a course would be impracticable since the Member State alone had the right to determine the composition of its delegation.[2] This argument appears to rest on sound legal grounds, since it is the State as a single entity that is a Member of the United Nations and is therefore entitled to be represented on the United Nations organs as such. There is no requirement in the Charter that sectional or interest groups within the Member State should be represented. In actual fact, the attempts to associate representatives of the non-self-governing territories in the work of the United Nations have not been successful.

• • • •

In spite of these attempts to produce a system to deal with non-self-governing territories under Chapter XI as similar as possible to the Trusteeship System, and in spite of the partial success of these attempts, the two systems remain separate. They were intended to be separate by the drafters of the Charter, and for this reason Chapter XI does not belong in a study of the United Nations Trusteeship System except in so far as this Chapter affects the trust territories themselves.

[2] *ibid.*, pp. 342–356.

Chapter 13

CONCLUSION

The trusteeship provisions of the Charter were designed to provide three things: a successor to the Mandates System of the League of Nations; a system to deal with territories detached from the enemy in the Second World War; and some recognition of the need 'to treat the welfare of dependent peoples as a matter not only of local but of international concern.'[1] These three purposes are reflected in the article of the Charter naming the categories of territories eligible for Trusteeship.[2] Therein provision is made for the placing under the Trusteeship System of former mandates, ex-enemy territories and 'territories voluntarily placed under the system by states responsible for their administration.'

As might have been expected, no state has viewed the Trusteeship System as an advance over its own colonial system, and, therefore, no use has been made of this third category. To the despair of the non-colonial Powers, the dependencies of Member States have remained outside the Trusteeship System—the object of international concern only to the extent that they are covered by the Declaration Regarding Non-Self-Governing Territories in Chapter XI of the Charter. For this reason there have been persistent attempts in the General Assembly to strengthen Chapter XI by assimilating it into the Trusteeship System. Whilst the attempts at assimilation have not been successful, Chapter XI has proved to be more than a mere declaration of general principles for the guidance of colonial powers. A system bearing strong similarities to the Trusteeship System has been created for non-trust dependent territories: non-permanent but nevertheless continuous committees have been established to receive and discuss information on the territories transmitted by the administering Powers—this information to be compiled on the basis of a Standard Form drawn up by the General Assembly. The similarities of these committees to the

[1] Mr. Francis Forde, Deputy Prime Minister of Australia at the San Francisco Conference. See Doc. 20, P/6 (*U.N.C.I.O. Docs.*, Vol. 1, p. 178).

[2] Article 77 (1). See further Chap. 3, p. 39 *et seq.*

Trusteeship Council, the information transmitted by the administering Powers to the Trusteeship System's annual reports, and the Standard Form to the Trusteeship Council's Questionnaire are apparent.[3] Nevertheless, the Trusteeship System and Chapter XI remain separate, and the vast majority of dependent territories remain outside the Trusteeship System.

The Mandates System had been created to reconcile the determination of the Allied and Associated Powers to detach certain territories from the enemy in the First World War, the fact that so many of these territories were unfit for immediate independence, and the non-annexation principle expounded in Wilson's Fourteen Points. Its creation was justified by the fact that by the end of 1923, fifteen mandates had emerged out of ex-enemy territory. With the example of the Mandates System before them, and with the declaration in the Atlantic Charter that no territorial aggrandisement was sought, it was not surprising that the drafters of the Trusteeship provisions of the Charter made provision for territories 'detached from enemy states as a result of the Second World War' to be brought under the Trusteeship System.

The surprising fact is that, with the exception of Somaliland, no use has been made of this provision. Two reasons may be considered partly responsible for this. The example of Japan's use of her mandate as a base from which to prepare and wage war had shown that international supervision of national administration was no guarantee of a territory's neutralisation. The split among the Great Powers which developed at the end of the war accentuated the importance of controlling dependencies for reasons of national security. In some cases, trusteeship was equated with sphere of influence or security zone, and no Power was willing to see another increase its sphere of influence through acquiring an ex-enemy territory to administer as a trusteeship. This interpretation of trusteeship was held especially by the Soviet Union, as is shown by a statement of Marshall Stalin's at the Berlin Conference, 1945, that the Soviet Union 'would like some territory of the defeated states.' His Delegation then submitted a paper proposing that the Soviet Union be named trustee of one of the Italian colonies.[4] Later, at the London Conference

[3] See further Chap. 12, p. 243 *et seq.*
[4] James Byrnes, *Speaking Frankly* (1947), p. 76.

of the Council of Foreign Ministers in September 1945, Mr. Molotov raised the question of a Soviet Trusteeship for Tripolitania. He said that 'the Soviet Union should take the place that is due it, and therefore should have bases in the Mediterranean for its merchant fleet. We do not propose to introduce the Soviet system into this territory apart from the democratic order that is desired by the people.'[5]

In the case of the United States, an interest in trusteeship for reasons of national security was shown in practice rather than words: she unilaterally transformed the Pacific Islands Mandate she had taken over from Japan into a 'strategic trust territory.' Provision was made in the trust agreement for the withholding of United Nations supervision from areas within the territory which the administering authority specifies as 'closed for security reasons'[6]; in practice, the territory has provided naval and military bases for the administering authority, as well as a field for the testing of nuclear weapons. More of a national strategic area than this trust territory would be hard to imagine.

The second reason for the lack of use of the Trusteeship System for ex-enemy territories is that trusteeship provides no permanent solution to the problem of strategically important areas. Even should the Organisation assume the role of administering authority,[7] and thus prevent the territory from falling under the sphere of influence of a single Power, trusteeship is not a permanent status: it is an intermediary stage leading to self-government or independence.[8] It is, thus, not suitable for a permanently neutralised territory.

Only as a successor to the Mandates System has the Trusteeship System been of any real importance. Of the eleven former Mandates which have not yet achieved independence, ten have been placed under the Trusteeship System. South-West Africa remains the only Mandate in existence; and there seems little likelihood that it will be brought under the Trusteeship System. As Mr. Huntington Gilchrist, the Executive Officer of Commission II on the General Assembly at San Francisco, has said of the Trusteeship System: 'Its first characteristic is that it is volun-

[5] *ibid.*, p. 96.
[6] Article 13 of the Trust Agreement.
[7] See above, Chap. 11, p. 208 *et seq.*
[8] See above, Chap. 3, p. 41, n. 11, and Chap. 4, pp. 62–63.

tary.'[9] Thus, territories, be they former Mandates, ex-enemy territories, or colonial dependencies, can only be brought under the System voluntarily. This was upheld by the International Court of Justice in its Advisory Opinion on the *International Status of South West Africa* (1950).[10] In the case of a Mandate, the Trusteeship System relied on the voluntary action of the Mandatory to bring a territory under trusteeship. It is here that the weakness of the Charter provisions in providing a successor to the Mandates System emerges, for should this action not be forthcoming, the Charter provides no system to supervise the Mandates. This became apparent when South Africa bluntly refused to place South-West Africa under trusteeship. It has taken two Advisory Opinions of the International Court to devise a system to supervise the Mandate of South-West Africa.[11] It still remains to be seen whether the Union of South Africa will co-operate with the United Nations to permit this supervision to be exercised.

The pre-occupation of the drafters of the Charter with the problem of international security is reflected in the avowed aims of the Trusteeship System, the furtherance of international peace and security being named as the first objective.[12] In practice, however, it is the 'development towards self-government or independence,'[13] especially independence, that has received the greatest attention. This is due partly to the fact that in practice 'international security' has been discarded in favour of national security: Thus, the achievement of independence by a trust territory is seen by some of the non-administering powers as a means for detaching it from the sphere of influence of the administering Power. Nor is it only the non-administering Powers who view the situation in this light. The administering Powers have been opposed to measures which might hasten the loosening of the tie between a trust territory and its Administering Authority, such as the fixing of a time limit for independence. In the case of British administered Togoland, the only trust

9 H. Gilchrist, *Colonial Questions at the San Francisco Conference* (39 *American Political Science Review*, October 1945, p. 982).

10 *I.C.J. Reports 1950*, p. 139. See further above, Chap. 3, pp. 42–45.

11 *International Status of South-West Africa* (1950) *loc. cit.*, and *South-West Africa—Voting Procedure* (1955) *I.C.J. Reports 1955*, p. 67 *et seq.*

12 Article 76 (a).

13 Article 76 (b).

territory (except for Somaliland where a time-limit for independence is inserted in the trust agreement) where the termination of the trusteeship status appears likely in the near future, the goal suggested by the Administering Authority is not independence, but unity with the Gold Coast when the latter attains self-government within the Commonwealth.

In line with the concern of the drafters of the Charter with the peace and security problem, trust territories were to be divided into categories not according to their stage of development as under the Mandates System, but according to their strategic importance. Not the welfare of the inhabitants but the strategic importance of the territory was to be the deciding factor. Those trust territories, or parts of trust territories, which were considered of strategic importance were to be designated as strategic trust territories, and were to come under the control of the Security Council. Presumably this was because the 'primary responsibility for the maintenance of international peace and security' was placed on the Security Council,[14] and, therefore, a trust territory which was especially important from this point of view should be placed at the disposal of the Security Council. In practice, however, it has not worked out in this way. The only strategic territory in existence, the Pacific Islands, is administered by the United States who has a permanent veto over Security Council action; and security in the case of this trust territory has been interpreted as United States security. Areas within the territory have, in accordance with Article 13 of the Trust Agreement, been declared 'closed for security reasons,' the security reasons being nuclear experiments by the United States. In these areas, at times, all supervision by the United Nations may be prohibited by the Administering Authority.

The application of the Trusteeship System to a particular territory depends on the prior conclusion of a trust agreement. This agreement provides the legal basis for the supervision of the trust territory by the United Nations and for its administration by an Administering Authority. It is the basic law for the application of United Nations trusteeship to the territory. Furthermore, no trust territory can reach its goal of 'self-government or independence' save through alteration of the

[14] Article 24.

trust agreement, unless a specific date for the achievement of this goal is set in the trust agreement. Only in the case of Somaliland has this been done; therefore, only Somaliland will achieve independence automatically without the alteration of the trust agreement.[15]

From the provisions of the Charter, it emerges that there are two agreements involved in the bringing of a territory under trusteeship: an agreement between the 'States directly concerned' on the terms of trusteeship; and the actual trust agreement between the United Nations and the Administering Authority by which they approve these terms and agree to play the roles assigned to them therein. Unfortunately the Charter provisions are so badly drafted that nowhere is it stated that there are two agreements; but when Articles 75, 77 (1), 77 (2) and 80 (1) are read together, this emerges as the most reasonable interpretation of the provisions. In practice, the agreement between the 'States directly concerned' did not take place correctly. This was not only due to the lack of a specific statement in the Charter that there were two agreements, but also to the lack of the identity of the 'States directly concerned.' Instead of an agreement on the terms by the latter, the administering authority drew up the terms of trusteeship, submitted them to a few chosen states for comment, and then informed the General Assembly or the Security Council that the provision regarding the 'States directly concerned' had been complied with. The United Nations was willing to acquiesce in this practice because of the voluntary nature of trusteeship, and because of the desire to get the territories concerned under trusteeship as quickly as possible so that the Trusteeship System could be established. It must not be assumed, however, that there will be the same urgency to alter or terminate the agreements as there was to conclude them; and since Article 79 provides the same process for alteration as for conclusion, the question of the 'states directly concerned' will arise once again. Without a final definition of the term 'states directly concerned,' it is not impossible that a trust territory will be delayed or prevented achieving the goal of the Trusteeship System—self-government or independence.[16]

One of the interesting things to emerge from the practice

15 See further above, Chap. 7, pp. 134–135.
16 See further above, Chap. 5, p. 80 *et seq.*, and Chap. 7, p. 137 *et seq.*

of the International Trusteeship System is that the separation of powers between administration and supervision which was a feature of the Mandates System has been maintained in the case of every trust territory. Although provision is made in the Charter for direct international administration, national administration under international supervision has been preferred in every case. This is due not only to the desire of the State submitting the territory to trusteeship to maintain control of the territory, but also to the inherent difficulties associated with direct international administration under the Trusteeship System.[17] Even in Somaliland, where direct international administration seemed the obvious solution to many, this was rejected for national administration by a former enemy State, a non-Member, and the State from whom the territory had been detached at the conclusion of the Second World War.

The obligations incumbent upon the Administering Authority arise out of the trust agreement and the Charter. They are greater for a Member than for a non-Member. Members of the United Nations accept certain obligations regarding all non-self-governing territories, including trust territories, under the provisions of Chapter XI—provisions not binding on a non-Member. The importance of this is that Chapter XI places primary emphasis on the welfare of the inhabitants, whereas the Trusteeship System stresses the 'maintenance of international peace and security.' In the case of the only non-Member designated as an administering authority to date, detailed obligations regarding the welfare of the inhabitants of Somaliland were undertaken in the trust agreement to compensate for the fact that Italy was not bound by Chapter XI. Yet, a Member's obligations are greater in other ways. Under Article 84, a Member Administering Authority 'may make use of volunteer forces, facilities and assistance from the trust territory' in carrying out its obligations towards the Security Council for the maintenance of international peace and security. Although the use of the volunteer forces, facilities and assistance is said to be permissive in this article, if the Security Council decides that the assistance of the trust territory is necessary for the maintenance of international peace and security, in accordance with Article 25[18] the

[17] See above, Chap. 11, p. 208 *et seq.*

[18] Article 25: 'The Members of the United Nations agree to accept and carry out the decisions of the Security Council in accordance with the present Charter.'

Member has an obligation towards the Security Council to make use of this assistance. A non-Member has undertaken no obligations towards the Security Council and, therefore, has no need of the assistance of the territory for this purpose. Finally, in the application of 'equal treatment . . . for all Members of the United Nations and their nationals' under Article 76 (d), the obligations of the Administering Authority are less in the case of non-Members than for Members. This provision permits discrimination by a non-Member Administering Authority in favour of itself and its nationals, and, therefore, requires only the granting of most-favoured-nation treatment to Members, rather than national treatment. An interesting point to note in the case of all the administering authorities is that they are all permitted to discriminate in favour of a non-Member and its nationals. The differences in the obligations of Members and of non-Members are due, in part, to the fact that the possibility of a non-Member becoming an Administering Authority was not anticipated at San Francisco. They also stem from a certain degree of carelessness in drafting the provisions of the Charter.

In the exercise of trusteeship administration, the administering authorities are subject to the international supervision of the United Nations. Whilst the Mandates System attempted to separate this supervision from politics through the provision of a commission composed of experts rather than government representatives, the United Nations has recognised that politics must inevitably enter into this supervision. Many instances in the practice of the Permanent Mandates Commission had illustrated this. An additional seat on the Permanent Mandates Commission was created for a German national when Germany joined the League; the German Member left the Commission when Germany withdrew its nationals from the League Committees in 1933; and the Italian chairman walked out of the Commission in June 1936 during a debate on sanctions against Italy, after making a speech on the subject expressing views identical to those of his government. Thus, when the question of a special Trusteeship organ came to be considered, it was decided that it should be a principal United Nations organ composed of representatives of States. Though a principal organ and theoretically equal with the General Assembly and the Security Council, it nevertheless operates under the authority of these two organs.[19]

19 Articles 87, 85 (2), and 83 (2).

The exact position of the Trusteeship Council in relation to other United Nations organs is not well defined in the Charter. Here, again, the uncertainty seems to be the result of careless drafting.[20]

The three means of exercising supervision over trust territories which the Charter specifies provide the United Nations with information from the three most interested parties. The Administering Authority's view is ascertained through consideration of its annual report; petitions provide the United Nations with first-hand information from the indigenous inhabitants; and the United Nations itself is empowered to dispatch its own visiting missions to a trust territory. These means of supervision have operated relatively smoothly because they are specifically provided for in the Charter, and were not assumed as the result of controversial resolutions which, in the words of Sir Gladwyn Jebb, 'seek amendment of the Charter by indirect methods.'[1] This becomes particularly apparent when the means of supervision of the Trusteeship System are viewed against those which the non-colonial powers have attempted to establish for non-self-governing territories subject only to Chapter XI of the Charter.[2]

20 See further above, Chap. 8.

1 *Official Records of the Economic and Social Council,* 14th Session, 666th Meeting, p. 730.

2 See further above, Chap. 12.

APPENDIX

CHARTER OF THE UNITED NATIONS

Chapter XI

Declaration Regarding Non-Self-Governing Territories

Article 73

Members of the United Nations which have or assume responsibilities for the administration of territories whose peoples have not yet attained a full measure of self-government recognise the principle that the interests of the inhabitants of these territories are paramount, and accept as a sacred trust the obligation to promote to the utmost, within the system of international peace and security established by the present Charter, the well-being of the inhabitants of these territories, and, to this end:

(a) to ensure, with due respect for the culture of the peoples concerned, their political, economic, social, and educational advancement, their just treatment, and their protection against abuses;

(b) to develop self-government, to take due account of the political aspirations of the peoples, and to assist them in the progressive development of their free political institutions, according to the particular circumstances of each territory and its peoples and their varying stages of advancement;

(c) to further international peace and security;

(d) to promote constructive measures of development, to encourage research, and to co-operate with one another and, when and where appropriate, with specialised international bodies with a view to the practical achievement of the social, economic, and scientific purposes set forth in this article; and

(e) to transmit regularly to the Secretary-General for information purposes, subject to such limitation as security and constitutional considerations may require, statistical and other information of a technical nature relating to economic, social, and educational conditions in the territories for which they are respectively responsible other than those territories to which Chapters XII and XIII apply.

Article 74

Members of the United Nations also agree that their policy in respect of the territories to which this Chapter applies, no less than in respect of their metropolitan areas, must be based on the general principle of good-neighbourliness, due account being taken of the interests and well-being of the rest of the world, in social, economic, and commercial matters.

Chapter XII

International Trusteeship System

Article 75

The United Nations shall establish under its authority an international trusteeship system for the administration and supervision of such territories as may be placed thereunder by subsequent individual agreements. These territories are hereinafter referred to as trust territories.

Article 76

The basic objectives of the trusteeship system, in accordance with the Purposes of the United Nations laid down in Article 1 of the present Charter, shall be:

(a) to further international peace and security;

(b) to promote the political, economic, social, and educational advancement of the inhabitants of the trust territories, and their progressive development towards self-government or independence as may be appropriate to the particular circumstances of each territory and its peoples and the freely expressed wishes of the peoples concerned, and as may be provided by the terms of each trusteeship agreement;

(c) to encourage respect for human rights and for fundamental freedoms for all without distinction as to race, sex, language, or religion, and to encourage recognition of the interdependence of the peoples of the world; and

(d) to ensure equal treatment in social, economic, and commercial matters for all Members of the United Nations and their nationals, and also equal treatment for the latter in the administration of justice, without prejudice to the attainment of the foregoing objectives and subject to the provisions of Article 80.

Article 77

1. The trusteeship system shall apply to such territories in the following categorics as may be placed thereunder by means of trusteeship agreements:

(a) territories now held under mandate;

(b) territories which may be detached from enemy states as a result of the Second World War; and

(c) territories voluntarily placed under the system by states responsible for their administration.

2. It will be a matter for subsequent agreement as to which territories in the foregoing categories will be brought under the trusteeship system and upon what terms.

Article 78

The trusteeship system shall not apply to territories which have become Members of the United Nations, relationship among which shall be based on respect for the principle of sovereign equality.

Article 79

The terms of trusteeship for each territory to be placed under the trusteeship system, including any alteration or amendment, shall be agreed upon by the states directly concerned, including the mandatory power in the case of territories held under mandate by a Member of the United Nations, and shall be approved as provided for in Articles 83 and 85.

Article 80

1. Except as may be agreed upon in individual trusteeship agreements, made under Articles 77, 79 and 81, placing each territory under the trusteeship system, and until such agreements have been concluded, nothing in this Chapter shall be construed in or of itself to alter in any manner the rights whatsoever of any states or any peoples or the terms of existing international instruments to which Members of the United Nations may respectively be parties.

2. Paragraph 1 of this Article shall not be interpreted as giving grounds for delay or postponement of the negotiation and conclusion of agreements for placing mandated and other territories under the trusteeship system as provided for in Article 77.

Article 81

The trusteeship agreement shall in each case include the terms under which the trust territory will be administered and designate the authority which will exercise the administration of the trust territory. Such authority, hereinafter called the administering authority, may be one or more states or the Organisation itself.

Article 82

There may be designated, in any trusteeship agreement, a strategic area or areas which may include part or all of the trust territory to which the agreement applies, without prejudice to any special agreement or agreements made under Article 43.

Article 83

1. All functions of the United Nations relating to strategic areas, including the approval of the terms of the trusteeship agreements and of their alteration or amendment, shall be exercised by the Security Council.

2. The basic objectives set forth in Article 76 shall be applicable to the people of each strategic area.

3. The Security Council shall, subject to the provisions of the trusteeship agreements and without prejudice to security considerations, avail itself of the assistance of the Trusteeship Council to perform those functions of the United Nations under the trusteeship system relating to political, economic, social, and educational matters in the strategic areas.

Article 84

It shall be the duty of the administering authority to ensure that the trust territory shall play its part in the maintenance of international peace and security. To this end the administering authority may make use of volunteer forces, facilities, and assistance from the trust territory in carrying out the obligations towards the Security Council undertaken in this regard by the administering authority, as well as for local defence and the maintenance of law and order within the trust territory.

Article 85

1. The functions of the United Nations with regard to trustee-

ship agreements for all areas not designated as strategic, including the approval of the terms of the trusteeship agreements and of their alteration or amendment, shall be exercised by the General Assembly.

2. The Trusteeship Council, operating under the authority of the General Assembly, shall assist the General Assembly in carrying out these functions.

CHAPTER XIII

THE TRUSTEESHIP COUNCIL

Composition

Article 86

1. The Trusteeship Council shall consist of the following Members of the United Nations:

(a) those Members administering trust territories;

(b) such of those Members mentioned by name in Article 23 as are not administering trust territories; and

(c) as many other Members elected for three-year terms by the General Assembly as may be necessary to ensure that the total number of members of the Trusteeship Council is equally divided between those Members of the United Nations which administer trust territories and those which do not.

2. Each member of the Trusteeship Council shall designate one specially qualified person to represent it therein.

Functions and Powers

Article 87

The General Assembly and, under its authority, the Trusteeship Council, in carrying out their functions, may:

(a) consider reports submitted by the administering authority;

(b) accept petitions and examine them in consultation with the administering authority;

(c) provide for periodic visits to the respective trust territories at times agreed upon with the administering authority; and

(d) take these and other actions in conformity with the terms of the trusteeship agreements.

Article 88

The Trusteeship Council shall formulate a questionnaire on the political, economic, social, and educational advancement of the inhabitants of each trust territory, and the administering authority for each trust territory within the competence of the General Assembly shall make an annual report to the General Assembly upon the basis of such questionnaire.

Voting

Article 89

1. Each member of the Trusteeship Council shall have one vote.

2. Decisions of the Trusteeship Council shall be made by a majority of the members present and voting.

Procedure

Article 90

1. The Trusteeship Council shall adopt its own rules of procedure, including the method of selecting its President.

2. The Trusteeship Council shall meet as required in accordance with its rules, which shall include provision for the convening of meetings on the request of a majority of its members.

Article 91

The Trusteeship Council shall, when appropriate, avail itself of the assistance of the Economic and Social Council and of the specialised agencies in regard to matters with which they are respectively concerned.

BIBLIOGRAPHY

Official Documents

Australia: *Parliamentary Debates.*

Hansard: *Parliamentary History of England.*

Parliamentary Debates.

International Court of Justice: *Reports.*

International Military Tribunal for the Far East: *Judgement* (1948), 3 vols. (mimeographed records).

League of Nations: *Official Journal* (1920–).

Records of the 20th and 21st Ordinary Sessions of the League Assembly (*Official Journal, Special Supplement 1946*).

Rules of Procedure in Respect of Petitions Concerning Inhabitants of Mandated Territories (Doc. *C.P.M.* 38 (I), 1923).

Permanent Mandates Commission: *Minutes.*

Permanent Court of International Justice: *Reports.*

United Kingdom: *Commentary on the Charter* (Cmd. 6666, 1945).

Report on the Disposal of the Former Italian Colonies in Accordance with the Terms of the Treaty of Peace with Italy of 1947 (Cmd. 8819, 1953).

Colonial Office: Information on Non-Self-Governing Territories: Memorandum by the Colonial Office on Proceedings in the General Assembly of the United Nations, 1947 (Colonial No. 228, 1948).

United Nations: *Official Records of the General Assembly* (1946–).

Official Records of the Economic and Social Council (1946–).

Official Records of the Preparatory Commission (1945).

Official Records of the Security Council (1946–).

Official Records of the Trusteeship Council (1947–).

Repertory of Practice of United Nations Organs, Vol. IV (1955).

Report by the Executive Committee to the Preparatory Commission of the United Nations (Doc. PC/EX/113/Rev. 1, 12th November 1945).

Rules of Procedure of the Economic and Social Council (Doc. E/2424, 1953).

Rules of Procedure of the General Assembly (Doc. A/520/Rev. 3, 1954).

Rules of Procedure of the Security Council (Doc. S/96/Rev. 4, 1952).

Rules of Procedure of the Trusteeship Council (Doc. T/1/Rev. 3, 1952).

Terms of League of Nations Mandates (Doc. A/70, 1946).

Treaty Series.

Secretariat: *The Question of Equal Treatment in Economic and Commercial Matters in Trust Territories: Memorandum prepared by the Secretary-General* (Doc. A/C.4/38, 1946).

The Question of Fortifications and Volunteer Forces in Trust Territories (Article 84): Memorandum prepared by the Secretariat (Doc. A/C.4/40, 3rd November 1946).

The Question of the 'States Directly Concerned': Memorandum prepared by the Secretariat (Doc. A/C.4/36, 1946).

Trusteeship Council: *The Ewe Problem* (Doc. E/1910/Add. 1, 5th February 1951).

Customs Union of the Cameroons under French Administration and French Equatorial Africa: Working Paper prepared by the Secretariat (Doc. T/AC.14/7, 9th February 1949).

Memorandum on Administrative Unions: Cameroons under British administration, Togoland under British administration (Doc. T/AC.14/4, 6th February 1949).

Memorandum on the Question of Administrative Unions during the Negotiation of the Eight Trusteeship Agreements in the General Assembly and its Fourth Committee in 1946 (Doc. T/AC.14/5, 8th February 1949).

United Nations Conference on International Organisation: *Documents*, 20 vols. (1945–1954).

United States, Congress: *Trusteeship of Pacific Islands: Summary of Congressional Proceedings* (U.S. A.3: April–July 1947, pp. 375–380).

United States: *Congressional Record.*

Dept. of State: *The Conferences at Malta and Yalta, 1945*, 2 vols. (1955).

Congress, Senate: *Hearings Before the Committee on Foreign Relations on the Charter of the United Nations . . . July 9–13, 1945 (Senate Executive Report 8, 16th July 1945).*

General Bibliography

Adam, L.: *Afrikaanse Gebieden onder Toezicht der Verenigde Naties—Trustgebieden* (1949).

Antonelli, E.: *Introduction à une Etude Juridique du Trusteeship* (57 *Penant*, decembre 1947, pp. 1–16).

Arangio-Ruis, G.: *I Sistemi Coloniali delle Nazioni Unite* (2 *Communita Internazionale* 1947).

Australian Institute of International Affairs: *Dependencies and Trusteeship in the Pacific Area* (1947).

Bailey, K. H.: *Dependent Areas of the Pacific* (*Foreign Affairs*, April 1946, pp. 494–512).

Bastid (S. Basdevant), Mme. Paul: *Le Territoire dans le Droit International Contemporain* (1954), pp. 363–369.

Bates, M. L.: *Tanganyika: The Development of a Trust Territory* (*International Organisation*, February 1955, p. 33 *et seq.*).

Bentwich, N.: *Colonial Mandates and Trusteeship* (32 *Transactions of the Grotius Society* 1946, p. 121 *et seq.*).

Bentwich, N. and Martin, A.: *A Commentary on the Charter of the United Nations* (1951).

Bernard, F.: *L'Institution d'un Trusteeship International et l'Evolution des Colonies Francaises* (1945).

Blom, N. S.: *De Trustschapsraad van de Verenigde Naties* (3 *Indonesie*, juli 1949, pp. 61–75).

The British Commonwealth and Trusteeship (22 *International Affairs*, April 1946).

Brugel, J. W.: *Trusteeship—The New Form of International Administration* (24 *Central European Observer*, December 1947).

Buckle, D.: *Eastern Europe and the U.N. Trusteeship System* (3 *New Central European Observer*, February 1950).

Bunche, R. J.: *Trusteeship* (*Annual Review of United Nations Affairs 1950*, pp. 139–155).

Trusteeship and Non-Self-Governing Territories in the Charter (United States, Department of State *Bulletin* XIII, 30th December 1945, pp. 1037–1044).

Burn, B. B.: *International Law and Colonies* (United States, *Foreign Service Journal,* October 1955, p. 30 *et seq.*).
'Bustamente y Rivero, J. L.: *La O.N.U. y los Territorios Dependientes* (Colleccion 'O Crece o Muere,' 45, 1953).
Chase, E. P.: *The United Nations in Action* (1950).
Chieh, Lui: *International Trusteeship System* (448 *International Conciliation,* February 1949).
Chowdhuri, R. N.: *International Mandates and Trusteeship Systems: a Comparative Study* (1955).
Commission to Study the Organisation of Peace: *Report on the Trusteeship System and Non-Self-Governing Territories* (1949).
The United States and the International Trusteeship System (1945).
Conforti, B.: *Sovranità sui paesi in amministrazione fiduciaria e rapporti tra gli ordinamenti dell'amministrante e dell'amministrato* (38 *Rivista di Diritto Internazionale,* fasc. 1, 1955, pp. 17–38).
Conover, H. H.: *Non-Self-Governing Areas, with Special Emphasis on Mandates and Trusteeships* (a selected list of references, 1947).
Crabbs, R. F.: *The Record of the Soviet Union in the United Nations with regard to Non-Self-Governing Territories* (Unpublished thesis, Stanford University, California, 1950).
Eggleston, F.: *The United Nations Charter critically Considered: the Trusteeship Provisions* (1 *Australian Outlook,* March 1947, pp. 43–52).
Eichelberger, Clark M.: *U.N.: the First Ten Years* (1955), pp. 64–74.
F. W.: *American Trusteeship in the Pacific Islands* (3 *World Today,* July 1947, pp. 317–322).
Finkelstein, L. S.: *Somaliland under Italian administration; a case study in United Nations trusteeship* (1955).
Gerig, B.: *Significance of the Trusteeship System* (*Annals of the American Academy of Political and Social Science,* January 1948, pp. 39 47).
Gilchrist, H.: *The Japanese Islands: Annexation or Trusteeship?* (XXII *Foreign Affairs,* pp. 634–642).
Trusteeship and the Colonial System (XXII *Academy of Political Science, Proceedings,* 1947, pp. 203–217).
Goodrich, L. and Hambro, E.: *Charter of the United Nations; Commentary and Documents* (1949).
Gross, L.: *United Nations Trusteeship and the League of Nations Mandates System* (4 *India Quarterly,* 1948, pp. 224–240).
Haas, E. B.: *The Attempt to Terminate Colonialism: Acceptance of the United Nations Trusteeship System* (7 *International Organisation,* February 1953, pp. 1–21).
Hailey, Lord: *Colonial Trusteeship* (*The Times,* October 3, 1945).
Trusteeship in Africa: How the New System Differs from the Old (*African World,* May 1946, pp. 16–18).
Hall, L. D.: *British Commonwealth and Trusteeship* (XXII *International Affairs* 1946, pp. 199–213).
Mandates, Dependencies and Trusteeship (1948).
The Trusteeship System (XXIV *British Yearbook of International Law* 1947, pp. 33–71).
Holcombe, A. N.: *The International Trusteeship System* (CCXLVI *Annals of the American Academy of Political and Social Science,* July 1946, p. 104 *et seq.*).
Holland, Sir Robert: *Trusteeship Aspirations* (XXV *Foreign Affairs,* 1946, pp. 118–129).
Homont, A.: *L'Application du Régime de la Tutelle aux Territoires sous Mandat* (6 *Revue Juridique et Politique de l'Union Francaise* 1952, pp. 149–188).
Hoo, V.: *Trusteeship and Non-Self-Governing Territories* (*Annual Review of United Nations Affairs* 1951, pp. 88–103).

Jevremović, B.: *Pravo Naroda na Samoopredeljenje i Kolonijalni Sistem* (5 *Medunarodni Problemi, januar–mart* 1953, pp. 3–17).
Johnson, D. H. N.: *Trusteeship: Theory and Practice* (5 *Yearbook of World Affairs* 1951).
Kelsen, H.: *The Law of the United Nations* (1951).
Lachs, M.: *Powiermetwo Kolonialne Zjednoczonyet narodow. Analiza Historyczno Prawna* (*Mysl Wspolczesma* (Poland), Febuary–March 1948, pp. 333–349).
Lapie, P.-O.: *Qu'est-ce que le Trusteeship* (*Revue Socialiste,* avril 1947, pp. 432–443).
Lawson, R.: *Trusteeship—1945–1950* (XIX *Current History,* 1950, pp. 261–266).
League of Nations: *The Mandates System—Origins—Principles—Application* (1945).
Leeper, D. S.: *International Law—Trusteeship Compared with Mandate* (49 *Michigan Law Review,* June 1951, pp. 1199–1210).
Logan, R. W.: *The System of International Trusteeship* (15 *Journal of Negro Education* 1946, pp. 285–299).
Mammucari, G.: *Note Sull'Amministrazione Fiduciaria Internazionale* (1954).
McHenry, D. E.: *The United Nations Trusteeship System* (19 *World Affairs Interpreter* 1948, pp. 149–158).
McKay, V.: *International Trusteeship* (XXII *Foreign Policy Reports,* 1946, p. 57 *et seq.*).
Messineo, A.: *Dal Mandato all amministrazione fiduciaria* (*Civilta Cattolica,* 18th December 1948, pp. 579–593).
Il Regime Tutelare delle Colonie e il Diritto Internazionale (*Civilta Cattolica,* 4th December 1948, pp. 477–489).
Mortimer, M.: *Trusteeship in Practice* (1951).
Narayan, C. V. L.: *United Nations Trusteeship of Non-Self-Governing Territories* (1951).
Nassif, A.: *Mandat ou Trusteeship* (2 *Revue Egyptienne de Droit International* 1946, pp. 30–44).
Novikov, N.: *Our Views on Trusteeship* (*Soviet News,* 19th December 1946, pp. 1–3).
Oppenheim, L. (ed. Lauterpacht): *International Law* (Eighth Edition), Part I (1955).
Pollux: *The Interpretation of the Charter of the United Nations* (XXIII *British Year Book of International Law* (1946).
Preuss, L.: *Article 2, paragraph 7 of the Charter of the United Nations and Matters of Domestic Jurisdiction* (L'Academie de Droit International de la Haye: *Recueil des Cours,* 1949, Part I, pp. 547–652).
La Question de 'l'International Trusteeship' (81 *Notes Documentaires et Etudes,* pp. 1–15).
Raggi, C. G.: *L'Amministrazione Fiduciaria Internazionale* (1950).
Rappard, W. E.: *League Mandates vs. United Nations Trusteeship* (I *Freedom and Union,* November 1946).
Mandates and the International Trusteeship System (61 *Political Science Quarterly,* September 1946, p. 409 *et seq.*).
La Régime International de Tutelle et le Conseil de Tutelle (1311 *La Documentation Francaise, Notes et Etudes Documentaires,* 12 avril 1950, pp. 1–27).
Riggs, F. W.: *Wards of the U.N.: Trust and Dependent Areas* (26 *Foreign Policy Reports,* No. 6, 1950).
Robbins, R.: *Trusteeship System and Non-Self-Governing Territories* (425 *International Conciliation* 1946).
Roche, J.: *La Soveraineté dans les Territoires sous Tutelle* (58 *Revue Generale de Droit International Public,* juillet–septembre 1954, pp. 399–437).
Royal Institute of International Affairs: *The Colonial Problem* (1937).

Sayre, F. B.: *Legal Problems arising from the United Nations Trusteeship System* (42 *American Journal of International Law,* April 1948, pp. 263–298).
Scelle, G.: *Cours de Droit International Public* (1948).
Schwarzenberger, G.: *Power Politics* (1951).
Shtein, B.: *The System of International Tutelage: Dual Tendencies in the Solution of the Colonial Problem in the United Nations Organisation* (1948).
Shurshalov, V. M.: *Rezhim Mezhdunarodnoi Opeki* (1951).
Singh, S. C.: *International Trusteeship System—Is it an Improvement on the Mandates System* (3 *India and World Affairs,* July–September 1947, pp. 70–74).
Five Years of Trusteeship (12 *Indian Journal of Political Science,* October–December, 1951, pp. 108–116).
The Trusteeship System under Operation (9 *Indian Journal of Political Science,* April–September 1948, pp. 74–81).
Smith, A.: *Trusteeship and Partnership in British Africa* (7 *Year Book of World Affairs* 1953, p. 170 *et seq.*).
Tempête à la Commission de Tutelle (2 *Revue de la Politique Mondiale,* 19 decembre 1951, pp. 11–12).
Thompson, David: *How International is Colonial Trusteeship?* (XVIII *The Political Quarterly,* No. 4, October–December 1947).
Toussaint, C. E.: *The United Nations and Dependent Peoples* (8 *Year Book of World Affairs* 1954, p. 141 *et seq.*).
The Trusteeship Problem (*Soviet News,* 18th December, 1946, p. 2).
The Trusteeship System: Dependencies in the New World Order (*The Round Table,* No. 142, March 1946, pp. 127–132).
United Kingdom: *General Assembly of the United Nations 20th September–10th December 1949: Memorandum on Proceedings Relating to Non-Self-Governing and Trust Territories* (Cmd. 8035, 1950).
British Information Services: *Britain and Trusteeship* (I.D. 697, 1946).
Colonial Office: *Territories in Africa under United Kingdom Mandate* (Cmd. 6840, 1946).
Webster, Sir Charles: *The United Nations Reviewed* (*International Conciliation,* No. 433, 1948).
Wieschoff, H. A.: *Trusteeship and Non-Self-Governing Territories* (*Annual Review of United Nations Affairs* 1952, pp. 117–134).
Trusteeship and Non-Self-Governing Territories (*Annual Review of United Nations Affairs* 1953, pp. 49–60).
Winkel, H. W. Te: *Financiële steun aan Overzeese Gebieden tegen de Achtergroud van de Trust-Gedachte* (1950).
Yearbook of the United Nations (Pub. United Nations Dept. of Public Information, 1946–).
Zhukov, Ye: *Problems of the National-Colonial Struggle Since the Second World War* (condensed from *Voprosy Ekonomiki,* No. 9, 1949, pp. 54–61: see *Current Digest of the Soviet Press,* Vol. I, No. 49, 3 January 1950, pp. 3–6).

Specialised Bibliography

PART ONE

THE ORIGINS OF THE TRUSTEESHIP SYSTEM

1. Historical Background

African Society: *Journal* (July 1919, pp. 249–261: Lord Keith's analysis of the Berlin Act of 1885).
Baroudi, M.: *Les Problèmes Juridiques concernant l'Administration des Communautés sous Mandat* (1949).
Bentwich, Norman: *Colonies and International Accountability* (XVI *The Political Quarterly,* No. 3, July–September 1945).

Clarkson, T.: *The History of the Abolition of the African Slave Trade by the British Parliament* (1808).
Cobban, A.: *National Self-Determination* (1945).
Crowe, S. E.: *The Berlin West African Conference, 1884–1885* (1942).
Fabian Society, Colonial Bureau: *Colonies and International Conscience* (1945).
Gerig, B.: *The Open-Door and the Mandates System* (1930).
Historicus: *Stalin on Revolution* (27 *Foreign Affairs,* No. 2, January 1949, p. 175 *et seq*).
Hurst, Sir Cecil: *Great Britain and the Dominions* (1928).
Lindley, M. F.: *The Acquisition and Government of Backward Territories in International Law* (1926).
Locke, J.: *Second Treatise on Civil Government* (1685).
Lugard, Lord: *Dual Mandate in British Tropical Africa* (1923).
Margalith, A. M.: *The International Mandates* (1930).
Miller, D. H.: *The Drafting of the Covenant* (1928).
Nys, E.: *Les Origines du Droit International* (1894).
Potter, P. B.: *Origins of the System of Mandates under the League of Nations* (16 *American Political Science Review,* November 1922, p. 563 *et seq.*).
Rousseau, J. J.: *Contrat Social* (1762).
Discours sur l'Inégalité (1754).
Schwarzenberger, G.: *Power Politics* (1951).
The Protection of Human Rights in British State Practice (1 *Current Legal Problems* 1948).
Scott, J. B.: *The Spanish Conception of International Law and* Sanctions (1934).
Sisco, J. J.: *The Soviet Attitude toward the Trusteeship System* (Unpublished thesis, University of Chicago, 1950).
Smuts, J. C.: *The League of Nations, a Practical Suggestion* (1918).
Upthegrove, C. L.: *Empire by Mandate* (1954).
Wortley, B. A.: *Idealism in International Law: a Spanish View of the Colonial Problem* (24 *Transactions of the Grotius Society* 1938, pp. 147–167).
Wright, Q.: *Mandates Under the League of Nations* (1930).
The Writings and Speeches of Edmund Burke (Pub. Little, Brown and Co., Boston).

2. The San Francisco Conference

Australia, Delegation to United Nations Conference on International Organisation: *Report . . . together with the Text of Agreements signed at San Francisco, 26th June 1945* (1945).
Parliament, House of Representatives: *Parliamentary Debates,* Vol. 184, pp. 5016–5039 (30th August 1945), pp. 5111–5144, 5156–5200, 5227–5242 (5–7th September 1945).
Senate: *Parliamentary Debates,* Vol. 184, pp. 5267–5273, 5344–5376, 5442–5451 (12–14th September 1945); Vol. 185, pp. 5542–5561 (19th September 1945).
Armstrong and Cargo: *Inauguration of the Trusteeship System of the United Nations* (Dept. of State *Bulletin* XVI, 23rd March 1947, pp. 511–521).
Council on African Affairs: *The San Francisco Conference and the Colonial Issue; statement by the Council on African Affairs, Inc.* (April 1945).
France, Ministere de l'Information, Sous-Direction des Services Etrangers: *Le 'Trusteeship' est-il realisable? La position de la France* (14 avril 1945).

Gilchrist, Huntington: *Colonial Questions at the San Francisco Conference* (XXXIX *American Political Science Review,* 1945, pp. 982–992).

Howard, P. W.: *Report on the United Nations Conference* (3 *National Bar Journal,* St. Louis, September 1945, pp. 291–295).

K. D.: *The Trusteeship Proposals at San Francisco* (*The World Today,* 1945, p. 76).

King, Francis P.: *International Trusteeship at San Francisco* (Dissertation 1948, Stanford University, California).

Maalem, A.: *Colonialisme, Trusteeship, Indépendence* (1946), pp. 133–158.

Mahony, T. H.: *Observations on the San Francisco Conference,* Part 9 (Catholic Association for International Peace, Washington D.C., 1945).

Schwarzenberger, G.: *Power Politics* (1951), pp. 652–660.

The Soviet Union at the San Francisco Conference (Published by *Soviet News,* 1945).

The Trusteeship Proposals at San Francisco (1 *World Today,* August 1945, pp. 76–86).

The United Nations Charter, with explanatory notes of its Development at San Francisco by the Executive Officers of the four Commissions in the Conference (413 *International Conciliation,* September 1945, pp. 437–538).

United Nations Conference on International Organisation, Documents (XX volumes, Pub. 1945–1954).

U.N.C.I.O., New Zealand Delegation to the United Nations Conference: *Report on the Conference held at San Francisco, 25th April–26th June 1945* (1945, Dept. of External Affairs Publication 11).

United Kingdom: *Crimea Conference* (Cmd. 7088, 1947).
Dumbarton Oaks Proposals (Cmd. 6580, 1944).
Parliamentary Debates (*House of Commons*), Vol. 413 22nd August 1945 *et seq.*
Parliamentary Debates (*House of Lords*), Vol. 137, 22nd August 1945 *et seq.*

United States: *Congressional Record* (*Senate*) (79th Congress, 1st Session, pp. 7941 *et seq.*), (1945).
Delegation to the San Francisco Conference: *Charter of the United Nations: Report to the President* (1945: Dept. of State Publication 2349).
Dept. of State: *Bulletin* (11th March 1945).
Bulletin (1st December, 1946, pp. 991–994: U.S. Position on Establishment of the Trusteeship System).
Post-War Foreign Policy Preparation 1939–1945 (Dept. of State Publication 3580, 1950).
The Conferences at Malta and Yalta 1945 (1955), Part, I, pp. 93, 101, 126–127.

Webster, Sir Charles: *The Making of the Charter of the United Nations* (32 *History,* March 1947, No. 115, p. 16).

PART TWO

SCOPE AND AIMS OF THE TRUSTEESHIP SYSTEM

3. Territories Subject to the Trusteeship System

Brinton, J. Y.: *Mandates, Trusteeships and South-West Africa* (6 *Revue Egyptienne de Droit International* 1950, pp. 82–89).

Colliard, C. A.: *Le Statut International du Sud-Ouest Africain* (5 *Revue Juridique et Politique de l'Union Francaise* 1951, pp. 94–112).

Fitzmaurice, G. G.: *The Law and Procedure of the International Court of Justice: International Organisations and Tribunals* (XXIX *British Year Book of International Law* 1952).

Gilchrist, Huntington: *Colonial Questions at the San Francisco Conference* (39 *American Political Science Review,* 1945, pp. 982–992).

Hall, L. D.: *The Trusteeship System and the Case of South-West Africa* (XXIV *British Year Book of International Law* 1947, p. 385 *et seq.*).

Jully, L.: *La Question Sud-Ouest Africain devant la Cour Internationale de Justice* (*Die Friedens-Warte,* Nr. 3, 1951).

Kahn, E.: *The International Court's Advisory Opinion on the International Status of South-West Africa* (4 *International Law Quarterly,* No. 1, 1951, pp. 77–99).

Kelsen, H.: *The Legal Status of Germany According to the Declaration of Berlin* (39 *American Journal of International Law,* 1949, pp. 518–526).

Lalive, J. F.: *Statut International du Sud-Ouest Africain* (77 *Journal de Droit International, octobre–decembre* 1950, pp. 1252–1271).

League of Nations: *The Council of the League of Nations: Composition, Competence, Procedure* (1938).

Mathiot, A.: *Le Champ d'Application du Statut de Tutelle* (5 *Revue Juridique et Politique de l'Union Francaise,* juillet–septembre 1951, pp. 373–398).

Le Champ d'Application du Statut de Tutelle; les Organes d'Application de Statut de Tutelle; le Contenue du Statut de Tutelle; le Contrôle de la Tutelle (7 *Revue Juridique et Politique de l'Union Francaise,* avril-juin 1953, pp. 242–261).

4. The Objectives of the Trusteeship System

Cheng, Bin: *Rights of United States Nationals in the French Zone of Morocco* (2 *International and Comparative Law Quarterly,* July 1953, p. 354 *et seq.*).

Commission to Study the Organisation of Peace: *Strategic Bases and the Problem of Security* (1945).

Cooper, J. C.: *United Nations Trusteeships* (*Cabotage under the Charter and the Covenant*) (2 *Air Affairs,* Washington D.C., Autumn 1947, pp. 115–127).

Gerig, B.: *The Open-Door and the Mandates System* (1950).

Huang, T. F.: *Trust Territories and Customs and Administrative Unions* (43 *American Journal of International Law,* October 1949, pp. 716–731).

Johnson, D. H. N.: *The Case Concerning Rights of Nationals of the United States of America in Morocco* (29 *British Year Book of International Law* 1952, pp. 401–423).

Kelsen, H.: *The Law of the United Nations* (1951).

Lauterpacht, H.: *International Law and Human Rights* (1950).

Maalem, A.: *Colonialisme, Trusteeship, Indépendence* (1946).

Mortimer, M.: *Administrative Unions* (4 *Venture,* No. 9, p. 8, 1952).

When is Self-Government not Self-Government? (4 *Venture,* No. 11, p. 8, 1953).

Sayre, F. B.: *Trust Territories' Program Toward Self-Government* (Department of State *Bulletin*, 24th December 1951, pp. 1024–1027).

PART THREE
THE TRUST AGREEMENTS

5. THE SUBMISSION OF A TERRITORY TO TRUSTEESHIP

Draft Convention on the Law of Treaties, Prepared Under the Auspices of the Faculty of the Harvard Law School (29 *American Journal of International Law*, 1935, Supplement, p. 870 *et seq.*).

Hansard: *Parliamentary Debates* (*House of Commons*), Vol. 418, 23rd January 1946, column 150.

Kelsen, Hans: *The Law of the United Nations* (1951), pp. 710–711.

Schwarzenberger, G.: *International Law*, Vol. I (1949), p. 143.

United States, Department of State: *Bulletin* (3rd February, 1946, and 1st December, 1946).

Wolfe, G. V.: *The States Directly Concerned: Article 79 of the U.N. Charter* (XLII *American Journal of International Law* 1948, pp. 368–388).

6. CONTENTS OF THE TRUST AGREEMENTS

Kelsen, H.: *The Law of the United Nations* (1951), p. 613.

Parry, C.: *The Legal Status of the Trusteeship Agreements* (XXVII *British Year Book of International Law* 1950, p. 164 *et seq.*).

United States: *Draft Trusteeship Agreement for the Japanese Mandated Islands with Article by Article Explanatory Comments, and Statements by President Truman and the U.S. Representative on the Security Council* (1947, Dept. of State Publication 2784).

Vedovato, G.: *Les Accords de Tutelle* (L'Académie de Droit International de la Haye: *Recueil des Cours*, Vol. 76, 1950 (I), pp. 609–697).

7. ALTERATION OR TERMINATION OF A TRUST AGREEMENT

Draft Convention on the Law of Treaties, prepared under the Auspices of the Faculty of the Harvard Law School (29 *American Journal of International Law*, 1935, Supplement, p. 870 *et seq.*).

Kelsen, H.: *The Law of the United Nations* (1951), pp. 653–656.

Lauterpacht, H.: *Restrictive Interpretation and the Principle of Effectiveness in the Interpretation of Treaties* (26 *British Year Book of International Law* 1949, p. 48 *et seq.*).

McNair, Sir Arnold: *La Terminaison et la Dissolution des Traités* (L'Académie de Droit International de la Haye: *Recueil des Cours*, 1928 (II), p. 456 *et seq.*).

Oppenheim, L. (ed. Lauterpacht): *International Law*, Vol. I (Eighth Edition) (1955), p. 841.

Pollux: *The Interpretation of the Charter* (23 *British Year Book of International Law* 1946, pp. 54–82).

Schwarzenberger, G.: *International Law*, Vol. I (1949), p. 208 *et seq.*

PART FOUR
MACHINERY OF SUPERVISION

8. ORGANS OF THE UNITED NATIONS CONCERNED WITH TRUSTEESHIP

Chu, T. F.: *La Compétence de l'Assemblée Générale des Nations Unies* (Unpublished Thesis, Faculté de Droit, University of Paris, 1952), pp. 60–76.

Kelsen, H.: *The Law of the United Nations* (1951), p. 689 *et seq.*
Sloan, F. B.: *The Binding Force of a Recommendation of the General Assembly of the United Nations* (23 *British Year Book of International Law* 1948, pp. 1–33).
Wieschhoff, H. A.: *Trusteeship and Non-Self-Governing Territories* (*Annual Review of United Nations Affairs* 1953, pp. 49–60).

9. THE TRUSTEESHIP COUNCIL

Cobanoglu, R.: *L'Evolution récente de la Notion de Souveraineté et les Procedures de Vote dans les Organisations Internationales* (Unpublished Thesis, Faculté de Droit, University of Paris, 1949), pp. 168–172.
Fraser, P.: *The Work of the Trusteeship Council* (445 *International Conciliation,* November 1948, pp. 651–666).
Hayden, S. S.: *Trusteeship Council: Its First Three Years* (60 *Political Science Quarterly,* June 1951, pp. 226–247).
Koo, W., jr.: *Voting Procedures in International Political Organizations* (1947), pp. 267–284.
League of Nations: *The Council of the League of Nations: Composition, Competence, Procedure* (1938).
Oddini, M.: *La Posizione dell'Italia nel Consiglio per l'Amministrazione Fiduciaria* (18 *Revista de Studi Politici Internazionali,* aprile–giugno 1951, pp. 225–228).
The United Nations Trusteeship Council and its Activities (*New Times,* No. 18, 1st May 1952, pp. 29–32).
Van Maanen-Helmer: *The Mandates System* (1929).
Wright, Quincy: *Mandates Under the League of Nations* (1930).

10. THE MEANS OF TRUSTEESHIP SUPERVISION

Finkelstein, L. S.: *Trusteeship in Action: the United Nations Mission to Western Samoa* (2 *International Organisation,* June 1948, pp. 268–282).
League of Nations: *The Mandates System: Origin—Principles—Application* (1945).
United States: *Foreign Relations: Paris Peace Conference* (1919), Vol. III.
Visiting Missions (448 *International Conciliation,* February 1949).
Wright, Quincy: *Mandates Under the League of Nations* (1930).

PART FIVE

THE ADMINISTRATION OF TRUST TERRITORIES

11. THE ADMINISTERING AUTHORITY AND ITS OBLIGATIONS

Becker, G. H., jr.: *The Disposition of the Italian Colonies; 1941–1951* (1952).
Communique of the Moscow Conference, 24th and 25th December, 1945 (Royal Institute of International Affairs: *United Nations Documents 1941–1945*).
Goodrich, L. and Hambro, E.: *The Charter of the United Nations; Commentary and Documents* (1949), pp. 107–108.
Hall, L. Duncan: *Mandates, Dependencies and Trusteeship* (1948).
The Italian Colonies (*United Nations Action,* 1945).
Kelsen, H.: *The Law of the United Nations* (1951), p. 91.
Oppenheim, L. (ed. Lauterpacht): *International Law,* Vol. I (Eighth Edition, 1955), p. 208.
Rivlin, Benjamin: *The Italian Colonies and the General Assembly* (III *International Organisation,* August 1949, p. 466f.).
The United Nations and the Italian Colonies (1950).

Schwarzenberger, G.: *Power Politics* (1951), pp. 407–411, 671–674.

Vedovato, G. and Moreno, N. and Mangano, G.: *The Question of the Administration of Italian Colonies in Africa under Trusteeship* (1947).

PART SIX

TRUSTEESHIP AND NON-SELF-GOVERNING TERRITORIES

12. The Trusteeship System and Chapter XI of the Charter

Asbeck, F. M. van: *International Law and Colonial Administration* (39 *Transactions of the Grotius Society,* 1953, pp. 5–37).

Le Statut Actuel des Pays Non Autonomes d'Outre-Mer (L'Académie de Droit International de la Haye: *Recueil des Cours,* Vol. 71, 1947 (II), pp. 349–475).

Armstrong, E.: *The United States and Non-Self-Governing Territories* (3 *International Journal,* 1948, pp. 327–333).

Benson, W.: *International Organisation and Non-Self-Governing Territories* (15 *Journal of Negro Education,* Summer 1946, pp. 300–310).

Bustamente y Rivero, J. L.: *La O.N.U. y los Territorios Dependientes* (*Coleccion 'O Crece o Muere,'* 45) (1953).

Chase, Eugene P.: *Dependent Areas and the Trusteeship System of the United Nations* (XVII *World Affairs Interpreter,* 1946, pp. 293–305).

Colonialism and the United Nations: Proposals for Charter Amendments (Chicago: Toward Freedom).

Constanzo, G. A.: *Lezioni di Diritto Coloniale Parte Speciale. L'Ordinamento dei Territori Non Autonomi nello Statuto dell'O.N.U.* (Roma: Edizioni dell'Ateneo).

Cordero Torres, J. M.: *La Evolucion de la Personalidad Internacional de les Paises Dependientes* (1930).

Council on African Affairs: *Text and Analysis of the United Nations Charter . . .* (1945).

Creech Jones,. A.: *United Nations Reform: Control of Dependent Territories* (25 *New Commonwealth,* 2nd March 1953, pp. 214–216).

Eagleton, C.: *Excesses of Self-Determination* (XXXI *Foreign Affairs,* July 1953, pp. 592–604).

Frazão, S. A.: *International Responsibility for Non-Self-Governing Peoples* (296 *Annals of the American Academy of Political and Social Science,* No. 1954, pp. 56–67).

Fox, A. B.: *The United Nations and Colonial Development* (4 *International Organisation,* May 1950, pp. 199–218).

Greenidge, C. W. W.: *The United Nations and Dependent Territories* (4 *Anti-Slavery Reporter and Aborigenes' Friend,* January 1949, pp. 75–78).

Hall, L. D.: *Mandates, Dependencies and Trusteeship* (1948).

Hayden, S. S. and Rivlin, B.: *Non-Self-Governing Territories; Status of Puerto Rico* (1954).

International Responsibility for Colonial Peoples—The United Nations and Chapter XI of the Charter (458 *International Conciliation,* February 1950).

Jovanović, B.: *Kolonijalna Klauzula u Posleratnim Ugovorima* (I *Arhiv za Pravne i Drustvene Nauke* 1952, pp. 88–102).

Kunz, J. L.: *Chapter XI of the United Nations Charter in Action* (48 *American Journal of International Law,* January 1954, pp. 103–110).

Langenhove, F. van: *Les Territoires Non Autonomes d'après la Charte des Nations Unies* (87 *Revue Générale Belge,* août 1952, pp. 505–525).

Logan, R. W.: *The United Nations and Dependent Territories* (2 *American Perspective,* No. 6, November 1948, p. 267 *et seq.*).

Louwers, O.: *L'Article 73 de la Charte et l'Anti-Colonialisme de l'Organisation des Nations Unies* (1952).

Mathiot, A.: *Le Contrôle de l'Organisation des Nations Unies sur l'Administration des Territoires Non Autonomes* (3 *Revue Juridique et Politique de l'Union Francaise,* janvier-mars 1949, pp. 26–59).

Le Statut des Territoires Dependants d'après la Charte des Nations Unies (*L'Revue Générale de Droit International Public,* 1946, pp. 159–206).

Les Territoires Non Autonomes et la Charte des Nations Unies (1949).

Les Questions Coloniales aux Nations Unies—L'Autonomie des Territoires Dependants et la Genèse de la 'Thèse Belge' sur les Populations Indigènes (6 *Chronique de Politique Etrangère,* No. 4, July 1953, pp. 474–478).

Menon, L. N.: *International Responsibility for Dependent Areas* (*India Quarterly,* July–September 1955).

Rao, B. S.: *The United Nations and Non-Self-Governing Territories* (6 *India Quarterly,* July–September 1950, pp. 227–234).

Rivlin, B.: *Self-Determination and Dependent Areas* (501 *International Conciliation,* January 1955, pp. 195–271).

Robinson, K.: *World Opinion and Colonial Status* (8 *International Organisation,* November 1954, pp. 468–483).

Rowley, C.: *United Nations, Colonialism and Australia* (7 *Australian Outlook,* June 1953, pp. 120–128).

Ryckmans, P.: *Questions Coloniales à l'O.N.U.* (52 *Revue Générale Belge,* fevrier 1950, pp. 525–534).

Situation Actuelle des Territoires Non-Autonomes à la Lumière des Articles 73 et 74 de la Charte des Nations Unies (Union Interparlementaire: *Compte Rendu de la XXXVII Conférence Tenue à Rome du 6 au 11,* septembre 1948, pp. 386–394).

Toussaint, C. E.: *The Colonial Controversy in the United Nations* (10 *Year Book of World Affairs* 1956).

The United Nations and Non-Self-Governing Territories (435 *International Conciliation,* November 1947).

CASES

National Courts

International Courts and Tribunals

TREATIES AND STATUTES

INDEX